Erotic Subjects and Outlaws

At the Interface/Probing the Boundaries

VOLUME 110

The titles published in this series are listed at *brill.com/aipb*

Erotic Subjects and Outlaws

Sketching the Borders of Sexual Citizenship

Edited by

Serena Petrella

BRILL
RODOPI

LEIDEN | BOSTON

Cover illustration: Person holding up a LGBT flag. Photographer: Yannis Papanastasopoulos. Retrieved from: https://unsplash.com/photos/if_29seD7tA. Used with permission.

The Library of Congress Cataloging-in-Publication Data is available online at http://catalog.loc.gov
LC record available at http://lccn.loc.gov/2018968429

Typeface for the Latin, Greek, and Cyrillic scripts: "Brill". See and download: brill.com/brill-typeface.

ISSN 1570-7113
ISBN 978-90-04-39228-1 (paperback)
ISBN 978-90-04-39229-8 (e-book)

This book is printed on acid-free paper and produced in a sustainable manner.

Contents

Notes on Contributors

Abidemi Fasanmi
is currently pursuing a Ph.D. in the Department of Women, Gender and Sexuality Studies at Emory University, in Atlanta, Georgia, U.S.A. Her interests are in the areas of Gender Violence, Bio-politics, Religion and Health, particularly in Africa.

René Hirsch
is an independent researcher who lives and works in The Netherlands. He is the author of the book *The Masculine Civilization*, and of various papers including 'Procreative Knowledge, Gender Roles, and Beliefs: Past and Present Parallels,' 'The Codes of Law and the Establishment of a Procreative Monopoly,' and 'Sex and Procreation in the Primitive World.'

Elene Lam
is a Ph.D. student at McMaster University, in Social Work. She is one of the founders and the Director of *Butterfly*, the Asian and Migrant Sex Workers Support Network in Canada, and co-director of the Migrant Sex Workers Project in Toronto. She has been involved in the sex work, migrant, and labour rights movement for more than 15 years. Ms. Lam has been a lecturer and course coordinator at colleges and universities. She is an accredited mediator and certified as a sex therapist.

Jaclyn Lanthier
is a Philosophy graduate student affiliated with the University of Western Ontario, in London, Ontario, Canada. Her area of interest and research is on methodological issues and the epistemic status of claims in cognitive neuroscience.

Todd G. Morrison
is a professor of Social Psychology at the University of Saskatchewan, in Saskatoon, Saskatchewan, Canada. He specializes in gay and lesbian psychology, body image, prejudice, discrimination, masculinity, and psychometrics. Morrison's research has appeared in various peer-reviewed journals including *Pain*, *Psychology of Men and Masculinity*, *Sexuality & Culture*, *Journal of Health Psychology*, and the *Journal of Homosexuality*.

Nick J. Mulé
is an associate professor at the School of Social Work and seconded to teach in Sexuality Studies at the School of Gender, Sexuality and Women's Studies both in the Faculty of Liberal Arts and Professional Studies at York University, in Toronto, Ontario, Canada. He is the founder and former chairperson of Queer Ontario and a psychotherapist in private practice serving the LGBT communities in Toronto.

Elly-Jean Nielsen
is a doctoral candidate in the Department of Psychology at the University of Saskatchewan, in Saskatoon, Saskatchewan, Canada. Her research interests include sexual diversity, queer identities, expressions of experience through art forms, and qualitative methodologies. Nielsen has published in various peer-reviewed journals including *Psychology & Sexuality*, *Psychology of Men and Masculinity*, *The Counseling Psychologist*, and the *Journal of Lesbian Studies*.

Serena Petrella
is an associate professor in Sociology and in Gender and Women's Studies at Brandon University, in Brandon, Manitoba, Canada. She specializes in sexuality, the evolution of relational norms and sexual regulation in the Law. She has been particularly engaged in exploring how the Canadian Judicial Systems deals with polygamy and polyamory.

Olivia Schuman
is completing her Ph.D in Philosophy at York University in Toronto, Ontario, Canada. Her research focuses on bioethics, especially on issues related to gamete donation and the "right to know" one's gamete donor. She is also interested in genetics, autonomy and reproductive freedom.

Deww Zhang
is currently doing a PhD on BDSM in Auckland at the University of Auckland, in Auckland, New Zealand. Her research focuses on BDSM communities and erotic dissidence.

Erotic Subjects and Outlaws: Sketching the Borders of Sexual Citizenship. An Introduction

Serena Petrella

1 Introduction: the Sex and the State and the Persons and Sexualities Projects

The Interdisciplinary.Net research hubs on *Sex and the State* (*SS*) and *Persons and Sexualities* (*PS*) have been active since 2004 and 2008 respectively, meeting over the years in diverse locations across the globe. They are just two of the many branches of the fruitful Interdisciplinary. Net tree, an international and interdisciplinary forum for the exchange and interaction of ideas, research and points of view on a wide range of issues of concern and interest in the contemporary world. *SS* and *PS* are international collaborative projects that span across disciplines and stretch beyond scholarly boundaries, engaging scholars, educators, policy makers, members of the medical and the therapeutic professions, and activists who do critical work on sexuality across a broad range of subject areas and institutional settings, using varied research methodologies, and operating in diverse national and international contexts.

The two hubs have become essential to the critical evaluation of debates on sexuality, and interrogate taken-for-granted attitudes and assumptions on erotic practice. They have been actively engaged in subverting the often tenacious and stereo-typified misunderstandings on gender identity, the orientation of desire, and the nature of sexual practices. Over the last twelve years, these research clusters have become irreplaceable hubs for the mobilization of critical research on sexuality, in many cultural settings, and across varied social contexts.

The *4th Global Conference on Sex and the State* and the *7th Global Conference on Persons and Sexualities* were held in Montreal in October 2014. The first conference focused on the regulation of sexuality by the state and government agencies' role in framing regulation on sexuality, enforcing prohibitions and extending permissions for sexual behaviour. The conference wished to flesh out the complex ways in which states and state governed social institutions regulate sexual conduct in contemporary societies. Specifically, it set out to explore the ways in which the Law and other forms of governance have been used to police and repress certain desires and pleasures, and the ways in which such prohibitions and regulations have been changed, subverted, challenged

 | DOI:10.1163/9789004392298_002

or transgressed, bringing about new and more inclusive versions of sexual citizenship.[1]

The themes explored in the meeting critically engaged with the ways in which proper sexual citizenship, or 'erotic civility,' and sex crime, or 'erotic incivility,' have been articulated and regulated, in ways that moved beyond a simple disciplinary focus on policy, social norms and values. Presentations delved into the ways in which the Law defined 'good' and 'bad' sexual behaviour in disparate national contexts, and explored the ways in which ethical considerations were mobilized to distinguish between licit and illicit sexual behaviour. At the hearth of this conference was the examination of sexual citizenship in terms of belonging and exclusion: many of the presentations examined the ways in which 'sexual outlaws' had challenged their marginalization and had eventually gained the status of full citizens, inevitably transforming the parameters of sexual citizenship itself.

The second conference, *Persons and Sexualities*, focused instead on the relationship between sexuality and personhood, and specifically sought to understand how sex and sexuality shape belonging, identity and expression. Presentations' themes gave primacy to practices related to sex, the interplay of identities, orientations, desires, pleasures, taboos, and sexual behaviours in a global context, and across a range of critical, contextual and cultural perspectives. The papers presented particularly addressed notions of embodiment and embodied practice, investigating how they were tied to social systems of belonging and exclusion, inevitably becoming part of political and legal debates on sexual citizenship.[2]

The issue of belonging was especially important: many of the presenters examined how desire and pleasure shape the identity that people take on, and the practices they engage in, by which they define who they are and how they interact with others, thus entering into social clusters framed through a certain kind of 'identity politics.' Some presentations troubled accepted sexual norms and probed the dichotomies of 'normal' and 'abnormal,' or 'deviant' or 'perverse.' Inevitably they questioned the ways in which desires, identities, behaviours and practices interplay in sexual expressions in contemporary life, making evident how power permeates these exchanges, and problematizing which bodies are afforded the 'right' to be sexual, and to participate in sex.

1 'Call for Presentations, 4th Global Conference on Sex and The State,' Interdisciplinary.Net, Viewed April 17, 2015,http://www.inter-disciplinary.net/critical-issues/gender-and-sexuality/sex-and-the-state/call-for-papers/

2 'Call for Presentations, 7th Global Conference on Persons and Sexualities,' Interdisciplinary.Net, Viewed April 17, 2015,https://call-for-papers.sas.upenn.edu/node/56634

They questioned the meaning of 'embodiment' through sexuality, making evident how such 'temporary crystallizations' could at times replicate cultural expectations that surrounded that particular sexuality or orientation, entrenching old structures, but in other instances they departed from the 'normal,' forging new possibilities for understanding and living sexuality. The delegates observed that our embodiment and sexual citizenship (or lack thereof) occur in the context of specific social spaces and social structures, such as gender, class, ability, age, and race and ethnicity.

It was at this junction that this collection fount its genesis: delegates became fascinated by the insight that the erotic dissident, the 'bad' illicit persona of the sexual outlaw, was always in discoursive and political struggle with and in juxtaposition to the erotically civil subject, the 'good' sexual citizen. These dichotomous figures, one inside, one outside, each struggling to 'get in' or to 'stay in,' brought each other to crisis, thus precipitating the reconfiguration of sexual citizenship itself. This insight became the guiding theme for our collection: participants embarked on many fruitful conversations on the topic of belonging, exploring the tropes of being 'inside' and 'outside,' with the promise that their musings would be published in a volume dedicated to exploring the 'borders' of sexual citizenship. The reflections that have emerged from their dialogues, which are compelling and vital, are found collected in this volume, which comprises a selection of essays drawn from both meetings.

The collection comprises nine chapters, each expanding and re-elaborating ideas originally presented at the conferences and debated at the forums. Sexual citizenship and exclusion are approached through diverse methodological and analytical lenses; some of the articles in the collection are theoretical and philosophical in nature, others are empirically based, and present the findings of sociological and ethnographic research projects; finally, some are textual analyses, of religious texts, film texts, and of legal discourse. These essays are the culmination of exchanges of ideas among the delegates during the conference and, in the months following, the additional conversations they had with one another. They are now presented to you, the reader and, as the title suggests, they attempt to trace the borders sexual citizenship, investigating the effects of what it means to be 'inside,' as erotic subjects, or outside, as 'sexual outlaws.'

2 The Chapters: Sketching the Borders of Sexual Citizenship

The collection is divided into four sections, organized thematically to cover the theorization of sexual citizenship, the exploration of case studies in Law, the relationship between sexual citizenship and bio-politics, and finally the erotic dissidence of sexual outlaws. The first section, titled 'Theorizing Shifting Sexual Citizenship Rights,' discusses the evolution of sexual rights politics from a theoretical perspective. The second section, titled 'Shaping and Constraining the Sexual Citizen in the Law,' closely analyzes legal texts, examining how sexual citizenship has been configured in different contexts over the course of human history; two case studies are examined, one that looks back into our distant past and one that studies present times. The third section, titled 'The Bio-political Governance of Sexual Citizenship,' is concerned with bio-politics, or the governance of life, and examines how 'experts' are able to mobilize specific definitions of sexual citizenship that in turn affect modes of intervention, that have real life effects on the lives of the people they have acted upon. Finally, the fourth and final section, titled 'The Erotic Dissidence of Kinksters and Queer Outlaws,' explores sexual 'abjection' and examines those left 'outside,' the 'sexual dissidents' and the 'erotic outlaws,' examining whether they hold aspirations for inclusion, thus problematizing the borders of sexual citizenship itself, through a process of generative mutual constitution.

3 Theorizing Shifting Sexual Citizenship Rights

Mulé's first contribution to the collection, titled 'Evolving Sexual Citizenry: Developing Queer Liberation Theory,' examines the evolution of the concept of sexual citizenship within theories on sexuality. The author pays particular attention to queer theory because, he argues, it has gained ascendancy and dominance in the realm of LGBTQ debates over the last two decades. A review of important currents within queer theory and LGBTQ social movements is undertaken, with special attention to a decidedly progressive and critical scion within queer theory, a politicized queer contingent that over the last decade has called into question trends of homonormativity and cisgenderism, in the context of Neoliberalism, espoused by a more conservative segment of the movement. In his chapter, Mulé outlines the political agendas of LGBTQ s on one hand and radical queers on the other, providing a critical analysis of each group's ideals for life, their emancipation goals and the praxes they choose to adopt to achieve them.

Departing from his experiences and involvement with the queer social justice group Queer Ontario, the author adopts an 'emergent' theorization approach that is firmly based in activist praxis, yet is intellectually conceptual. He is thus able to sketch the frame of a new form of sexual citizenship that can maintain revolutionary impetus and transformative power, even in the precarious climate of Neoliberalism. Mulé proposes a framework that is respectful of the movement's historical past and returns to the tenets and principles of gay liberation, yet masterfully re-contextualizes them so that the multiplicities that make up gender and sexual diversity in present times are taken into account. Mulé's engagement and effort to 'theorize anew' are particularly meaningful in a period that has seen a strong trend of homogenization in the LGBTQ movement, a turn towards 'homonormativity.'

Increasingly the movement has lost its radical edge and is being assimilated, professionalized, and mainstreamed, or co-opted into the political agendas of privatization of Neoliberalism, that tout a specific form of self-governing citizenship based on personal responsibility. In the conclusion of his chapter, Mulé reminds us that progressive, critical, and radical queer voices, striving for emancipation and liberation hold an important place in the movement: they not only espouse the value of political engagement, but also provide the occasion and drive to reimagine sexual citizenship anew, for the benefit of all members of society.

The second chapter of the collection, by Jaclyn Lanthier, tackles the issue of same-sex marriage, which has come to signify one of the most important thresholds for inclusion into sexual citizenship. Titled 'Broadening and Complicating Sexual Citizenship by Applying the 'Post-Gay' Third Way and the Minimal Marriage Model,' this essay opens by discussing the polarization of the LGBTQ movement into two scions, that coalesce around a pro-marriage stance on one hand and an anti-homogenization position on the other, echoing Mulé's analysis of the evolution of sexual citizenship proposed in the first chapter of this collection. Lanthier reflects on political processes of polarization that have crystallized same-sex marriage debates in North America into a struggle between two socio-political factions, represented on one hand by 'traditionalists' demanding traditional marital rights, and on the other by 'progressivists,' radical queers fighting for the abolition of marriage, considered oppressive, homonormative and undesirable.

In light of what appears to be an irreconcilable tension, the author proposes a possible way forward from the ideological impasse that separates the two groups politically, and, finding her roots in philosophy, she focuses on ethics. Lanthier suggests a model that combines Alan Sinfield's concept of the 'Post-Gay Third Way' and Elizabeth Brake's concept of 'Minimal Marriage,' to move political debates forward. Having shown the usefulness of adopting this combined framework to resolve the ideological gridlock on same-sex marriage debates in North America, she proceeds to explore its usefulness in an international context, pondering whether it can be appropriate for advancing the struggle for sexual citizenship in non-Western countries, using South Africa,

Uganda and Zimbabwe as case studies. Drawing on the research carried out by Butler, Alpaslan, Strümpher and Astbury on the struggles towards emancipation for legal recognition, and the multiple paradoxes that are encountered by LGBTQ activists in these countries, she concludes that the 'Post-Gay Third Way' and the 'Minimal Marriage' model can be helpful in advancing their political struggles, despite very important differences in the North American and African contexts, provided human rights education be the essential and seminal first step to guide its implementation.

Sometimes the debates on the legitimacy of same-sex marriage are not put to rest, even if a nation has passed laws to protect its legality. This is the case in Canada: same-sex marriage legislation was passed in 2005, and still ethicists continue to debate its legitimacy, especially in relation to the issue of reproduction. An influential Canadian ethicist, Margaret Sommerville, has proposed arguments against same-sex marriage, by leveraging another contested topic, the right of same-sex parents to have children. The third chapter of this collection, by Olivia Schuman, addresses these issues and is titled 'Sexual Citizenship and Reproduction: Do Children Have a Right Not to Be Conceived *via* New Reproductive Technologies (NRT s)?' This essay delves into debates on the legitimacy of same-sex marriage as they are complicated by reproduction.

As a bioethicist, specializing in the study of the ethical challenges that the science of medicine faces as new technologies emerge, Schuman chooses to analyze the legitimacy of same-sex marriage in terms of sexual rights, as the basis for inclusion into sexual citizenship. Sexual citizenship, she argues, is a status that entails specific rights claims, related to sex and sexuality, bundling together conduct-based claims as well as identity-based claims. For instance, in Canada same-sex marriage has already been buttressed by more than a decade of legal recognition, not only legalizing a specific form of sexual conduct, but also extending marital status to same-sex couples, thus awarding full sexual citizenship to individuals who identify according to a specific sexual orientation.

Nevertheless, debates on its legality are far from over, especially in cases where the rights claims of one group cannot be upheld because they come into conflict and violate the rights claims of other groups. According to ethicist Somerville, the legality of same-sex marriage precisely finds itself into this kind of conflict and thus should be repealed. She argues that same-sex marriage is unethical because it affects the rights of the potential future children that might be born to these unions. Inevitably, reproduction for these couples would require the use of new reproductive technologies (NRT s), which in turn would 'unlink' the direct biological bond of the parents to their children. This 'unlinking,' for Somerville, is unavoidably harmful, because it violates what she considers to be two fundamental human rights of children: the right to know their biological origins, and the right to be bonded with those biological parents. Taking these arguments to their most extreme logical conclusion, she calls for the annulation of same-sex marriage and the repealing of laws that currently extend full sexual citizenship to same-sex couples.

In this chapter, Schuman seriously engages with Somerville's argument, closely examining the main thesis that same-sex marriage should not be allowed because it undermines the basic 'biological origins rights' of children. She proceeds to tease out the inconsistencies in Somerville's arguments, illustrating how she applies ethical standards inconsistently among heterosexual and same-sex couples, also pointing out the problematic outcomes of her position when it is taken to its logical conclusions. Schuman refutes Somerville's claim that all children have a right to have 'unmodified biological origins,' making evident the incoherence of this argument, and proving that this right is not automatic, and that its retraction is not inherently harmful to them. She goes on to refute Somerville's second claim that all children have a biological origins right to know their biological parents, demonstrating that the implications of this right are much more limited than Somerville suggests. She concludes by fully rejecting Somerville's assessment that same-sex marriage is unethical and harmful to children, and thus should not be allowed.

4 Shaping and Constraining the Sexual Citizen in the Law

The second section of this collection examines how sexual citizenship is defined in the Law. The section presents two case studies, from very different historical periods and contexts. The fourth chapter of the collection, by René Hirsch, explores the very first codes of Law from Asia Minor, Babylonia, Mesopotamia, Assyria and Ancient Israel, including *The Oresteia, The Laws of Lipit-Ishtar, The Laws of Hammurabi, Hittite Laws, Middle Assyrian Laws, The Laws of Ur-Nammu,* including *The Old Testament* and *Deuteronomy.* Hirsch's contribution, the fourth chapter of the collection, is titled 'Gender Procreative Roles in the First Codes of Law.' The essay discusses the procreative principle around which sexual citizenship was organized and legislative institutions' understanding of proper gender behaviour in the East between the 3rd and the 1st millennium BCE of our history.

The 'procreative vision' that dominated antiquity, according to Hirsch, probably found its origins in animal and plant domestication: procreation was believed to be a uniquely male ability, and attributed solely to his seed; conversely, women were not believed to have any creative role, were reduced to a passive nurturing function, and conceived as 'the soil' in which the seed was planted. The first books of law that appeared in this period in the East collectively confirmed this gendered order of subordination imposed on women. Hirsch provides a detailed analysis of the laws that regulated sexual offences, revealing how lawmakers conceived of gender roles according to the prevailing procreative principle of the times. Sexual citizenship was extended solely to males: they were considered to be the sole creators of a child, and thus the law granted men exclusive procreative rights. Women, conversely, were stripped of any exclusive access and control to their progeny. In order to demarcate paternal procreative activity with the utmost certainty, Hirsch argues, the law sought to impose very strict boundaries on female sexual activities, considered 'necessary' to prevent women from engaging in any promiscuous relationship.

The books of law clearly outlined gender roles according to the procreative functions of each sex, entrenching and consecrating the normative foundations of the patriarchal family, and eradicating previously tolerated marital practices, such as polygamous marriage structures. For instance, a law dating to around 2,400 BCE forbid the practice of polyandry, which had been previously tolerated in Sumer until that period. Hirsch speculates that the particularly high number of laws regulating sexual offences in the first Eastern codes of law indicate that the enforced norms might not have been completely shared or accepted. Additionally, he reasons, the fact that the laws in the *Old Testament* were more extensive and restrictive than the laws preceding them might indicate a process of crystallization and stricter regulation of the sexual interaction between men and women.

And yet, Hirsch argues, such a regulatory intensification might have been influenced by shifts in the membership of the population for which they were intended. While the older codes were meant to regulate sexual behaviour in the first kingdoms and empires of Antiquity, Hirsch explains, the laws found in the *Old Testament* were written for a pastoral people who lived at the margins of the 'urban revolution,' and whose sexual heritage might have been less 'normalised' and regulated than that of their urban contemporaries. The author concludes that further study of the sexual mores of the last millennium BCE in Eastern Mediterranean regions might shed more light on these legal trends.

The second contribution of the section dedicated to the examination of the Law skips ahead many centuries to present time in Canada, and examines a legislative area that strongly constrains the sexual citizenship of sex workers, Municipal Regulation, effectively circumventing and neutralizing the protections that Federal Law affords them. The fifth chapter of the collection, by Elene Lam, wishes to bring attention to the plight of Asian sex workers employed in massage parlours in the city of Toronto, whose struggles are ignored and voices go unheard. The essay, titled 'Micromanaging the Massage Parlour: How Municipal Bylaws Organize and Shape the Lives of Asian Sex Workers,' is an essential contribution to sex work research and aims to alleviate a serious lacuna in the literature in the juridical space of the municipality.

Lam opens her discussion by making the point that debates on sex work in Canada have focused on its criminal aspects, its harms, and the 'nuisance' it posits for communities. Not much attention, she argues, has been devoted to more subtle forms of regulation that take place in other juridical spaces, such as the legal apparatus of municipalities. And yet a growing number of cities are restricting sex work and using micro-regulation to police, constrain and control the activities and lives of sex workers: local governments use bylaws to constrain sex work and prosecute sex workers, using a myriad of rules that severely constrain the range of activities that can take place in massage parlours, effectively crating barriers to sex work. Lam reminds us that the power to legislate on and regulate sex work does not fall to municipal constituencies, because its governance is the responsibility of Federal jurisprudence: cities do not have the power to prohibit or constrain in any way the sale of sexual services, which is decriminalized and legal. Lam presents ethnographic data collected during a practice-based research study conducted in Toronto in 2014. Her findings show that municipal bylaws have been draconically used to crate barriers to the practice of sex work in the context of holistic centres, barriers that push sex work underground, endangering sex workers and exacerbating their stigmatization and exploitation. She sheds light on the impact such micro-regulation has on the lives of Asian women who work in massage parlours, effectively making the case that these bylaws create barriers to the practice of sex work.

In conclusion, Lam argues that municipal micro-regulation has a very different ideological basis from Federal regulation of sex work, which supposedly is attempting to mitigate its harms and the levels of exploitation of sex workers. The irony, Lam shows, is that current criminal federal laws assume that sex workers are 'victims' and their primary goal is to specifically reduce victimization and the risk of exploitation. Municipal regulation, in contravention of the latest iteration of the *Federal Criminal Code*, opts instead to conceive sex work as a 'nuisance' and sex workers as a 'criminal element;' it assumes that the exchange of money for sex is problematic and should be curbed, conflating the culpability and criminality of the recipient of sex services and the sex worker providing them. Municipal law creates barriers to the practice of sex work in the context of the massage parlour, barriers that ultimately endanger, stigmatize and push sex work underground, generating conditions of greater and more severe exploitation for the sex workers involved.

5 The Bio-political Governance of Sexual Citizenship

The third section of collection examines how the medicalization of sexuality has shaped sexual citizenship, by investigating processes of bio-politics and the exercise of bio-power. It is necessary to provide a short digression in the works of influential philosopher and historian Michel Foucault, to clarify the meaning of these terms, in order to give context and provide a frame to Fasanmi's and Mulé chapters in the collection, which explore how sexual citizenship has been organized through the medicalization of sexuality. Foucault has argued that sexuality, over the last two centuries, has become the entry point for multiple and decentred forms of governance, processes that he has described as a deployment of 'bio-politics' and the exercise of 'bio-power.'[3] For Foucault governance through bio-politics takes place along two modes of intervention, or bio-power, which allow the control of individual lives as well as entire societies.[4] The first practice is 'the anato-politics of the human body,' which is primarily concerned with economics and aims to maximise an individual's usefulness; the second practice is 'the bio-politics of populations,' and is primarily concerned with biology, and is characterised by all practices concerned with health, life expectancy and longevity of a population; it specifically intervenes into reproduction.[5] Bio-power then can be thought of as an 'explosion' of interventions and practices, justified through bio-political ideologies, or 'techniques for achieving the subjugations of bodies and the control of populations.'[6]

Since the 1850s sexuality has been under increasing scrutiny and the object of rigorous scientific study. This has gone hand in hand with a massive proliferation of management practices for its amelioration, as well as a great explosion of systems of control and surveillance strategies. The management of sexuality has become essential, because it provides an entry point for the exercise of bio-power not only into every person's individual life, but also to the well-being of the entire species.[7] Governance of sexual practices is thus tied to the economic

---

3 Serena Petrella, 'Only with You – Maybe – *If* You Make Me Happy: A genealogy of Serial monogamy as Governance and Self-Governance,' in *Genealogies of Identity. Interdisciplinary Readings on Sex and Sexuality*, eds. Margaret Sorensen Breen and Fiona Peters (Amsterdam: Radopi, 2005), 174.

4 Michel Foucault. *Security, Territory, Population: Lectures at the Collège de France 1977–1978*, trans. Graham Burchell (Basingstoke: Palgrave Macmillan, 2007), 243.

5 Michel Foucault, *The History of Sexuality Vol. 1* (London: Penguin, [1978]1998), 139–40.

6 Ibid., 140.

7 Petrella, 'Only with You,' 174.

maximisation of the individual's body, and the overall fostering of the populace,[8] and medical science has been one of the most effective authorities over such practices, gaining ascendancy in the production of knowledge on sex and its 'care.' Foucault argued that these operate at the abstract level as 'speculative discourses,' and take the form of concrete arrangements, or 'technologies of power,' which have colonised our social, political and economic lives.[9]

This section presents two case studies of the bio-political management of sexuality, showing the negative effects that the deployment of bio-power may have and questioning the ways in which the two practices combined have fashioned the parameters for 'proper' sexual citizenship. These have ended up marginalizing without cause a section of the populace, creating barriers to the healthcare of some of the most vulnerable groups in society. The sixth chapter of the collection examines the manner in which the scientific discipline of psychiatry has defined sexual perversion, and specifically delves into its definition of the 'paraphilias,' or those acts that are now known as BDSM practices, offering a critique of the its diagnostic manual. The seventh chapter of the collection looks at the United Nations and the World Health Organization's global interventions on reproduction for the reduction of mother-to-child transmission of HIV, practices that have the 'benign' goals to maximize the health of the world's populations. Fasanmi offers a critique of such strategies, discussing the high failure rates of these programs, and addressing the barriers they inadvertently set and their harmful effects on the most at-risk groups that they attempt to help, mothers and children.

The advent of the era of bio-power during the eighteen century was marked by the emergence of the sciences of life,[10] disciplines that produced knowledge on subjects, and that were equipped with diverse techniques to achieve the subjugation of bodies and the control of populations. These functioned, in Rose's terms, as 'great machines of morality,'[11] working both at the abstract level, by producing knowledge in the form of speculative discourses, and at the concrete level, in the form of programs for intervention.[12] This marked the beginning of the medicalization of sexuality and one of the most influential

8 Foucault, *The History of Sexuality*, 145–46.

9 Ibid.

10 Hubert Dreyfus and Paul Rabinow. *Michel Foucault. Beyond Structuralism and Hermeneutics.* (Chicago: Chicago University Press, 1982).

11 Nikolas Rose, 'Authority and the Genealogy of Subjectivity,' in *Detraditionalization: Critical Reflections on Authority and Identity*, eds. Paul Heelas, Scott Lash and Paul Morris. (Cambridge: Blackwell, 1996a), 298.

12 Foucault, *The History of Sexuality*, 139–140.

among these disciplinary machines are what Rose has termed the 'psy sciences.'[13] Psychiatry was particularly influential in the governance of sexuality because it introduced the first 'taxonomies of perverse behaviour,' making deviance not simply a discrete event or temporary aberration, but a perversion of the moral fibre of an individual, one that needed intervention and treatment.[14] Psychiatry then was instrumental in categorizing perversion and offering the first portraits of 'sexual abjection,' while at the same time outlining its desirable licit opposite, 'erotic civility.'[15] As such, Psychiatry helped to form and presently continues to define the healthy, desirable and licit parameters of 'sexual citizenship,' while inevitably also setting up the contours of abject sexuality, postulating on all the perverse behaviours that should be repressed, controlled or criminalized, thus codifying 'erotic lawlessness.'

In his second contribution to this collection, chapter six, titled 'Regulation of Kink: Pathologization of BDSM in the DSM-V,' Nick Mulé takes on the Scientific discipline of Psychiatry. He examines its bio-political efforts by studying the American Psychiatric Association's (APA) medical knowledge production, and offering a critique of its diagnostic tools. Mulé shows how effectively the authority of Psychiatry has been in shaping sexual citizenship, especially through the production of its diagnostic tools, including the series of Diagnostic and Statistical Manuals of Mental Disorders that it has been publishing since the 1950s. They remain today some of the most influential texts used by medical professionals and other experts in the therapeutic sciences, by criminal investigators and legal adjudicators, to identify and treat, but also to criminalize and discipline those who suffer from these mental 'disorders.'

Mulé deconstructs the fifth edition of the American Psychiatric Association's *Diagnostic and Statistical Manual of Mental Disorders* (DSM-5), to tease out the classist, racist and heteronormaiteve biases found therein. He particularly focuses on the section of the manual on the Paraphilias, which encompass fetishistic sex, forms of sexual activities and practices that APA deems to be 'abnormal' 'pathological.' Mulé interrogates the APA's heteronormative and cisgender notions of sexuality, gender identity and expression, offering a queer liberationist analysis and critique. He buttresses his arguments by discussing at length the works of other researchers who have found little substantiation to the claims

13 Nikolas Rose, *Inventing Our Selves. Psychology, Power and Personhood* (Cambridge: Cambridge University Press, 1996b), 151.

14 Rose, Inventing Our Selves, 152.

15 Serena Petrella, 'Erotic Civility: Normative Monogamy as a Technology of Governance in North America, 1850s to the Present.' (PhD diss., Carleton University, 2008).

that BDSM sex is harmful or pathological. Such findings seem to severely undermine the legitimacy of including paraphilia-based desires in the DSM-5: this diagnostic 'over-reach' is not only unnecessary, Mulé argues, but dangerous.

The author goes on to examine the disagreements that exists on the putative 'harms' of paraphilias both within and outside the APA, debates that took place during the review process of the manual before it was published in its present form, as well as debates that are currently ongoing. He points out that the mere inclusion of such fetishistic paraphilias in the DSM-5 can have labelling consequences: individuals who end up being diagnosed with these conditions, are inevitably classified as 'deviant' and in need of therapeutic intervention and 'care.' Such diagnostic labels participate in the oppression of alternate forms of sexuality, through pathologisation; they contribute to the regulation of sexual desire that serve to further marginalize kinksters and LGBTQ populations, in particular through systemic forms of stigmatisation. Mulé calls for the APA to end the conflation of BDSM with pathology, and demands that all forms of paraphilic and fetishistic behaviours be removed from the DSM, because there are other forms of regulation through criminal Law that are already able to catch and prosecute any BDSM acts that are inappropriate or harmful.

The seventh chapter of the collection, titled 'Bio-Politics in Sub-Saharan Africa: Re-Examining Prevention of Mother-to-Child Transmission Strategies for HIV,' by Abidemi Fasanmi, offers a systematic analysis of PMTCT strategies' 'benign' bio-political agendas and their effects on the lives of marginalized women. Fasanmi courageously undertakes a critique of some of the most influential governance bodies in the world, the United Nations (UN) and the World Health Organization (WHO), who engage in the bio-political governance of populations. Adopting a Foucaultian lens, Fasanmi approaches bio-politics as all practices that seek to improve the health, life expectancy and longevity of a population, and she specifically focuses on reproduction.

Since the discovery of HIV, the UN and WHO have benignly put in place medical intervention strategies that attempt to maximize the health of the world's populations. One such strategy has been the fight to reduce the rate of transmission of HIV in the developing world, but alas – HIV infection has continued to spread unabated despite these efforts, especially in Sub-Saharan Africa, and has reached pandemic proportions. An insufficient decrease in the rate of infection has led authorities to go through cycles of re-examinations of their strategies and numerous revisions in their programming and guidelines for prevention and the treatment of HIV infection in many countries. Still, Fasanmi argues, what appears to be missing from these new strategies is the resolve and willingness to take seriously the fact that infection is taking place in specific socio-cultural contexts, through local norms for sexual behaviour, that impact infection rates. As long as the specific cultural practices and traditional values that impact infection are ignored, the most vulnerable groups in these societies, especially women and children, will continue to be disadvantaged and make choices that put them at increased risk for HIV infection.

Fasanmi offers a systematic analysis of PMTCT strategies' 'benign' bio-political agendas and their effects on the lives of marginalized women. She teases out their ideological and epistemological shortcomings, and their dire and harmful effects on the vulnerable populations that they seek to help. She offers an intersectional examination of the societal norms, the marital and familial structures, the traditional customs, and the moral and religious values of the region, to illustrate the ways in which biomedical interventions fail to address the socio-cultural contexts that shape the sexual and reproductive choices that place women and their children at greater risk of HIV infection, providing an exhaustive explanation of how and why PMTCT strategies, so far, have had such low success rates.

Fasanmi powerfully illustrates the effects of bio-political interventions in the lives of women living with HIV in the administration of PMTCT care. To a certain extent, these programs have been able to provide some opportunity for agency and have improved the survival rates of women and their babies living with HIV, but on the other hand, these programs have made possible the subjugation of their bodies to a set of disciplinary interventions and actions, informed by narrow definitions of 'sexual citizenship,' 'proper' sexual behaviour, 'good' health, and 'desirable' reproductive choices. In conclusion, Fasanmi calls for a critical dialogue for the development of appropriate and sustainable interventions that address the socio-economic, cultural and political peculiarities that these women face, so that PMTCT interventions and public health strategies can better serve one of the most vulnerable groups in Sub-Saharan Africa.

6 The Erotic Dissidence of Kinksters and Queer Outlaws

The final section of the collection explores erotic dissidence, and delves into two case studies about those who inhabit the liminal spaces of sexual lawlessness. Chapter eight presents an ethnographic study of the world of BDSM and the kinksters of New Zealand; the ninth and final chapter studies the film text *Bottom*, an ethnographic documentary that gives a rare glimpse into one of the most secretive and misunderstood sub-cultures within the gay community, barebackers, or men who purposely choose to have unprotected anal sex with one another. These essays provide accounts of the ways in which these erotic dissidents negotiate their experiences of being 'outside,' at times fully embracing their status of outlaws, at times expressing ambivalence. Inevitably, the 'bad' and 'illicit' persona of the sexual outlaw comes into discoursive conflict with the 'civil' and 'civic' erotic subject, the 'good' sexual citizen. The mere existence of the outlaw inevitably calls into question the processes though which its doppelganger is constituted, interrogating the exclusionary practices that have solely given legitimacy to sexual citizenship in the first place, precipitating a reconfiguration of erotic citizenship itself.

The eighth chapter of the collection, titled 'Kiwi Kinksters: An Ethnographic Exploration of the Auckland BDSM Scene,' by Deww Zhang, presents the testimony of twenty-one self-identifying BDSM practitioners in the Auckland scene. They shared their kinky journeys with the author and reflected on their status of 'outsiders.' They offered their thoughts on the mainstreaming of kink, pondering whether this would soon translate into full acceptance into sexual citizenship. Zhang provides an analysis of the trajectory of BDSM from lawlessness into 'pseudo-legitimacy.' She departs for the rise of sexology and psychiatry in the 1860s, which saw the pathologization of kinksters and BDSM practices. These sciences produced the first taxonomies of 'perverse sexual behaviour,' and marked the advent of the vilification of paraphilic practices in psychiatry and medicine first and to society at large soon after. The consequences, to present times, have been dire for BDSM practitioners: kinksters have experienced social, legal, and medical persecution and prosecution, the ramifications of which have included losing jobs and child custody battles, the breakup of marriages and other intimate relationships, the dissolution of friendships, and even a denial of medical treatment for fear of outing if the body presented the marks of kink. Zhang argues this pathologization continues to haunt BDSM, and even though there has been a positive turn in the representation of kink in popular media, it continues to pose barriers to the inclusion of BDSM practitioners into legitimate sexual citizenship.

Should kinksters strive towards sexual citizenship? Will they organize and engage in a struggle for recognition to achieve this ultimate goal? Zhang sets out to establish whether this movement 'into the light' is something Auckland kinksters are interested in pursuing. She discovers that the issue of identity politics is fraught with difficulties for kinksters, because differently from other sexual minorities who are more publicly visible, BDSM practitioners can inhabit an 'invisible closet.' The ability that kinksters have to 'blend in' with the heteronormative mainstream has fragmented the community: not all are interested in joining a political struggle for sexual emancipation and recognition into sexual citizenship. Zhang explores the ways in which Auckland kinksters grapple with the status of 'sexual outlaw,' testing out to what extent they have reached the status of 'sexual borderline acceptable minority.'

Aware of the more positive 'aura' that kink currently enjoys in the mainstream, Zhang shows, this paradigmatic attitude shift is monitored with some ambivalence and caution. The author closely analyzes how kinky 'outlaws' perceive and navigate the 'vanilla' world, and their attitudes on popular (mis)representations of kink, what she terms the *Fifty Shades of Grey* 'effect.' In some cases, Zhang argues, kinksters engage in their own forms of stereotyping, exaggerating the differences between practitioners and non-practitioners, to maintain a separation between the 'in' group and the 'out' group, thus enhancing and celebrating the 'specialness' of BDSM practices. In conclusion, Zhang finds contradictory attitudes about emancipation, and discovers a resistance to full recognition into sexual citizenship, because the status of 'outlaw' would be unavoidably compromised, and it is essential and constitutive to kinksters' sense of self.

The ninth and final chapter, titled 'Barebacking as a Form of Homosociality? Notes on *Bottom*,' by Elly-Jean Nielsen and Todd Morrison explore the practice of bareback sex, the deliberate omission of condoms during anal intercourse between men. There has been no shortage of backlash against this practice, propelled by the belief that gay men should 'know better' given their recent history and the devastation that the AIDS virus waged on the community, until the introduction of antiretroviral drugs. Barebacking has been the object of moral panics, which have added to the demonization of gay men's sexuality and bodies, already the targets of a long history of vilification: what could possibly make such a persecuted community risk the mortal dangers of purposeful contagion?

Medical experts and researchers are puzzled: some have harshly condemned this practice as 'suicidal,' but some have taken a more permissive attitude, and attempted to unearth the logic or function this seemingly irrational recalcitrance might have for gay men. Nielsen and Morrison approach the issue from this second optic, and explore the discourse surrounding bareback sex beyond the initial monolithic view of this sexual practice as 'dangerous' and 'destructive,' to the more nuanced view of bareback sex as a form of communal bonding and a challenge to gay assimilation and homonormativity. They explore various theories on barebacking, effectively extracting from these a grid for analysis that they then project onto the ritualized sex acts depicted in a filmic ethnography, the pornographic documentary *Bottom*. Basing themselves on the practices portrayed in the film, they are able to provide essential insights into this greatly misunderstood subculture. The authors devote a significant hermeneutical effort to the spoken word among barebackers: they discover that the local subcultural vernacular is ontologically constitutive, and integral to the often unacknowledged intersection between homosocial bonding and homosexual identity.

The authors offer the concluding argument that sex is foundational to gay male identity and gives them a sense of community. Men who fuck each other without rubbers are not just 'misguided' sexual outlaws who engage in dangerous sex to get 'high' on risk; their acts deliberately create a new sub-culture, their bonds to one another forge a new community, an outlaw socio-cultural enclave in which, finally, they can feel a sense of belonging. In this sub-culture the true reality of current or impending seropositivity can be transcended: it is no longer a 'death sentence,' and it no longer means the 'end' of their erotic lives. The label 'barebacker' becomes an ontological affirmation and is, in and of itself, a source of pleasure. The barebacker is a new 'sexual outlaw,' a new option for alterity, a transgressive form of queer sexual citizenship, one that openly resists and contests the ever present heteronormative gaze. Barebackers' outrageous sexuality is purposeful, it is an act of emancipation from bourgeois respectability: their agentic transgression allows them to re-invent their erotic destinies, take charge, and create new circumstances and possibilities. In conclusion, Nielsen and Morrison call for a change in the management of HIV prevention, asking that it be reframed in view of the creation of new modes of identity that are organized around homosociality, given also that there has been a significant survival rate increase thanks to the introduction of new treatments. The medical community should desist its facile and reductionist pathologization of sexual risk-takers and consider the ways in which these communities negotiate a sense of communal belonging and intimate friendship.

Acknowledgments

I would like to thank the contributors to this volume, both for their essays and for their willingness to answer my numerous questions during the editing process. Jan Mahoney and Shari Maguire patiently edited and formatted the volume; I wish to express my deep gratitude for their kindness and their keen eye for details. Finally, I would like to extend my warmest thanks to Dr. Rob Fisher, Founder and Network Leader at Interdisciplinary.Net. He is the mind and the engine behind each of our projects, and this volume would not be a reality without his devotion and his unwavering support.

Bibliography

Breen, Margaret Sorensen, and Fiona Peters, Eds. *Genealogies of Identity. Interdisciplinary Readings on Sex and Sexuality*. Amsterdam: Radopi, 2005.

Dreyfus, Hubert, and Paul Rabinow. *Michel Foucault. Beyond Structuralism and Hermeneutics.* Chicago: Chicago university Press, 1982.

Foucault, Michel. *The History of Sexuality Vol. 1.* London: Penguin, [1978] 1998.

Foucault, Michel. Security, *Territory, Population: Lectures at the Collège de France 1977–1978*, trans. Graham Burchell. Basingstoke: Palgrave Macmillan, 2007.

Interdisciplinary.Net. 'Call for Presentations, 4th Global Conference on Sex and The State,' Viewed April 17, 2015. http://www.inter-disciplinary.net/critical-issues/gender-and-sexuality/sex-and-the-state/call-for-papers/

Interdisciplinary.Net. 'Call for Presentations, 7th Global Conference on Persons and Sexualities,' Interdisciplinary.Net, Viewed April 17, 2015. https://call-for-papers.sas.upenn.edu/node/56634

Petrella, Serena. 'Only with You – Maybe – *If* You Make Me Happy: A genealogy of Serial monogamy as Governance and Self-Governance.' In *Genealogies of Identity. Interdisciplinary Readings on Sex and Sexuality*, edited by Margaret Sorensen Breen and Fiona Peters, 169–184. Amsterdam: Radopi, 2005.

Petrella, Serena. 'Erotic Civility: Normative Monogamy as a Technology of Governance in NorthAmerica, 1850s to the Present.' PhD diss., Carleton University, 2008.

Rose, Nikolas. 'Authority and the Genealogy of Subjectivity.' In *Detraditionalization: Critical Reflections on Authority and Identity*, edited by Paul Heelas, Scott Lash and Paul Morris, 294–327. Cambridge: Blackwell, 1996a.

Rose, Nikolas. *Inventing Our Selves. Psychology, Power and Personhood.* Cambridge: Cambridge University Press, 1996b.

CHAPTER 1

Evolving Sexual Citizenry: Developing Queer Liberation Theory

Nick J. Mulé

Abstract

Sexuality theories and the concept of sexual citizenship have evolved over time. Over the past two decades, queer theory has gained ascendancy and dominance in the realm of LGBTQ debates. In our diverse world, rich with a complexity of varied perspectives, new contemporary theories and concepts are arising that challenge long established theoretical concepts and notions. This chapter undertakes a critical review of homonormativity, cisgenderism, neoliberalism and queer theory distinguishing and highlighting the world views of a decidedly progressive, critical segment of the broad LGBTQ movement, being that of a politicized queer contingent. I outline the differences between LGBT s and Queers and the respective social agendas of each group, providing a critical, progressive understanding of LGBTQ populations and communities. Premised on activist motivations, and based on the experiences of the queer social justice group Queer Ontario, this chapter theorizes a new political perspective that is intellectually conceptual, yet practically applied in one segment of the broader LGBTQ movement. This approach involves respecting the historical past by returning to the tenets and principles of gay liberation, re-contextualizing them to take into consideration the multiplicities that make up gender and sexual diversity, and resurrecting such world views into a modernized queer liberation theory. The focus on 'theorizing anew' in this conceptual chapter is particularly significant in an era in which the broad LGBTQ movement is being increasingly assimilated, professionalized, mainstreamed and bent to the political agendas of neoliberalism. Progressive, critical, radical queer voices that are politically driven towards liberation, hold an important place in the movement, not only in ensuring a politicized world view from within, but also because they provide creative opportunities for restructuring sexual citizenship in society at large.

Keywords

cisgenderism – gay liberation – homonormativity – LGBTQ – neoliberalism – queer liberation theory – queer theory – sexual citizenship – social justice

 | DOI:10.1163/9789004392298_003

1 Introduction

The lesbian, gay, bisexual, transgender and queer (LGBTQ) movement, as with all social movements and by the very nature of our collective structures, experience internalized tensions as to mission, goals and objectives, as well as the methods adopted to pursue them. Although initially launched in the late 1960s and early 1970s from the premise of gay liberation (itself an antecedent of the black and feminist movements), I argue that over the next five decades the Canadian LGBT movement has increasingly veered towards a rights-based, assimilationist perspective.[1] Yet, within the movement, progressive and radical elements exist that often feel marginalized but continue to champion the *ethos* of liberation. This self-defined 'queer' segment of the movement is engaged in a process of questioning whether the principles and tenets of gay liberation can be resurrected and re-contextualized within a contemporary queer discourse in beginning to develop a queer liberation theory as an alternative to the movement's current assimilationist directions. This project, similar to the initial modern-day gay liberation movement, first arose at the grassroots community level and is currently in development. Also, the motivations behind such an intellectual project are not merely and solely academic, but driven by the desires of queer activists to articulate our political discourse so that our perspective-based actions are theoretically expounded.

In this chapter I review some of the prominent theories that are influencing the LGBTQ movement and define terminology that play a crucial role in positioning a movement's socio-political *ethos*. I outline ethical principles and tenets of gay liberation that represent touchstones for a modern day queer liberation movement. I discuss today's issues challenging queer liberationists, and as such, the importance of taking up the queer liberation project in light of current homonormative and assimilationist trends. Finally, I conclude the chapter by discussing the potential such a project provides in developing a queer liberation theory, which grapples with some concepts similar to queer theory, yet is informed by a grassroots community movement.

1 Barry Adam, *The Rise of a Gay and Lesbian Movement*. (Boston: Twayne Publishers, 1987), 28; Miriam Smith, *Lesbian and Gay Rights in Canada: Social Movements and Equality-Seeking, 1971–1995*. (Toronto: University of Toronto Press, 1999), 124; Tom Warner, *Never Going Back: A History of Queer Activism in Canada*. (Toronto: University of Toronto, 2002), 43.

2 Development of Sexual Theory and Discourse

Heavily influenced by other social movements of the time such as the black and feminist movements, gay liberationists initially took up the challenge of confronting homophobia by 'coming out,' resisting heterosexism by living their lives as they chose to and contesting straight hegemony by exposing individualized and systemic discrimination based on sexual orientation.[2] In essence, gay liberationists were defining for themselves the kind of lives they wanted to live based on a shameless confidence in their sexual orientation, without interest in assimilating into mainstream society for a false sense of tolerance, respectability or acceptance.[3] Also, Marxist perspectives and the questioning of capitalism and our relationship to it were and continue to be debated.[4]

A new and influential theoretical perspective made its entrance in academic circles in the 1990s: queer theory. The theory arose out of a social constructionist paradigm influenced by the works of Michel Foucault, who traced the historical genealogy of erotic desire in the West, illustrating its complex and multiple articulations over the last 2,000 years. Foucault effectively showed that sexuality, and its related modes of being, are socially constructed, historically specific and culturally contingent. The sodomite's activities, for instance, went from being an unproblematic sexual proclivity of the Classical Greek citizen, to a temporary sinful aberration in the Middle Ages, to a problem of 'essence' with the birth of the social sciences of Sexology and Psychiatry. Since the 1850s, same-sex desires have been framed as a feature of an individual's 'basic nature,' transforming from a simple yet 'questionable' act, to a feature of one's subjective identity. Arguing the contextual malleability of desire, Foucault posited that sexuality is not tied to any irreducible 'natural' aspect of the body: sexual orientation, he concluded, is a social construct, and he rejected essentialism, providing the key insight and departure point for queer theory.[5]

Jagose sees 'identity as fluid, the effect of social conditioning and available cultural models for understanding oneself.'[6] Sexuality is discursively

2 Brian Waite, 'A Strategy for Gay Liberation,' *The Body Politic*, March/April 1972, 17.

3 Dennis Altman, *Homosexual Oppression and Liberation.* (New York: Outerbridge & Deinstfrey, 1971), 37.

4 Alan Sears, 'Queer Anti-Capitalism: What's Left of Lesbian and Gay Liberation?' *Science & Society* 6.1 (2005): 95.

5 Michel Foucault, *The History of Sexuality Volume I.* (New York: Random House Press, 1978), 182.

6 Annamarie Jagose, *Queer Theory: An Introduction.* (New York: New York University Press, 1996), 8.

constructed within cultural and historical contexts.[7] 'Queer,' as understood in queer theory, is critical of identity focused movements, as it values fluidity and flexibility, yet cannot escape being an identity category even if it chooses not to consolidate or stabilize.[8] Over the past two decades, queer theorists themselves have grappled with tensions of the non-essentializing features of queer theory and how it links to other theories such as Marxism and social locations, for example, gender.[9] More recently attention has turned to possibilities from the very contradictory nature of queerdom to using subjective failure to illuminate systemic hypocrisies in pursuit of freedom to the idea that we may not be fully conscious of the true potentiality of 'queer' and its possibilities for our future.[10]

A major critique of queer theory is its lack of applicability in the advocacy work of social movements regarding social change. This is not to say that queer theory does not have resonance in radical, progressive queer movements. Today's grassroots level queer activists understand and embrace the fluidity of 'queer,' both in terms of its varying sexualities and inclusive of other social locations and positions such as gender, gender identity, race, (dis)Ability, class, etc. Not restricting themselves to the non–essentializing notions of queer theory, queer activists self-define as 'queer' in a politicized way, that centres their non-normative sexuality and gender identity as a salient aspect of their being (whether essential identity or fluid experience). Queer activists thus take up 'queer' as a centralizing, salient identity, proudly being different within social and positional intersections, living their lives as they choose, contributing to society's diversity and freeing others to do the same. In essence, this is a form of grassroots, progressive, radical, applicable queer liberationism.[11]

---

7 Nikki Sullivan, *A Critical Introduction to Queer Theory*. (New York: New York University Press, 2003), 21.

8 Jagose, *Queer Theory*, 78.

9 Kevin Floyd, *The Reification of Desire: Toward a Queer Marxism*. (Minneapolis, MN: University of Minnesota Press, 2009), 56; Judith Butler, *Gender Trouble: Feminism and the Subversion of Identity*. (New York: Routledge, 1990), 43; Valerie Traub, 'The Psychomorphology of the Clitoris,' *GLQ: A Journal of Lesbian and Gay Studies*, 2.1-2 (1995): 86.

10 Heather Love, *Loss and the Politics of Queer History*. (Cambridge, MA: Harvard University Press, 2007), 121; Judith Halberstam, *The Queer Art of Failure*. (Durham, NC: Duke University Press, 2011), 147; Jose. E. Munoz, *Cruising Utopia: The Then and There of Queer Futurity*. (New York: New York University Press, 2009), 70.

11 Nick Mulé, 'Queer' in Name.' *Queer Ontario*, 2010. Accessed, September 17, 2012, http://thinktank.queerontario.org/about/founding-ideas/queer-in-name/

In its collective form, queer liberation also has the ability to contribute to sexual citizenry by expanding its parameters. An attempt to stake out one's place in society, based upon a valued and acknowledged sexual identity, is a means of establishing a sexual citizenship. Claims for citizenship are a pursuit of belonging,[12] a means of demarcating a legitimate place in society. For queer communities, such claims represent a transition from a private (closeted) existence, to one that is more public and challenges society to be more inclusive, while simultaneously protecting one's private life.[13] Citizenship can indicate a marker of inclusion/exclusion, the shaping and distribution of economic and social power, as well as accessibility to political power.[14] The public/private dichotomy is extremely complex with regards to the concept of the sexual citizen, challenging at once society and its resident sexual dissidents, whom Bell describes as 'citizen-pervert,'[15] as they often need to oscillate between the public and private, constantly redefining themselves. Regardless of the existence of 'citizen-perverts,' the concept of citizenship tends to be ensconced in the public realm and contained within the traditional boundaries of nation-states, organized religions, and government structures, each with its own history of discrimination towards sexual minorities.

A lesbian/feminist perspective highlights concerns regarding traditional notions of citizenship being associated with patriarchy, heterosexism and the nuclear family.[16] Richardson cautions that Western notions of citizenship status are associated with heterosexism and male privilege and their institutionalization.[17] The effects of these forms of discrimination are a particular kind of heterosexuality, a strict version of marriage, and a closed traditional, middle-class nuclear family, bundled together to form a crystallized version of 'good citizenship.' Provided that one stays within the boundaries of tolerance, as defined by a heterosexist public/private divide, then one will in essence be

---

12 Jeffery Weeks, 'The Sexual Citizen,' *Theory, Culture and Society* 15.3–4 (1998): 39.

13 Ibid, 44.

14 Brenda Cossman, 'Sexing Citizenship, Privatizing Sex,' *Citizenship Studies* 6.4 (2002): 487; Ann Field, 'Contested Citizenship: Renewed Hope for Social Justice,' *Canadian Woman Studies* 20.2 (2000): 80; David Taylor, 'Citizenship and Social Power,' *Critical Social Policy* 9.26 (1989): 24.

15 David Bell, 'Pleasure and Danger: The Paradoxical Spaces of Sexual Citizenship,' *Political Geography* 14.2 (1995): 141.

16 Diane Richardson, 'Claiming Citizenship? Sexuality, Citizenship and Lesbian/Feminist Theory,' *Sexualities* 3.2 (2000a): 263.

17 Diane Richardson, 'Sexuality and Citizenship,' *Sociology* 32.1 (1998): 91.

tolerated. Taylor notes that heterosexuality is directly associated with nation-states citizenship.[18]

Recent trends in sexually diverse community activism have been slanted towards a rights claims/assimilationist stance,[19] such as the pursuance of same-sex marriage,[20] and have sought out acceptance through a normalized form of respectability, adopting precisely the kind of 'citizenship concept' articulated by Richardson and Taylor.[21] Such a concept is premised on 'similarities' rather than 'equity,' the latter of which would leave space to recognize differences.[22] Both feminists and queers have critiqued the politics of normalcy and the mainstreaming of the sexually diverse movement, which equal rights claims inevitably end up limiting.[23] Yet, the political goals of societal assimilation and integration as 'normal gays' are being interrogated, exposed, and questioned because they achieve an imaginary equality and an illusion of progress,[24] as gender and sexually diverse populations continue to experience prejudice and discrimination.[25] The limitations of equality rights claims and gains based on

18 David Taylor, 'Citizenship and Social Power,' *Critical Social Policy: A Reader*, ed. David Taylor (London: Sage, 1996), 20.

19 Matthew Waites, 'Equality at Last? Homosexuality, Heterosexuality and the Age of Consent in the United Kingdom,' *Sociology* 37.4 (2003): 644.

20 Jaclyn Lanthier, 'Broadening and Complicating Sexual Citizenship by Applying the 'Post-Gay' Third Way and the Minimal Marriage Model,' in this volume.

21 See also Shane Phelan, *Sexual Strangers. Gays, Lesbians and Dilemmas of Citizenship*, (Philadelphia, PA: Temple University Press, 2001), 147.

22 Alexandra Chasin, *Selling Out: The Gay and Lesbian Movement Goes to Market*, (New York: St. Martin's Press, 2000), 52.

23 Phil Hubbard, 'Kissing is Not a Universal Right: Sexuality, Law and the Scales of Citizenship,' *Geoforum*, 49 (2013): 228; Nick J. Mulé, 'Equality's Limitations, Liberation's Challenges: Considerations for Queer Movement Strategizing,' *Canadian Online Journal of Queer Studies in Education*, 2.1, (2006), accessed February 17, 2007, http://jqstudies.oise.utoronto.ca/journal/viewarticle.php?id=26; Diane Richardson. 'Claiming Citizenship?,' 261; Diane Richardson. 'Desiring Sameness? The Rise of a Neoliberal Politics of Normalisation,' *Antipode*, 37.3 (2005): 519; Steven Seidman, *Difference Troubles: Queering Social Theory and Sexual Politics*, (Cambridge: Cambridge University Press, 1997), 126; Steven Seidman. (Ed.) *Queer Theory/Sociology*. (Oxford: Blackwell, 1996), 147; Michael Warner, *Fear of a Queer Planet: Queer Politics and Social Theory*, (Minneapolis: University of Minnesota Press, 1993), 82.

24 Shane Phelan, *Sexual Strangers*, 49; Urvashi Vaid, *Virtual Equality: The Mainstreaming of Gay and Lesbian Liberation*, (New York, NY: Doubleday, 1995), 209.

25 David Bell and Jon Binnie, *The Sexual Citizen: Queer Politics and Beyond*, (Blackwell Publishing, 2000), 55; Maya Mikdashi, 'Queering Citizenship, Queering Middle East Studies,' *International Journal of Middle East Studies* 45.2 (2013): 350; Michael Warner,

legal 'protections,' is that they do not extend to the civil, political and social rights associated with citizenship.[26]

Queer liberation is a sex positive progressive form of LGBTQ activism that borders on radicalism, due to its critique of current LGBT assimilationism. In the next section, I discuss definitions of major concepts associated with queer activism, and outline the key principles and tenets of the original gay liberation movement, illustrating how they are bridged with today's queer liberation movement. I also analyze the challenges that mainstreaming and neoliberalism pose to this movement. The final aim of my exploration is to open a discussion on how Queer Ontario in Canada is theorizing queer liberation as a means to inform not only queer activism, but to contribute to society at large, following the intent of the founders of the gay liberation movement.

3 Terminology and Their Meanings

In this chapter, terms are used to illuminate arguments which require some contextual definitions. Herein, the term 'queer' takes a decidedly temporal and politicized meaning, whereas it represents the more progressive, radical members of the movement that more or less find comfort in liberationist rather than assimilationist perspectives. Furthermore, 'queer' is used here as a term that has increasingly gained currency at the grassroots, community-based activist movement level, rather than in the echelons of academic queer theory. Self-identified 'queers' understand and utilize the term as a means of identity politics, both in distinguishing ourselves – from the 'gaystreamed' neoliberal that seeks to reshape itself to fit the *status quo* – to *us* politically representing a pronounced difference that resists and challenges the *status quo*. This latter point also represents the essence of 'queer culture,' a sensibility that questions, resists and challenges mainstream sensibilities towards the 'liberation' of the queer movement, and society in general from the constraints of a highly oppression-based society.

For the purposes of this chapter, the term 'neoliberalism' refers to an economic theory emphasizing deregulation, privatization, and limiting state intervention. The governmental apparatus removes itself from the lives of its citizenry as much as possible, only interested in satisfying the economic needs

---

The Trouble with Normal: Sexual Politics and the Ethics of Queer Life, (Cambridge, MA: Harvard University Press, 1999), 122.

26 Cossman, 'Sexing Citizenship, Privatizing Sex,' 497; Field, 'Contested Citizenship,' 80.

of a 'free' market, which should regulate itself as it pursues maximum profits. Chomsky identifies the key actors and the insidious effects of this new kind of capitalism:

> The 'principal architects' of this neoliberal 'Washington Consensus' are the masters of the private economy, mainly huge corporations that control much of the international economy and have the means to dominate policy formation as well as the structuring of thought and opinion.[27]

The social agenda of the ideology of neoliberalism is to erase any notion of constituency, substituting it with a privatized and individualized 'citizen:' it aims to create and preserve 'equality of opportunity,' or equal legal treatment of all members of society, but steadfastly refuses to recognize that people might have different and unequal needs. Concepts of the 'public good' and 'community' are replaced with 'individual responsibility.' Hence, there is no recognition of the disenfranchised and marginalized, any collectivist effort to better their plight, which is the reason why neoliberals seldom consider the social consequences of their reforms.[28] Systemically, neoliberalism has had debilitating effects on community and citizenship. A culture of apathetic consumerism has been created, marginalizing discourse that includes an ideal of 'commons' or 'the common good.'[29] Hence, neoliberalism has a governing rationality that mediates the construction of the very normativity queer liberationists oppose. The desire for sexual and gender freedom, allowing space for diversity and fluid expression, is one that can be applied to all, regardless of sexual orientation or gender identity. This is at the core of what the queer liberation movement can contribute to sexual citizenship. The intent of the collective of queer liberation activists is to posit our ideas, perspectives and discourse as a sexual citizenry in the hope that the benefits will be recognized and adopted by society at large, broadening and accommodating of what is understood as sexual citizenship.

---

27 Noam Chomsky, *Profit Over People: Neoliberalism and Global Order*. (New York: Seven Stories Press, 1999), 20.

28 James Petras and Henry Veltmeyer, *Beyond Neoliberalism: A World to Win*. Surrey, (UK: Ashgate Publishing Limited, 2011), 70.

29 Kalle Lasn, *Culture Jam: How to Reverse America's Suicidal Consumer Binge – And Why We Must*. (New York: Quill, 2000), 22; Linda McQuaig, *All You Can Eat: Greed, Lust and the New Capitalism*. (Toronto: Penguin Viking, 2001), 107.

4 Linking Past Gay Liberation to Today's Queer Liberation

The gay liberation movement, during its time, operated from an ethical, principled and progressive position that influenced thought and, to some extent, actions. Queer liberation activists and I are in the process of developing queer liberation theory in engagement with the progressive, sex-positive, critical, queer liberationist group Queer Ontario in Canada. This project has involved interviewing academics, activists and artists in the LGBTQ communities with a queer sensibility. Quilting together the narratives of activists involved at the start of the gay liberation movement, academics engaged in thinking through the issues and shaping theory, and artists who creatively interpret them, this project has collected together the general tenets for gay liberation, that include the following principles:

- Liberation begins at the micro level with the individual as the core unit of concern, and provides a macro perspective that goes beyond liberating the individual, to altering society as a whole for the better.
- The omnipresence of heteronormativity must be disrupted by declaring one's 'fringe' (minoritized) sexuality.
- The importance of identity politics in the powerful act of 'coming out' must be recognized, particularly for collectivist reasons, yet never losing sight of the multiplicities that make up the queer communities.
- Winning equality and legal rights are necessary steps but smaller victories on the journey towards the larger goals of transforming the social order and achieving social justice.
- An analysis of power dynamics must take place to re-contextualize all stakeholders and the kind of society we want to live in.
- All of these processes are the essence of liberation – the freedom to live our lives as we choose to.

Although these principles and tenets of the gay liberation movement capture the *ethos* of its time, they also represent a departure point that can be built upon. Today's queer liberation activists are engaged in precisely this process. By forging links, they are bridging the temporal, intersectional, political or social locations: the relevance and significance of these guiding points continue to inform the structuring of thought and personal, relational and communal lives, with the possibility of a new liberated sexual citizenship. Yet the pursuit of such a liberated vision is one that is fought against a backdrop of formal legal rights claims, the limitations of equality, neoliberalism and mainstreaming.[30]

30 Richardson, 'Desiring Sameness?' 521.

5 Rights Claims and Social Justice

In current times queer liberationists are highly critical of equality seeking measures, assimilationist agendas and the pursuit of respectability on heterosexual terms. Centred on sex positivity, queer liberationists recognize equity, celebrate diversity and are committed to emancipation via a notion of empowerment that promotes autonomy and freedom to express one's sexuality and gender identity, and challenge norms which privilege heterosexuality and the generally accepted female/male binary. Placing a queer lens on such a critical liberationist perspective brings into focus ongoing inequities, equality-based limitations and assimilationist restrictions. Therein queer liberationists recognize, and as such, grapple with the tense relationship between legal justice and social justice and how each implicates the other. A critical queer liberationist perspective acknowledges the points of progress the movement has made over the past fifty years, yet can also identify the deleterious effects that have occurred to liberationist principles, caused by some of the directions taken. To this end, queer liberationists critically examine, deconstruct, analyze and provide alternative solutions to issues and laws affecting queer populations, in order to preserve personal and community integrity. Sometimes, this kind of activism takes the form of 'strategic essentialism' in order to assert a collective identitarian stance, while not losing sight of the specificities within the queer movement.[31]

Legal victories that secure LGBTQ rights are commendable, but we should be under no illusions that this represents an end, as it moves us closer to equality in a cisgendered and heteronormatively defined world, a process that can compromise our uniqueness and diversity. It will continue to be important for LGBTQs to pursue legal and social changes based on equity, which recognizes the uniqueness and diversity of LGBTQ communities while simultaneously preserving them. To do so requires ongoing work toward social change, beyond mere legal victories. Although liberation strategists take this approach, we are under threat by the insidiousness of neoliberalism and the desire of factions in the LGBTQ communities to gravitate towards and pursue assimilationist equality.[32] Cracks in LGBTQ community relations are beginning to show, as those more invested in mainstreaming vs. progressive change become increasingly

31 Judith Butler, 'Imitation and Gender Insubordination.' In *Women, Knowledge and Reality: Explorations in Feminist Philosophy*, edited by Ann Garry and Marilyn Pearsall, (New York: Routledge, 1996), 376.

32 Lisa Duggan, *The Twilight of Equality?: Neoliberalism, Cultural Politics, and the Attack on Democracy*. (Boston: Beacon Press, 2003), 140.

divided. As such, the work of queer liberation activists has had to focus on devising a critique that is not only directed at mainstream society, but also the LGBTQ movement itself. It is no surprise that the queer segment of the movement can be perceived as radical, and a threat both internally and externally.

To embody the dual critical voice, as critical queer liberationist activists do, requires the ability to constantly deconstruct heteronormative and cisnormative societal perspectives, and the insidious ways in which they infiltrate the broad LGBTQ movement. These in turn manifest themselves into homonormative and transnormative perspectives. What are of particular concern to queer liberation activists is that such perspectives influence the agendas, goals and actions of the movement, with neoliberal mainstreaming results. Yet this work must incorporate a reflexive approach in which queer liberationists engage in self-reflection and think about ways to best contribute to our communities and society in general. The work of liberationists, if it is going to be faithful to its critical, progressive *praxis* to question, resist, and challenge – I argue – must take on the larger work of social change that transforms society into one that is inclusive of LGBTQ communities, as defined by the multitude of constituencies that are part of it. This larger work would in turn contribute to a restructuring of sexual citizenry, devising new, more inclusive and liberating structures of sexual citizenship, benefitting both individuals and communities, regardless of sexual orientation, gender identity and gender expression. In other words, a liberated sexual citizenry free to be what it chooses without the constraints of neoliberalized normativity, is the larger project premised on social justice.

6 From 'Gay' to 'Queer' Liberation Discourse

What can be considered refreshing is the openness and level of expansive thought undertaken by those on the frontlines of the queer liberation movement. Queer liberation activists are not preoccupied with essentialist and social constructionist paradigms, but rather how to apply their alternative perspective, coming from a salient position of queerdom, which includes both those who essentialize their social location as well as those who are more fluid. As such, queer liberationists today continue with identity politics, but with one in which 'queer' is more encompassing than 'gay' used to be, and continues to be more progressive and challenging in light of where 'gay' has gone. 'Queer' is a more deliberate and distinguishing politicized identity, compared to the more mainstream, equality-seeking 'gay' or 'LGBT.' Due to their strong progressive political affiliation, some go so far as to self-identify as 'queer' over any of what the 'LGBT' acronym represents. Theoretically, queer liberation activists do not allow themselves to be restricted by the far swung pendulum of queer theory that elevates fluidity and an anti-identitarian stance. Queer liberation, true to its history, is grounded in the grassroots, respecting diversity including those who consider themselves essentialists or fluid, whether they choose to label themselves or not.

Yet, within 'queer' sensibility today, there is an inclusiveness of non-heterosexual sexualities and non-cisgendered gender identities, in addition to other social and positional locations. The term captures such intersectionalities because it emphasizes the complexities of difference they represent, and the depth of diversity they contribute to society. It borrows from gay liberation the understanding that our sexuality is distinct, in that it is different from that found in dominant heterosexual society.

Yet it is also capable of evolving, growing, for instance, to include transsexual and transgender people, and recognizing their distinct experience of identifying with or transitioning to another gender, (or disposing of gender binaries altogether). Further nuancing this recognition, is the awareness of other structures, such as race, ethnicity, age and (dis)ability, and a special attention to the ways in which culture complicates their relationship. Queer liberation anarchist writings have been focusing on class struggle, usually from a Marxist perspective, challenging capitalism, patriarchy and the non-profit industrial complex's (NPIC).[33] Additionally, attention has been paid to co-optation of intersectionality (e.g. diversity programs that merely address representation but not power differentials), as well as the difficulties in bringing our private lives into the public realm of work.[34]

LGBTQ communities are non-monolithic, and as such, individual subjectivities vary. The radical, progressive perspectives of queer liberationists stand in great contrast to those in the movement. For Duggan:

33 Gayge, 'A Critique of Anti-Assimilation, Part 1,' *Autonomous Struggle of the Glittertariat*, August 11, 2011a, accessed May 28, 2013, http://glittertariat.blogspot.ca/2011_08_01_archive.html . Blog; Gayge, 'A Critique of Anti-Assimilation, Part 2,' *Autonomous Struggle of the Glittertariat*, September 4, 2011b, accessed May 28, 2013, http://glittertariat.blogspot.ca/2011_09_01_archive.html . Blog; JOMO. 'Queer Liberation is Class Struggle.' 2010, accessed September 11, 2012, http://gatheringforces.org/2010/01/08/queer-liberation-is-class-struggle/

34 Benjamin Shepard, 'DIY Politics and Queer Activism,' *Uses of a Whirlwind: Movement, Movements, and Contemporary Radical Currents in the United States*, ed. Team Colors Collective (Oakland, CA: AK Press, 2010), 167.

> New neoliberal sexual politics ... might be termed the new homonormativity – it is a politics that does not contest dominant heteronormative assumptions and institutions, but upholds and sustains them, while promising the possibility of a symbolized gay constituency and a privatized, depoliticized gay culture anchored in domesticity and consumption.[35]

These homonormative individuals seek to 'fit in,' want to be accepted and respected as equals to heterosexuals and would rather choose to engage with the capitalist system and its neoliberal influences, rather than question them. Neoliberalism with its market-driven, capitalist, corporatizing influences, is affecting the notions of community development in LGBTQ populations.[36] Such agents of capitalism are increasingly commercializing our communities (Pride festivities, bars, clubs, bathhouses, travel industry, social events, publications, online websites, etc.).[37] This includes financial sponsorships and associated logos shaping the message, and crowding out political discourse. More and more LGBTQ organizations are becoming 'professionalized,' increasingly dependent on public or private sector funds, muting their political mandates and voices. Whether through public-private social enterprises, or public funding/project funding, and oftentimes out of financial necessity, LGBTQ groups and organizations need to abide by the 'non-advocacy' stance of their funders, sacrificing their political voice in the process.[38]

The challenge for queer liberation activists is staking out a place in the movement that does not merely rest upon a rights-claims agenda, but is in continuous pursuit of social change, while at the same time resisting neoliberalism and assimilationism, and not losing sight of its critical liberationist focus. Adding to this challenge is that temporally, the queer liberation movement of today is at a very different place than the gay liberation movement was 50 years ago. While the former was on the frontlines of publicly organized activism based on an identity that mainstream society oppressed on all major fronts (religion/sinful, law/criminal, medical/sick),[39] today queer liberation is required to capture multiple identities and experiences and a nuanced

---

35 Lisa Duggan, *The Twilight of Equality?*, 176.

36 Ibid., 181.

37 Sears, 'Queer Anti-Capitalism,' 102.

38 Nick J. Mulé, 'Advocacy Limitations on Gender and Sexually Diverse Activist Organisations in Canada's Voluntary Sector,' *Canadian Journal of Nonprofit and Social Economy Research* 2.1 (2011): 11.

39 Adam, *The Rise of a Gay and Lesbian Movement,* 41. Smith, Lesbian and Gay Rights in Canada, 132; Warner, Never Going Back, 160.

understanding of gender and sexual diversity in its commitment to uphold liberationist values and principles. Yet, despite this temporal difference, interestingly there is a strong similarity with what anarchists theorized and fought for in the 19th and 20th centuries, in the sex positive movement, regarding positive and negative liberty. Positive liberty involves freedom to sexual expression and diversity and negative liberty that involves freedom from oppressive sexual norms and expectations, and importantly how the latter relates to the former is still very relevant today.[40]

7 Developing Queer Liberation Theory

Given the current mainstreaming and assimilationist direction of the LGBTQ movement, the queer liberation project is of utmost importance. Principles and tenets of the gay liberation perspective continue to apply today. The work of mainstreaming LGBTs, and their pursuit of equality, must be challenged and its limiting and marginalizing effects exposed. Queer activists must put forth a counter-cultural voice that resists assimilationist mainstreaming agendas, instead upholding diversity and the importance of the latter's contribution to society. We must be cognizant of the effects of neoliberalism and its attempts at exploiting the LGBTQ movement. Queer liberation is a commitment to change society to meet our needs as we define them, not to re-shape ourselves to fit into a cisgendered, heteronormative society, contrasting greatly with an assimilationist perspective. At the core of queer liberation work, I argue, is the undertaking of a critical perspective that is reflexively engaged at inner (queer liberationists), inter (LGBTQ communities) and intra (mainstream society) levels. A progressive, critical, queer liberationist sensibility recognizes through acknowledgment, decontextualizes through interrogation, disrupts through resistance, challenges through contestation, and diversifies through creation.

How then does all of this contribute to the development of a queer liberation theory project? First of all, it must be recognized as a work in progress. Understanding 'queer' as a politicized umbrella term, that captures sexualities and gender identities and expressions outside of heteronormative and cisgendered notions, broadens the scope from traditional understandings of 'gay' (think male 'homosexuals') and mainstreaming (captured by the slang neologism 'gaystreaming') assimilationist notions. Queers at the politicized

40 Breanne Fahs. "Freedom To" and "Freedom From": A New Vision for Sex Positive Politics.' *Sexualities*, 17(3), (2014): 284.

community activist level, borrow from queer theory in terms of understanding fluidity therein, yet respect that for some there is an essentialist social positioning of one's sexuality and/or gender identity. To this end, queer activists embrace 'queer' as a social and political identity in activating our liberationist ethics, principles and tenets. Queer liberationist activism is underscored by a critical theoretical perspective that engages in questioning, in resisting, and in challenging the ongoing heterosexism and cisgenderism of mainstream society, as well as the neoliberal assimilationism of the LGBT movement, while at the same time reflexively undertaking an internal critique of queer liberation itself as a means of ongoing accountability.

Queer Ontario puts in practice the work of developing queer liberation theory, by engaging in a dialogical process with academics, activists and artists known for their liberationist perspectives and sensibilities. This includes a cross range of diversities and intersectionalities of the various social locations people hold. Deserving of special attention is the input received by senior activists who were present during the heady days of the gay liberation movement. They have provided information and feedback to the work of this project, including a historical perspective that is key to our understanding of the *ethos*. Those of a younger generation provide modern day issues and concerns that challenge us as to the applicable ways and means queer liberation can respond. Insights from ethno-racial groups bring an updated, sensitized approach, redressing concerns that were not taken up by the gay liberation movement in the early days. Trans communities contribute greatly to our understanding of liberating one from the binary confines of gender. This dialogical process spans the generations and various social locations, temporally addressing the shifts from gay to queer liberation – a kind of insight that contributes greatly to our ongoing development and understanding of queer liberation discourse/theory with on-the-ground implications for queer activism. This latter point is important in keeping with the original intentions of gay liberation, as a discourse with practical implications for society in general.

Gay liberation activists of the late 1960s and early 1970s were engaged in real on-the-ground activism with serious implications on their daily lives, given how the society of the time stigmatized them and labelled them as 'sick,' 'criminal,' 'immoral,' and 'sinners.' Although they developed a political *ethos* to guide their activism, at the time it was not an exercise in theory development. At this time, some of us queer liberation activists are returning to the past, given the insidiousness of neoliberalism, the current assimilationist state of the LGBT movement and dominance of queer theory, to theorize the important principles and tenets of what gay liberation taught us, and re-contextualizing it into a sensitized queer liberation theory that is applicable via social action and mobilization relevant to today.

8 Conclusion

Because of the pressures that neoliberalism places on us today, the *praxis* of liberationism becomes ever more relevant. Indeed, the LGBT movement has fought numerous battles throughout its history, sometimes with a liberationist perspective, other times focusing instead on equality, and at other times again adopting a combination of the two political agendas. The focus of this chapter has not been a chronology of the battles, rather a discussion of the approaches the movement has taken, how those approaches were influenced by outside forces (neoliberalism) and how they may implicate our communities (assimilationism). Given that gay liberation has suffered a degree of erosion during the past five decades, the greatest threat it faces presently is to keep its purpose alive. In essence, a maturation process has occurred in which queer liberationists have become increasingly sensitized to neoliberal influences, the limits of equality and the slide towards assimilation.

Queer liberation is a commitment to change society to meet our needs as we define them, not to re-shape ourselves to fit into a rights claims-premised, heteronormative, cisgendered environment. Therefore, queer activists, similar to the generation of gay activists before them, carry forth the evolutionary pattern of putting forth a counter-cultural voice that resists neoliberal mainstreaming powers. This resistance, backed with alternative perspectives based on gender and sexual diversity and inclusivity, maps an evolving sexual citizenship that goes far beyond equality rights claims (i.e. formal legal rights) and engages in a continuous striving towards social justice. By engaging in a theory development project, queer liberation activists seek to learn from our history, recontextualize for the present, and fashion a new *praxis* to bring about a more inclusive future.

This is a multi-level work in progress. Queer liberation activists are charged with monitoring and addressing issues in mainstream society, within the LGBT movement and internally within queer liberation circles. Additionally, each of these levels intersect and influence the other, creating a complicated yet creative context in which the dialectical relationship between theory and practice is constantly exercised. A modern era queer liberation movement thrives in Canada, in its small and fledgling way, keeping a progressive, critical discourse alive and challenging any threats to our diversity and its promise to society as a whole.

Bibliography

Adam, Barry D. *The Rise of a Gay and Lesbian Movement*. Boston: Twayne Publishers, 1987.

Altman, Dennis. *Homosexual Oppression and Liberation*. New York: Outerbridge & Deinstfrey, 1971.

Bell, David. "Pleasure and Danger: The Paradoxical Spaces of Sexual Citizenship." *Political Geography*, 14.2 (1995): 139–153.

Bell, David and Binnie, Jon. *The Sexual Citizen: Queer Politics and Beyond*. Blackwell Publishing, 2000.

Butler, Judith. *Gender Trouble: Feminism and the Subversion of Identity*. New York: Routledge, 1990.

Butler, Judith. "Imitation and Gender Insubordination." In *Women, Knowledge and Reality: Explorations in Feminist Philosophy*, edited by Ann Garry and Marilyn Pearsall, 371–87. New York: Routledge, 1996.

Chasin, Alexandra. *Selling Out: The Gay and Lesbian Movement Goes to Market*. New York: St. Martin's Press, 2000.

Chomsky, Noam. *Profit Over People: Neoliberalism and Global Order*. New York: Seven Stories Press, 1999.

Cossman, Brenda. "Sexing Citizenship, Privatizing Sex." *Citizenship Studies*, 6.4 (2002): 483–506.

Duggan, Lisa. *The Twilight of Equality?: Neoliberalism, Cultural Politics, and the Attack on Democracy*. Boston: Beacon Press, 2003.

Fahs, Breanne. " 'Freedom To' and 'Freedom From': A New Vision for Sex Positive Politics." *Sexualities* 17(3), (2014): 267–290.

Field, Ann. "Contested Citizenship: Renewed Hope for Social Justice." *Canadian Woman Studies* 20.2 (2000): 78–83.

Floyd, Kevin. *The Reification of Desire: Toward a Queer Marxism*. Minneapolis, MN: University of Minnesota Press, 2009.

Foucault, Michel. *The History of Sexuality Volume I*. New York: Random House Press, 1978.

Garry, Ann and Marilyn Pearsall, Eds. *Women, Knowledge and Reality: Explorations in Feminist Philosophy*. New York: Routledge, 1996.

Gayge. "A Critique of Anti-Assimilation, Part 1," *Autonomous Struggle of the Glittertariat*, August 11, 2011a. Viewed on May 28, 2013. http://glittertariat.blogspot.ca/2011_08_01_archive.html.Blog.

Gayge. "A Critique of Anti-Assimilation, Part 2," *Autonomous Struggle of the Glittertariat*, September 4, 2011b. Viewed on May 28, 2013. http://glittertariat.blogspot.ca/2011_09_01_archive.html.Blog.

Halberstam, Judith. *The Queer Art of Failure*. Durham, NC: Duke University Press, 2011.

Hubbard, Phil. "Kissing is Not a Universal Right: Sexuality, Law and the Scales of Citizenship." *Geoforum*, 49 (2013): 224–232.

Jagose, Annamarie. *Queer Theory: An Introduction*. New York: New York University Press, 1996.

JOMO. "Queer Liberation is Class Struggle."2010. Viewed 11 September 2012. http://gatheringforces.org/2010/01/08/queer-liberation-is-class-struggle/.

Lasn, Kalle. *Culture Jam: How to Reverse America's Suicidal Consumer Binge – And Why We Must*. New York: Quill, 2000.

Love, Heather. *Loss and the Politics of Queer History*. Cambridge, MA: Harvard University Press, 2007.

McQuaig, Linda. *All You Can Eat: Greed, Lust and the New Capitalism*. Toronto: Penguin Viking, 2001.

Mikdashi, Maya. "Queering Citizenship, Queering Middle East Studies." *International Journal of Middle East Studies*, 45.2 (2013): 350–352.

Mulé, Nick. "Queer' in Name." *Queer Ontario*, 2010. Viewed September 17, 2012. http://thinktank.queerontario.org/about/founding-ideas/queer-in-name/.

Mulé, Nick. "Equality's Limitations, Liberation's Challenges: Considerations for Queer Movement Strategizing," *Canadian Online Journal of Queer Studies in Education*, 2.1, (2006):http://jqstudies.oise.utoronto.ca/journal/viewarticle.php?id=26.

Mulé, Nick. "Advocacy Limitations on Gender and Sexually Diverse Activist Organisations in Canada's Voluntary Sector." *Canadian Journal of Nonprofit and Social Economy Research*, 2.1 (2011): 5–23.

Munoz, Jose. E. *Cruising Utopia: The Then and There of Queer Futurity*. New York: New York University Press, 2009.

Petras, James and Henry Veltmeyer. *Beyond Neoliberalism: A World to Win*. Surrey, UK: Ashgate Publishing Limited, 2011.

Phelan, Shane. *Sexual Strangers. Gays, Lesbians and Dilemmas of Citizenship*. Philadelphia, PA: Temple University Press, 2001.

Richardson, Diane. "Sexuality and Citizenship," *Sociology*, 32.1 (1998): 83–100.

Richardson, Diane. "Claiming Citizenship? Sexuality, Citizenship and Lesbian/Feminist Theory." *Sexualities*, 3.2 (2000a): 255–272.

Richardson, Diane. "Constructing Sexual Citizenship: Theorizing Sexual Rights," *Critical Social Policy*, 20.1 (2000b): 105–135.

Richardson, Diane. "Desiring Sameness? The Rise of a Neoliberal Politics of Normalisation," *Antipode*, 37.3 (2005): 515–535.

Sears, Alan. "Queer Anti-Capitalism: What's Left of Lesbian and Gay Liberation?" *Science & Society* 6.1 (2005): 92–112.

Seidman, Steven. (Ed.) *Queer Theory/Sociology*. Oxford: Blackwell, 1996.

Seidman, Steven. *Difference Troubles: Queering Social Theory and Sexual Politics*. Cambridge: Cambridge University Press, 1997.

Shepard, Benjamin. "DIY Politics and Queer Activism." In *Uses of a Whirlwind: Movement, Movements, and Contemporary Radical Currents in the United States*, edited by Team Colors Collective, 163–82. Oakland, CA: AK Press, 2010.

Smith, Miriam. *Lesbian and Gay Rights in Canada: Social Movements and Equality-Seeking, 1971–1995*. Toronto: University of Toronto Press, 1999.

Sullivan, Nikki. *A Critical Introduction to Queer Theory*. New York: New York University Press, 2003.

Team Colors Collective, eds. *Uses of a Whirlwind: Movement, Movements, and Contemporary Radical Currents in the United States*. Oakland, CA: AK Press, 2010,

Taylor, David. "Citizenship and Social Power." *Critical Social Policy*, 9.26 (1989): 19–31.

Taylor, David. "Citizenship and Social Power." *Critical Social Policy: A Reader*, edited by David Taylor, 19–31. London: Sage, 1996.

Traub, Valerie. "The Psychomorphology of the Clitoris." *GLQ: A Journal of Lesbian and Gay Studies*, 2.1-2 (1995): 81–113.

Vaid, Urvashi. *Virtual Equality: The Mainstreaming of Gay and Lesbian Liberation*. New York, NY: Doubleday, 1995.

Waite, Brian. "A Strategy for Gay Liberation." *The Body Politic*, March/April 1972.

Waites, Matthew. "Equality at Last? Homosexuality, Heterosexuality and the Age of Consent in the United Kingdom," *Sociology*, 37.4 (2003): 637–655.

Warner, Michael. *Fear of a Queer Planet: Queer Politics and Social Theory*. Minneapolis: University of Minnesota Press, 1993.

Warner, Michael. *The Trouble with Normal: Sexual Politics and the Ethics of Queer Life*. Cambridge, MA: Harvard University Press, 1999.

Warner, Tom. *Never Going Back: A History of Queer Activism in Canada*. Toronto: University of Toronto, 2002.

"We Demand, 1971." *Canadian Lesbian and Gay Archives* (*CLGA*). 1998. Viewed 7 January 2012,http://www.clga.ca/Material/Records/docs/wedemand.htm.

Weeks, Jeffery. "The Sexual Citizen." *Theory, Culture and Society*, 15.3–4 (1998): 35–52.

CHAPTER 2

Broadening and Complicating Sexual Citizenship by Applying the 'Post-Gay' Third Way and the Minimal Marriage Model

Jaclyn Lanthier

Abstract

In large part, sexual citizenship can be defined as a struggle between two socio-political sides; one side is represented by traditionalists and the other by progressivists. With respect to same-sex marriage debates in North America, the struggle is articulated between the position of the gay and lesbian community demanding same-sex marriage and traditional marital rights, and the queer community fighting for the abolition of marriage, considered to be oppressive and fundamentally contrary to its needs and concerns. In light of what appears to be an irreconcilable tension, I propose a model that combines a new avenue, combining Alan Sinfield 'Post-Gay Third Way' and Elizabeth Brake's 'Minimal Marriage.' In this chapter, I investigate the application of this model in an international context, asking whether or not it is appropriate for advancing the struggle for sexual citizenship in non-Western countries. Drawing on Butler et al.'s 'Gay and Lesbian Youth Experiences of Homophobia in South African Secondary Education,' I focus on the African LGBTTTQQIAA struggle and various paradoxes faced.[1] Ultimately, I will argue, the Post-Gay Third Way/ Minimal Marriage model is compatible with the human rights framework that Butler et al. propose. Further, I will contend that despite important differences in the North American and African contexts, the model can be helpful to advance African LGBTTTQQIAA struggles, with the *caveat* that human rights education (guided by the principles of the Post-Gay Third Way) is adopted as the first stage of the model, with Minimal Marriage being introduced later.[2]

---

1 Allister H.Butler, A.H. Alpaslan, J. Strümpher, Gaynor Astbury, 'Gay and Lesbian Youth Experiences of Homophobia in South African Secondary Education,' *Journal of Gay and Lesbian Issues in Education, Vol. 1* (2) (The Haworth Press, Inc., 2003), 3–28.

2 'What Does LGBTQ+ Mean?' by KW Counselling Services, *OK2BME*, Viewed January 19th, 2016, <http://ok2bme.ca/resources/kids-teens/what-does-lgbtq-mean/>. The choice of acronym 'LGBTTTQQIAA' stands for: Lesbian, Gay, Genderqueer, Bisexual, Transgender, Transsexual, Two-Spirited, Queer, Questioning, Intersex, Asexual, Ally. This is one of the more common and currently most used acronyms.

 | DOI:10.1163/9789004392298_004

Keywords

belonging – exclusion – marriage laws – assimilation – transgression – the post-gay third way – Minimal Marriage – sexual citizenship – the African LGBTTTQQIAA community

1 Introduction

The struggle for sexual citizenship, especially with respect to the same-sex marriage debate, has been generally organized into two diametrically opposed poles and has crystallized into opposite political positions: on one side is the gay and lesbian community, asking for the legalization of same-sex marriage, seen as a basic, fundamental human right; on the other side is the queer community, demanding that the institution of marriage be abolished, as it is considered to be oppressive and heteropatriarchal. In order to realize the goals and concerns of the gay and lesbian community, a politics of sameness and of assimilation is advocated; conversely, the goals and concerns of the queer community have been advocated through a politics of difference and transgression. Thus, the debate is comprised of two differing positions whose goals and political tactics have been polarized into opposites. The pursuit of these two radically different positions has resulted in an impasse, whereby neither position on its own is properly equipped to deal with the wide spectrum of concerns held by *both* sides. The challenge for sexual citizenship is to conceptualize (and then implement) a model for broadening citizenship such that the concerns of both sides are equally met, and where neither side feels alienated nor threatened.

In 'Neurobiology and Performativity: Finding the Middle Ground in the Politics of Sexual Citizenship,'[3] I considered this debate, with a focus on two different conceptions of the 'gay brain' and the way in which those play into the politics of assimilation and transgression. I examined the impasse these two positions create, and considered a conceptual model for navigating around this discoursive obstacle. I argued that Alan Sinfield's alternative proposition, which he termed the 'Post-Gay,'[4] is an appropriate model for broadening the

3 Jaclyn Lanthier, 'Neurobiology and Performativity: Finding the Middle Ground in the Politics of Sexual Citizenship,' (paper presented at the 3rd Global Conference on *Sex and the State*, Montreal, Quebec, Canada, October 17–19, 2014).

4 Alan Sinfield, *Gay and After* (London, Serpent's Tail, 1998), 199.

parameters of sexual citizenship, since it synthesizes both political positions.[5] While this model appears to offer the best possible resolution, by combining politics of assimilation and transgression, one could object that these kinds of hybrid approaches merely look attractive in theory, but fail to be applicable in 'real world' situations. I suggested that one way to practically implement Sinfield's model was the adoption of Elizabeth Brake's notion of 'Minimal Marriage.'[6]

In this chapter, I extend this proposal by elaborating on what is meant by Minimal Marriage and the way in which it is compatible with the Post-Gay Third Way. While the benefits of this model are clear when the debate is considered with respect to Canada and the United States, it is less clear whether it would be beneficial in an international context. I will contend that such a model is indeed beneficial internationally, and could be compatible with the kind of human rights framework Butler, Alpaslan, Strümpher, and Astbury advocate in 'Gay and Lesbian Youth Experience of Homophobia in South African Secondary Education,' and the position that Butler takes in his conference paper 'Redefining Sexual Citizenship and Spaces for LBGTI Communities in Africa: Examining the Implications of Uganda's Anti-Homosexuality Legislation.'[7]

In the coming paragraphs I shall propose that there would be certain *caveats* for an international application of the model, given the specific historical and socio-political contingencies found in a non-Western context. In the next section, I outline the various features of Elizabeth Brake's Minimal Marriage; in section three I go on to sketch the general structure of the Post-Gay Third Way, introduced by Alan Sinfield. In the fourth section of the chapter, I illustrate the ways in which the two are compatible and argue that the Post-Gay Third Way/ Minimal Marriage model is the best way to broaden sexual citizenship and move beyond the impasse frequently encountered in political debates. In the fifth section of the chapter, I adopt an international lens and, using South Africa, Uganda and Zimbabwe as case studies, I highlight some of the current struggles for sexual citizenship occurring in these countries, relying on the

5 This third option, the 'Post-Gay,' developed by Sinfield, is referred to by David Bell and Jon Binnie as 'the Post-Gay Third Way,' in *The Sexual Citizen: Queer Politics and Beyond* (Cambridge, Polity Press, 2000); I adopt their terminology in this chapter.

6 Elizabeth Brake, 'Minimal Marriage: What Political Liberalism Implies for Marriage Law,' *Ethics* 120, 2, 305.

7 Butler et al., 'Gay and Lesbian Youth Experiences,' 24; Allister Butler, 'Redefining Sexual Citizenship and Spaces for LBGTI Communities in Africa: Examining the Implications of Uganda's Anti-Homosexuality Legislation,' (paper presented at the *7th Global Conference on Persons and Sexualities*, Montreal, Quebec, Canada, October 20–22, 2014).

work of Butler, and Butler et al. as well as making references to news stories on various injustices and struggles that have taken place in these regions.

In order to see whether the Minimal Marriage/Post-Gay Third Way model has any international merit, I will outline the ways in which sexual citizenship dilemmas in some African contexts mirror North American ones. In the sixth section, I will show that both dilemmas take the form of a struggle between the traditional and the non-traditional, creating a seemingly irreconcilable impasse; I will highlight the ways in which the dilemma in the South African, Zimbabwean and Ugandan contexts are importantly distinct from those in North America, and how the Post-Gay Third Way/Minimal Marriage model ought to be altered according to this unique cultural and social positioning. In the final part of the chapter, section seven, I will make the case that the Post-Gay Third Way/Minimal Marriage model is compatible with human rights educational reform, with some important *caveats*. I will conclude by outlining some complications and provide some suggestions to move this political project forward.

2 Considering Minimal Marriage

According to Brake, Minimal Marriage does away with the legal restrictions usually placed on marriage by the state. With this model a liberal state '[…] can set no principled restrictions on the sex or number of spouses and the nature and purpose of their relationships, except that they be caring relationships.'[8] Further, Brake argues, the state '… cannot require exchanges of marital rights (shorthand for various entitlements, powers and obligations) to be reciprocal and complete, as opposed to a symmetrical and divided.'[9] This means that the members of a Minimal Marriage should be allowed to personally manage how rights, obligations and exchanges are organized within the relationships, allowing for a certain degree of asymmetry.

With this model the types of relationships that would be legally recognized are significantly broadened. For example, marriage could be extended to a straight man and a straight woman, or two gay men, or two lesbian women, or a bisexual woman and a transitioning woman; a two-spirited individual could marry a gay man, and so on. Further, an individual may have more than one spouse, thus expanding dyadic marriage and allowing multiple *types* of relationships including, for example, polyamorous relationships as well as

8 Brake, 'Minimal Marriage,' 305.

9 Ibid., 305.

Mormon polygyny. Additionally, various types of friendships and caretaking relationships could count as 'marriage' under this new framework. Minimal Marriage does not champion one ideal type of relationship over another; all are equally supported insofar as the relationship in question is a *caring relationship*.[10] For Brake, this broad construction of 'care' '...may involve physical or emotional caretaking or a caring attitude;' a 'relationship' requires that '[...] parties know and are known to one another, have ongoing contact, and share a history.'[11]

When one examines the issue of exchange of marital rights under this model, it becomes clear that it would be necessary to break away from the current exchange and/or receipt system (such as being covered by each other's health, disability or life insurance plans, or qualifying for special statuses or benefits, such as immigration status or veteran's benefits) as being a *closed package* that can *only* be shared amongst two individuals who are married to each other. Brake argues that contrary to the way marriage currently functions, Minimal Marriage would *not necessarily* entail reciprocal exchanges of a complete bundle of rights (although, it could certainly be the case that a married couple *chooses* this kind of exchange). Instead, the package of marital rights could be divided up and shared in such a way that it may support any of the various types of caring relationships an individual may have throughout his or her lifetime.[12]

In order to elucidate the difference between current reciprocal marital rights and the system under Minimal Marriage (let us call the former the 'current framework' and the latter the 'minimal framework'), let us consider a hypothetical life situation: Jane has been married to Jake for 16 years. While the marriage has been amicable and romantic, later in their life together they both reach the decision to have an open marriage. Jane is now involved in an intimate partnership with Samantha, who is an academic, currently employed part time (as a guest lecturer at various universities and colleges) in addition to tutoring students part-time. Samantha also lives with primary progressive multiple sclerosis, and struggles to pay her medical expenses due to lack of professional job security. Both Jane and Jake have professional jobs with full benefits and pensions. Under the current-framework, the complete package of marital rights would be exchanged between Jane and Jake *exclusively*. Under a minimal framework, however, because Jane's employer provides health

10 Ibid., 305.
11 Ibid., 307.
12 Ibid., 307.

benefits to whoever Jane's spouse is, Jane would be able to transfer these rights over to Samantha (instead of Jake, who already has his own health benefits).

This brief example helps to delve into the minimal marriage framework in more detail and make evident that rights/benefits configurations under this model can range from simple (i.e. resembling the reciprocal and complete exchange of marital rights between two people as seen under the current-framework) to complex (i.e. dividing marital rights amongst various partners in a polyamorous relationship). This wide range is due to the fact that Minimal Marriage does not endorse any one ideal way to divide up one's marital rights. In a similar manner, Minimal Marriage does not restrict access to marriage, and in terms of the sex of the individuals involved, or the number of spouses, or the nature of each relationship.[13]

3 The Structure of Sinfield's Post-Gay Third Way

Let us now discuss in detail Alan Sinfield's Post-Gay Third Way, before connecting it to the concept of Minimal Marriage. Recapping briefly, the debate between the essentialist and the constructivist positions, with respect to same-sex marriage, is articulated along these lines: the gay conservative-assimilationist side argues that same-sex marriage is essential for attaining full citizenship, with the ultimate goal being '... invisibility and total assimilation into the mainstream.'[14] The queer-transgressive-constructivist side, on the other hand, argues for the elimination of marriage altogether, because it is oppressive to all those who fall outside heteronormativity. David Bell and Jon Binnie conclude: '... marriage serves to reprivatize queer desires, pushing them back into the monogamous couple-form.'[15]

Under the assimilationist model, the needs and desires of queer individuals are left unaccounted for (leading to their exclusion from sexual citizenship) and under the transgressive model, those who have strong assimilationist needs and desires end up excluded. Accordingly, neither side is adequately equipped to deal with the complexities of demands and concerns made by various individuals. I term this impasse the 'navigation dilemma.' In order for sexual citizenship debates to progress, it is necessary to find a model that allows the concerns of both sides to be addressed.

13 Ibid., 305.

14 Bell and Binnie, *The Sexual Citizen*, 46.

15 Ibid., 54.

In response to this impasse, Alan Sinfield proposed moving away from the polarizing dichotomy of an 'us' and 'them,' and instead opt for a 'Post-Gay' intermediary position, which strives to '...build on the diverse strengths of our constituency, to enlarge it, and to politicize it.'[16] The Post-Gay Third Way synthesizes both sides of the debate by assuming both politics of assimilation and of transgression:

> What this seems to mean is accommodating some elements of assimilation (in recognition that 'in-your-face' visibility is not an option for everyone, and very much depends on material circumstances) together with some of the principles of queer politics (inclusiveness without homogeneity, the personal as political).[17]

Presumably the logic behind this model is to integrate the beneficial aspects of both sides and discard their respective problems (that each group left the other alienated, threatened and excluded from citizenship). Due to this inclusivity, this structure should be taken as the theoretical basis for an alternative model that broadens sexual citizenship.

4 Broadening Sexual Citizenship by Merging the 'Post-Gay Third Way' with 'Minimal Marriage'

In this section, I will demonstrate that the Post-Gay Third Way and Minimal Marriage are compatible with one another, and further argue that a merged model is the best avenue to broaden sexual citizenship.

Sinfield has proposed a theoretical paradigm that provides the conceptual components to be applied and used in real world contexts. It is meant to address the concern that neither gay and lesbian assimilationist politics, nor emancipatory queer politics, are sufficient to address the needs of both sides *at the same time*. Further, it implies that the discoursive dichotomy of 'us' *versus* 'them' needs to disappear from political dialogue: such a dichotomy reinforces the desire for a constituency made up of separate groups of people who focus solely on how their individual concerns can be addressed. As long as this kind of dialogue persists, progress will be stunted. Sinfield reminds us that the goal of the Post-Gay Third Way is not to envision '... an exclusive group of

16 Alan Sinfield, *Gay and After*, 199.
17 David Bell and Jon Binnie, *The Sexual Citizen*, 52.

like-minded people, but to build on the diverse strengths of our constituency, to enlarge it, and to politicise it.'[18]

It seems, then, that Sinfield's aims are to bring the two groups together under one umbrella (erasing the 'us' and 'them' borders) in such a way that would allow both a politics of assimilation and of transgression to take place simultaneously. While this model seems advantageous, it is unclear how it might work in practice. Would this mean that we appeal to assimilationist goals and politics in some situations, and progressive goals and politics in others? And, if so, how would we go about discerning which situation calls for the former position or the latter, or when one particular political goal is more attractive than the other? Or would it be a fully inclusive approach where everyone's aspirations are pursued along with their personal concerns and desires?

With respect to the first question, it seems to me that this would likely reinforce the initial dichotomy of 'us' *versus* 'them,' and exacerbate the impasse that sexual citizenship discourse needs to overcome. Those with strong assimilationist desires would not want to pursue progressive goals or politics in *any* situation, and thus opt to further their own goals and politics, and *vice versa*. With respect to the second question, it is not clear how both could be pursued simultaneously. If one considers that the goals and politics of each group are polar opposites, how would it be possible to simultaneously strive for 'marriage' and 'not-marriage'? Can the two positions be reconciled? It might be concluded that although Sinfield's model seems to be an option at least theoretically, in practice it brings us no further from the political impasse of before.

I think that far from being a pragmatic impediment, this model is useful in a practical and applicable way, if one returns to Brake's notion of Minimal Marriage. Specifically, Minimal Marriage provides us with a practical way to apply the theoretical structure that Sinfield has introduced, as well as gives us examples of practices of how this model would be implemented in real-life situations. The ideal of Minimal Marriage assumes that a liberal egalitarian state would not be able to restrict the sex, number of spouses or type of relationship available to its citizenry. Further, marital rights (such as immigration status or disability insurance) could be exchanged either reciprocally or asymmetrically, as a complete or fragmented package. Under this model both the gay-conservative-assimilationist and the queer-transgressive-constructivist's political concerns could be satisfied.

Since the state can place no restrictions on the sex of the parties to be married, gay conservatives would be satisfied as they could easily fulfill their

18 David Bell and Jon Binnie, *The Sexual Citizen*, 52, citing Alan Sinfield, *Gay and After*, 199.

desire for a two-party, same-sex marriage, where marital rights are exchanged reciprocally. And queer activists could be satisfied as well, as they would be able to enter into relationships of their choice without any state's oversight. Though they generally advocate the abolition of marriage as an institution, the Minimal Marriage model would allow them to circumvent the need for a total abolition, as it makes legitimate a wide range of relationship types and rights exchanges, so that the rights of all groups are respected. At the same time, because the state places no restrictions on the sex, number and type of relationships involved, it welcomes all needs and rights of the queer community. Queers, gays, lesbians, bisexuals, transgendered people, transsexual people, intersex people, asexual people, two-spirited people, asexual people, pansexual people and questioning people would all be able to pursue the kinds of relationships that they desire without being denied some of the fundamental rights that traditionally are available exclusively to those engaged in hetero-monogamous marriages.

'Urban tribalists' and 'quirkyalones' are examples of types of individuals who seek caring relationships that go beyond traditional monogamous binaries.[19] Instead of seeking care and affection from traditional monogamous coupledom or marriage, '... their conceptions of good relationships involve networks, 'tribes,' or groups of friends.'[20] Under the Post-Gay Third Way/Minimal Marriage model, these types of caring adult networks could flourish. Finally, because the number of 'spouses' is unrestricted, polyamorous relationships could also be included in this 'enlarged constituency.'[21] This would have the effect of loosening constraints for some queer relationships. For example, a bisexual woman, Danica, who has been in a long term partnership with an asexual lesbian, Isabel, could share certain marital rights. And yet Danica could also be engaged in other caring relationships, which are equally important to her. Under the Minimal Marriage model, Danica could pursue multiple caring relationships and transfer certain rights or entitlements asymmetrically, as she sees fit.

Minimal Marriage, with its significantly reduced state restrictions, addresses the concerns of both political positions, without undermining the other, or creating a distinct discoursive dichotomy of 'us' and 'them.' To quote Brake: 'Minimal Marriage is a law of adult care networks, including 'traditional'

19 Brake, 'Minimal Marriage,' 321.

20 Ibid., 322.

21 Bell and Binnie, *The Sexual Citizen*, 52.

marriages.'[22] It is thus compatible with both the structure and vision of the Post-Gay Third Way; this vision is a broadened constituency encompassing elements of both positions, and thus extending sexual citizenship beyond its current boundaries. Minimal Marriage is flexible enough to accommodate the many demands that would be present in this broadened, dynamic community. Those who desire a more traditional dyadic marriage continue to have access to this marital form, while those who want a more open relationship form, can do so as well.

This model also seems to be in line with the arguments made by Nick Mulé in chapter 1, on Queer liberation theory, in this volume, to advance the progress and evolution of sexual citizenship.[23] Mulé argues that it is possible to recover many of the principles of gay liberation as long as they are re-cast in such a way that considers the various complexities that comprise contemporary gender and sexual identity. By grappling seriously with these considerations, queer liberation can expand upon and thus improve sexual citizenship. Queer liberation theory similarly involves a synthesizing process, one that looks back at the past but at the same time looks forward into the future to consider what could be, or *should be*, by taking into account all new configurations of gender identity and sexual desire of the present.[24]

While this theory and the model I advocate do not closely mirror each other, they nevertheless share strong structural similarities that I think are critical for the evolution of sexual citizenship. The Post-Gay Third Way/Minimal Marriage framework seems like the best option for moving beyond the impasse currently blocking progress with respect to sexual citizenship, as it allows traditional relationships and marriages to persist alongside alternative relationships and marriages. Now that I have shown the ways in which the two models fit together and how, once combined, they are the best option available for advancing sexual citizenship from a Western perspective, I would like to reconsider this model at an international level, focusing on some LGBTTTQQIAA communities in Africa and their struggle for sexual citizenship.

---

22 Brake, 'Minimal Marriage,' 312.

23 Nick Mulé, 'Evolving Sexual Citizenry: Developing Queer Liberation Theory,' Chapter 1, in this volume.

24 Ibid.

5 Considering Sexual Citizenship Struggles in a Non-Western Context: Recent Developments in South Africa, Uganda and Zimbabwe

The coming discussion is based on the analysis of the status of sexual citizenship in three African countries carried out by Allister Butler in his presentation at the *7th Global Conference on Persons and Sexualities*, Montreal, Quebec, Canada, in October, 2014. I shall also rely on the article 'Gay and Lesbian Youth Experience of Homophobia in South African Secondary Education,' by Butler, Alpaslan, Strümpher, and Astbury to provide further details about the experiences of queer youth in South Africa. I shall go on to discuss the applicability of the Post-Gay Third Way and Minimal Marriage model to non-western contexts, specifically making reference to three countries: South Africa, Uganda and Zimbabwe.

Butler et al. carried out extensive ethnographic research on the coming out experiences of queer South African youth, setting them against the backdrop of the evolving debates of citizenship rights in contemporary post-apartheid South Africa.[25] The experiences of these young people reflect the different socio-political paradoxes and challenges that African LGBTTTQQIAA people and communities face in navigating and negotiating their sexual citizenship. Across the African continent, members of the LGBTTTQQIAA community are fighting to gain inclusion into sexual citizenship and be extended the rights and protections associated with it. An emblematic example of these struggles was the organization of the Gay Pride march in Uganda (which took place for the first time in August 2014), during which participants actively proclaimed the right to access public space and freedom to marry, among other rights.[26]

However, despite open demonstrations and public activism, and at least at the policy level, seemingly progressive legislative reform (for example, the passing of South Africa's new *Constitution*, Act 108 in 1996) the LGBTTTQQIAA community is far from achieving their goals. Its members continue to be the victims of human rights violations and experience large scale hate crimes.[27] For example, Ugandan gay rights activist Dave Kato, who had been prosecuted for his homosexuality in the courts, was murdered shortly after being acquitted

25 Butler, et al., 'Gay and Lesbian Youth Experiences,' 3.

26 Chris Johnston 'Uganda Holds First Pride Rally after "Abominable" Anti-Gay Law Overthrown,' *The Guardian*, August 9th, 2014, Viewed June 6th, 2015,<http://www.theguardian.com/world/2014/aug/09/uganda-first-gay-pride-rally-law-overturned>

27 Butler, et al., 'Gay and Lesbian Youth Experiences,' 4.

of any crimes as charges were dropped against him.[28] In South Africa women who are openly lesbian, particularly in rural areas, continue to be at risk of being subjected to 'corrective rape,' whereby they are forced into heterosexual intercourse in order to be 'cured' of their 'disease.' This distressing phenomenon at times takes place in urban settings as well: AIDS activists Sizakele Sigasa, outreach coordinator for the Positive Women's Network, was gang-raped and murdered, alongside her friend, Salome Masooa in Soweto, South Africa in 2009.[29]

The experiences of gay and lesbian youth in secondary and tertiary schools discussed by Butler et al. show that much remains to be done. The new sexually inclusive Constitution and the country's efforts to become a more inclusive and tolerant nation remain grossly insufficient and fail to protect queer individuals: there is a significant gap between protective legislation and its enforcement. The authors documented the complex ways in which homophobia is experienced, outlining six distinct areas that require improvement:

> ...school environment; peer harassment; harassment in the form of homophobia inflicted by teachers and school administrators; school counsellors; feelings of being avoided/rejected/isolated; lack of information; and curriculum content.[30]

Gay and lesbian youth spoke of an unwelcoming and intolerant school environment, in which a pervasive negativity towards homosexuality was perpetrated by teachers and students alike: being gay is 'wrong,'[31] and this master discourse made gay and lesbian students feel vulnerable and humiliated. A participant commented:

> Like [sic] a teacher would say something derogatory about being gay. I would feel...it would hit me hard. It would like [sic] hit a vein in me. And the whole class was supporting her. And I felt how am I, all by myself,

28 Xan Rice, 'Ugandan Gay Rights Activist David Kato found Murdered,' *The Guardian*, January 27th, 2011, Viewed June 15th, 2015,<http://www.theguardian.com/world/2011/jan/27/ugandan-gay-rights-activist-murdered>.

29 Tanya Braun, 'South African Lesbians Live in Fear of "Corrective Rape'", *The Independent*, August 29th, 2009, Viewed June 15th, 2015,<http://www.independent.co.uk/news/world/africa/south-african-lesbians-live-in-fear-of-corrective-rape-1779261.html>

30 Butler, et al., 'Gay and Lesbian Youth Experiences,' 9.

31 Ibid., 10.

> going to stand up against the whole class, and the teacher, who should know better.[32]

Further, a lack of educational curriculum content on queer minorities and library materials on 'alternative lifestyles' reinforced the heteronormative belief that '… gay and lesbian youth do not exist in South African schools.'[33] Given the distressing status of sexual citizenship in South Africa, the unwelcoming and intolerant school environments teeming with homophobia, the disregard of instances of mental and physical harassment, and the refusal by police to properly address the beatings, kidnappings, rapes and murders of members of the LGBTTTQQIAA community, makes evident that much remains to be done.

There are three themes that emerge out of Butler's presentation and Butler et al.'s article that are relevant to the discussion at hand. The first is the trope of 'othering': this is a discoursive binary that sets up an ontological distinction between an 'I,' the normative heterosexual citizen, and an 'other,' the queer, illicit and abject subject. The second theme addresses the issue of 'authenticity:' this discoursive utterance posits that 'homosexuality is essentially un-African,' against the political demand made by the progressive LGBTI movement, which is attempting to broaden the terms of sexual citizenship. For them, all sexualities should be included as 'African.' The third theme has to do with the slippage between legislation and enforcement, and addresses the paradox of ongoing homophobia and homophobic violence in even those African states that have passed specific legislations aimed at to protecting the LGBTTTQQIAA community from violence and discrimination.[34]

I will begin by addressing the first two themes and tease out the similarities in the developments in sexual citizenship debates in Canada and in the USA. Following this, I will highlight critical differences in Western and African citizenship struggles, focusing on the paradox of the introduction of protective legislation but a lack of effective enforcement, and the ongoing homophobia taking place in countries that have made efforts to protect LGBTTTQQIAA rights. Despite these differences, I will argue that the Post-Gay Third Way/Minimal Marriage model is still a viable option in non-western contexts and that it is compatible with Butler's human rights framework.[35]

Given the highlighted differences, there may be a strong focus, initially, on human rights reform and education, and then a transitional shift towards the

32 Ibid., 13.

33 Ibid., 18.

34 Ibid., 5.

35 Butler, 'Redefining Sexual Citizenship.'

Post-Gay Third Way/Minimal Marriage model. Specifically, I maintain that the vision and structure of the Post-Gay Third Way would be fruitful at every level and that Minimal Marriage would likely be applied at later stage (and this would differ depending on the country and its salient socio-cultural, political, economic, religious and legal specificities).

Butler et al. note that there is a strong sense of 'who is self' and 'who is other' at play in the struggle for sexual citizenship in South Africa, Uganda and Zimbabwe. This discuoursive dichotomy can be interpreted in two ways: firstly, it might refer to the 'straight' population *vis a vis* the LGBTTTQQIAA community; alternatively, it might refer to the utterances that 'homosexuality is un-African,' set against the statement that 'homosexuality is a part of African sexuality.'[36] To illustrate this, let us consider the position on homosexuality adopted by the Zimbabwean government and the manner in which it has been translated into law.

Zimbabwean President Robert Mugabe, representing the Zanu-PF government, has warned Zimbabweans to be wary of gay rights activism. Mugabe's secretary of education, Sikhanyiso Ndlovu, has been quoted saying:

> Our Zimbabwean cultural values, which abhor homosexuality, must be enshrined in our Constitution and we must guard against the smuggling of homosexuality in the constitution by other parties and NGOs under the euphemism or disguise called 'sexual preferences' or 'sexual orientation.'[37]

What I have termed the 'trope of othering' is at work here: from the Zimbabwean government's perspective, 'us' is strictly defined as 'heterosexual Africans' while the 'other' is the queer subject, member of the LGBTTTQQIAA community. The two positions are set up as an excluding dichotomy, with no possibility of ever allowing membership to both terms: if one is in, inevitably the other is out.

The general form of this dichotomy mirrors that of the North American struggle for sexual citizenship. In both cases there is a strong sense of 'us' and 'them' at play in the goals and politics of each group. In the North American case, the conservative position wishes to protect its heteronormative 'tradition' and maintain exclusive access to sexual citizenship by closing access to the

---

36 Butler, et al., 'Gay and Lesbian Youth Experiences,' 5.

37 'September 17th, 2010, Lawyers of Gays and Lesbians of Zimbabwe (GALZ) Employee File for Discharge,' *African Activist Archive*, Viewed June 15th, 2015,<http://africanactivistarchive.blogspot.ca/2010/09/lawyers-of-gays-and-lesbians-of.html>.

legal status of its rights. In the African context examined, a similar discourse is used: traditionalists wish to protect their 'cultural tradition,' framed as 'African and heterosexual' at the exclusion of all other claims, especially those made by LGBTTTQQIAA individuals, because they are deemed 'un-African.' Broadly speaking, in both the North American and the non-Western context examined, progressivists claim the right to fight for *all* sexualities to be extended sexual citizenship rights under the law, and protected from harm through the exercise of such protective laws.

6 Examining How Sexual Citizenship Struggles in a Non-Western Context Differ from the Western Dilemma

Since the African context examined points to a struggle for sexual citizenship that in some ways mirrors the North American struggle, as discussed above, one might be tempted to straightforwardly recommend the immediate adoption of the Post-Gay Third Way/Minimal Marriage model. That is, if the trope of 'othering,' (the discoursive binary that sets up the distinction between an 'I,' the normative heterosexual citizen, and the 'other,' the queer, illicit and abject subject) is stunting the progress for sexual citizenship, then one may want to apply the same vision – Sinfield's enlarged constituency of diverse sexualities – for sexual citizenship in the African context examined.

Furthermore, if the rift between traditionalists and progressivists is creating an impasse for the rights of the African LGBTTTQQIAA community, then perhaps the synthesizing model of the Post-Gay Third Way/Minimal Marriage, allowing the rights and concerns of both groups to exist simultaneously, might be warranted. However, we should proceed with caution and consider the important differences in the African contexts examined, which may posit barriers to the adoption of the Post-Gay Third Way/Minimal Marriage model.

There is a sense that what is taking place in South Africa, Zimbabwe and Uganda is a more a fundamental struggle for basic human rights than what is taking place in the North American context. Although it is true that in North America a number of hate crimes continue to take place, particularly against transgender and transsexual individuals, the inclusion of sexual minority issues is starting to be implemented in some schools and the ball has started to roll with the legalization of same-sex marriage. I develop the latter further in the chapter. With respect to the former, consider the following report on sex education in North America:

> Most parents, medical organizations, and educational organizations support the teaching of LGBT-inclusive, comprehensive sex education in schools. National surveys reveal that 93 percent of parents of junior high school students and 91 percent of parents of high school students believe it is important to teach sex education in schools, and that 80 percent of parents of junior high school students and 73 percent of parents of high school students believe sexual orientation is an appropriate topic for inclusion. Parental support for comprehensive sex education cuts across political and religious lines. Additionally, many organizations, including the American Medical Association, the National Education Association, and the U.S. Department of Health and Human Services, all support LGBT-inclusive, comprehensive sex education.[38]

North American and African sexual citizenship movements thus seem to be at different stages, making the hate crimes in these African countries all the more pressing.

Even liberal sovereign states such as South Africa, where significant social, constitutional and legislative reforms have been passed to protect the rights of LGBTTTQQIAA people, continue to experience persistent homophobia and violent homophobic hate crimes. This is important, given that South Africa claims to be a country that is 'unified in diversity,' which in theory follows Sinfield's vision of sexual inclusivity outlined in the 'Post-Gay' Third Way.[39] South Africa, at least on paper, ostensibly seems to satisfy the conditions for Sinfield's broadened constituency built upon *diversity*. However, as Butler et al. rightly note, simply ratifying protective legislation is not sufficient to transform and change the deep-seated homophobic attitudes and traditional beliefs of an entire population.[40]

Despite claims of diversity and belonging for all, the idea that 'homosexuality is un-African' is still dominant. This attitude has destructive consequences for the queer community that can be ascertained in the staggeringly high rates of homophobic hate crimes and violence, including the murders of more than 30 black lesbian women, continuing the phenomenon of 'corrective' rape in urban and rural settings, as well as the emotional abuse and discrimination

---

38 Hannah Slater, 'LGBT-Inclusive Sex Education Means Healthier Youth and Safer Schools,' *Center for American Progress*, June 21st, 2013, Viewed 15th, 2015, <https://www.americanprogress.org/issues/lgbt/news/2013/06/21/67411/lgbt-inclusive-sex-education-means-healthier-youth-and-safer-schools/>.

39 Butler, 'Redefining Sexual Citizenship..'

40 Butler, et al., 'Gay and Lesbian Youth Experiences,' 6.

that a large part of the African LGBTTTQQIAA community continues to suffer.[41]

The fact that the government and courts choose to overlook these crimes demonstrates how the battle for sexual citizenship is far from being over. Further, the slippage between legislation and its enforcement signals a peculiarity about the nature of the hate crimes. It seems that the hate which forms the core of this homophobic attitude is complex and multifaceted, and its complexity finds its root in the colonial past that these countries have experienced. The utterance that 'homosexuality is un-African' points to an ideological stance motivated by political resistance and a rejection of what is conveniently construed as a 'foreign pollution.' Particularly, to say that homosexuality is 'un-African,' is to assume that it is inherently and biologically impossible for African people to be homosexual. Thus homosexuality is posited as a 'condition' of whiteness, an 'abomination' that the colonizers brought with them and left behind, to 'contaminate' native Africans.

Butler powerfully makes this point in his discussion of the 'multi-woundedness' experienced by many countries that have suffered colonization.[42] He argues that the struggle for broadening the terms of sexual citizenship in the African context examined is cast against a backdrop of a past of colonization, and all its noxious consequences, including brutal dictatorships, genocide, civil wars, endemic poverty and sickness, and so on. This complex history makes the struggle for sexual citizenship in the African context importantly distinct from the struggles that are taking place in the West in general and North America specifically.

Another important difference worth mentioning is the fact that the struggles for broadening the terms of inclusion into sexual citizenship seem to be at different stages of development. Same-sex marriage has been legal in Canada since 2005, and the *Obergefell v. Hodges* Supreme Court Case in 2015 has finally resolved the long debate that had been raging for years, giving same-sex couples the right to marry in the United States of America.[43]

Legal processes are at a very different stage in the African context, with homosexuality still illegal in 38 out of 54 African countries.[44] There is a long hard

---

41 Braun, 'South African Lesbians Live in Fear of 'Corrective Rape.'

42 Butler, 'Redefining Sexual Citizenship.'

43 Ariane de Vogue and Jeremy Diamond, 'Supreme Court rules in favor of same-sex marriage,' *CNN Politics*, June 27th, 2015, Viewed January 14th, 2015, <http://www.cnn.com/2015/06/26/politics/supreme-court-same-sex-marriage-ruling/>

44 Mark Grevisser, 'Homosexuality and the Battle for Africa's Soul,' *Mail and Guardian*, June 4th, 2010, Viewed July 3rd, 2015,<http://mg.co.za/article/2010-06-04-homosexuality-and-the-battle-for-africas-soul>.

road ahead in the struggle to broaden sexual citizenship, and the first step is to focus on combatting this deep-seated homophobia. And yet, as discussed above, the healing process that will foster such developments needs first to address the harm and divisiveness that a colonial past has wrought on the countries now engaging in the struggle to make sexual citizenship available to queer people.

7 Bringing Together Butler's Human Rights Framework and the Post-Gay Third Way/Minimal Marriage Model

The impasse that inhibits the progress of sexual citizenship, then, is quite different in the cases examined. Historical complexities complicate the impasse in ways that are distinct from the North American struggles and further, such struggles appear to be at difference stages. Does this mean that the Post-Gay Third Way/Minimal Marriage model has no advantages – theoretical or otherwise – for the African LGBTTTQQIAA communities examined? I contend there are still advantages to adopting the Post-Gay Third/Minimal Marriage model, and further, that it is compatible with Butler's and Butler et al.'s human rights framework. However, the application of this model should be carried out with caution and follow certain *caveats* in virtue of the socio-historical differences highlighted in the past section

Butler argues that the situation in South Africa, Uganda and Zimbabwe should be assessed through a human rights lens, and work must begin by addressing the numerous human rights violations of queer individuals in the African context examined. Specifically, Butler adds, in order to progress it is necessary to implement Human Rights Education (hereafter HRE) at every level in society, beginning at the governmental level and its leaders, and proceeding to the education system and other institutional realms.[45] I argue that the Post-Gay Third Way/Minimal Marriage model is compatible with these recommendations and concerns.

First, both the Post-Gay Third Way approach and the Minimal Marriage model are geared to address human rights disparities: within the LGBTTTQQIAA community, there are groups whose rights are being violated or ignored. Fundamentally, the Post-Gay Third Way/Minimal Marriage model is specifically organized around human rights considerations. Namely, the Post-Gay Third Way approach accommodates traditionalists and progressivists, thus ensuring

45 Butler, 'Redefining Sexual Citizenship.'

that *the rights of both groups* are addressed and respected. Minimal Marriage is also deeply concerned with human rights and the equal distribution of such rights for upholding socio-political justice.

Since Minimal Marriage reduces the restrictions that the state can place on the direction of sexual desire, the range of gender identity, the number of spouses, and the types of relationships permissible, a greater number of individuals' rights can be incorporated into the legal system. In other words, both the Post-Gay Third Way and Minimal Marriage approaches encourage a system that accepts a larger spectrum of genders identities, sexual orientations and relationships, and facilitate access to rights and services in a manner that is horizontal and unrestrictive to all. By bringing together the polar opposite political positions of the traditionalist and progressive stances under one umbrella, this model strives to ensure that the rights of neither side are violated, undermined or ignored.[46] Given that the impetus of this model is the full realization of human rights for all, it is in line with Butler's and Butler et al.'s recommendations that human rights be the first area of concern in advancing queer rights activism in the African contexts examined. Second, the Post-Gay Third Way/Minimal Marriage model is also compatible with HRE and a restructuring of the education system for sexual inclusivity, in the sense that nothing in this model would create a barrier to the institutionalization of these kinds of programs.

An important issue for consideration is at what point it would be best to implement such programming and the manner in which it would unfold. Given the historical contingencies and complexities that make the African LGBTTTQQIAA struggles for sexual citizenship taken into consideration unique, the first area of action might indeed focus on HRE. This would mean that instead of starting with marriage reform in the legislature as the first step, by implementing a Minimal Marriage model in Marriage, Divorce and Family Law, efforts would instead focus on the creation of policies and programs to combat the deep-seated homophobic attitudes present in these societies, and creating an integrated HRE education in every institutional realm, including the education, health and government system.

This would include providing up-to-date health information and sexual education.[47] I add that such education would be augmented by taking as its foundational principles of the Post-Gay Third Way, diversity and tolerance. Additionally, education efforts might further be augmented by another important

46 No model, of course, can ever fully guarantee this. This is why it is of outmost importance to return to this issue time and again, a process to which I allude to in the conclusion of this chapter.

47 Butler, 'Redefining Sexual Citizenship.'

principle at the heart of the Minimal Marriage model, the ethics of care, which would broaden appreciation and acceptance of all forms of caring relationships.

8 Conclusion: Final Thoughts and Further Concerns for Consideration

While I think the Post-Gay Third Way/Minimal Marriage model has advantages for advancing the struggle for sexual citizenship both with respect to North American and African communities (and by extension, the larger global context), I want to conclude this chapter by highlighting some complications, gray areas, and directions for future research.

The first complication I wish to flag relates to the nature of care inherent in Minimal Marriage. Minimal Marriage does not endorse any one ideal type of relationship; instead, it holds that all types of relationships (heterosexual, same-sex, polyamorous, pansexual, polygamous, quirkyalones etc.) are equally legitimate, so long as they all comprise of caring adult relationships.[48] Let us be reminded of the fact that Brake defines 'care' as involving a physical and/or emotional caring attitude, defined as 'an attitude of concern for a particular other.'[49]

Three issues arise from this type of consideration. First, in the context of Minimal Marriage and sexual citizenship a detailed understanding of what care is and what caring relationships consist of is required; second, moral education courses in high schools should dedicate a portion of the curriculum to the ethics of care and caring relationships; third sex education should similarly concern itself in emphasizing the importance of care in all relationships.

Another question that is necessary to confront is whether or not a liberal state is required to implement the Post-Gay Third Way/Minimal Marriage model and the implications for this consideration. Answering this question falls beyond the scope of this paper, though it is a critical part of assessing Minimal Marriage; accordingly, I wish to flag this question as an area that needs development and consideration.

It may be that a liberal state is necessary, and, if this is the case, this may discourage the use of the Post-Gay Third Way/Minimal Marriage model at an international level. Further, it should be noted that simply having a liberal

48 Brake, 'Minimal Marriage,' 320.

49 Ibid., 307.

state does not guarantee that equal rights are respected. As in the case of South Africa, a liberal state may codify in law the protection against discrimination for all, and yet allow homophobia and homophobic hate crimes to continue at alarming rates. Further, the fact that there are persistent homophobic and transphobic hate crimes occurring in liberal North American states indicates that perhaps the Post-Gay Third Way/Minimal Marriage model is *not enough*. While it may help bridge the gap between traditionalists and progressivists, it is not sufficient in itself in addressing hate crimes and homo/transphobic attitudes.

One might be tempted to say that the Post-Gay Third Way/Minimal Marriage model can function well in an ideal world, but fails to be applicable in the real world. This discrepancy between ideal and non-ideal worlds is what makes theorists of oppression suspicious of liberalism.[50] And while theorists of liberalism and theorists of oppression tend to work in parallel, perhaps one implication of this discussion is that the two fields ought to actively engage with one another in a manner that acts as a constraint on the other, and *vice versa*.

These are just some of many complications that arise when the Post-Gay Third Way/Minimal Marriage model is seriously considered in respect to advancing and broadening sexual citizenship debates. In sum, I have argued that despite differences between the North American and the African dilemmas about sexual citizenship rights, the Post-Gay Third Way/Minimal Marriage model can still be beneficial for South African, Ugandan and Zimbabwean LGBTTTQQIAA communities. Specifically, I showed how this model is compatible with the human rights framework Butler et al. have discussed and the educational reform Butler advocated.[51] The fact that the Post-Gay Third Way/Minimal Marriage model enables progress for sexual citizenship does not entail that *all* the needs and concerns of every group will be addressed. It also does not necessarily bring about the eradication of hate crimes, homophobic and transphobic attitudes, and discrimination. Nevertheless, given the current stalemate between traditionalists and progressivists, the Post-Gay Third Way/Minimal Marriage model provides the best avenue for advancing sexual citizenship by synthesizing the goals of both political sides.

However, if the Post-Gay Third Way/Minimal Marriage model were implemented, it would be necessary to question who remains at risk of marginalization in this new model. Perhaps, as José Esteban Muñoz urges, an 'infusion

50 Ibid., 303.

51 Butler, et al., 'Gay and Lesbian Youth Experiences,' 24; Butler, 'Redefining Sexual Citizenship.'

of utopianism' is required for queer politics: the Post-Gay Third Way/Minimal Marriage model provides *a critique of what currently is* while offering *a vision for what could be*, by combining the positive elements of assimilation and transgression, moving beyond the impasse currently experienced in the debates for broadening of sexual citizenship rights.[52]

Bibliography

African Activist Archive. 'Lawyers of Gays and Lesbians of Zimbabwe (GALZ) Employee File for Discharge.' Viewed June 15th, 2015. http://africanactivistarchive.blogspot.ca/2010/09/lawyers-of-gays-and-lesbians-of.html.>

Bell, David and Jon Binnie. *The Sexual Citizen: Queer Politics and Beyond*. Cambridge: Polity Press, 2000.

Brake, Elizabeth. 'Minimal Marriage: What Political Liberalism Implies for Marriage Law.' *Ethics* 120 (2010): 302–337.

Braun, Tanya. 'South African Lesbians Live in Fear of "Corrective Rape".' *The Independent*. August 29th, 2009. Viewed June 15th, 2015.http://www.independent.co.uk/news/world/africa/south-african-lesbians-live-in-fear-of-corrective-rape-1779261.html>.

Butler, Allister. 'Redefining Sexual Citizenship and Spaces for LBGT I Communities in Africa: Examining the Implications of Uganda's Anti-Homosexuality Legislation.' Paper presented at the *7th Global Conference on Persons and Sexualities*, Montreal, Quebec, Canada. October 20–22, 2014.

Butler, Allister H., A.H., Alpaslan, J., Strümpher, and Gaylor, Astbury. 'Gay and Lesbian Youth Experiences of Homophobia in South African Secondary Education.' *Journal of Gay and Lesbian Issues in Education* 1, 2 (2003): 3–28.

Cossman, Brenda. 'Sexing Citizenship, Privatizing Sex.' *Citizenship Studies* 6, 4 (2002): 483–506.

KW Counselling Services. 'What Does LGBTQ+ Mean?.' Viewed January 19th, 2016. http://ok2bme.ca/resources/kids-teens/what-does-lgbtq-mean/.

Gevisser, Mark. 'Homosexuality and the Battle for Africa's Soul.' *Mail and Guardian*, June 4th, 2010. Viewed May 5, 2015.<http://mg.co.za/article/2010-06-04-homosexuality-and-the-battle-for-africas-soul>.

Johnston, Chris. 'Uganda Holds First Pride Rally after 'Abominable' Anti-Gay Law Overthrown.' *The Guardian*. August 9th, 2014. Viewed June 6th, 2015. <http://www.theguardian.com/world/2014/aug/09/uganda-first-gay-pride-rally-law-overturned>.

52 Bell and Binnie, *The Sexual Citizen*, 50.

Phelan, Shane. *Sexual Strangers: Gays, Lesbians and the Dilemmas of Citizenship* (2001). Philadelphia: Temple University Press, 2001.

Richardson, Diane. 'Constructing Sexual Citizenship: Theorizing Sexual Rights.' *Critical Social Policy 20, 1* (2000): 105–135.

Rice, Xan. 'Ugandan Gay Rights Activist David Kato found Murdered.' *The Guardian*. January 27th, 2011, Viewed June 15th, 2015.<http://www.theguardian.com/world/2011/jan/27/ugandan-gay-rights-activist-murdered>.

Sinfield, Alan. *Gay and After*. London: Serpent's Tail, 1998.

Slater, Hannah. 'LGBT-Inclusive Sex Education Means Healthier and Safer Schools.' *Center for American Progress*. June 21st, 2013, Viewed 15th, 2015.<https://www.americanprogress.org/issues/lgbt/news/2013/06/21/67411/lgbt-inclusive-sex-education-means-healthier-youth-and-safer-schools/>.

CHAPTER 3

Sexual Citizenship and Reproduction: Do Children Have a Right Not to Be Conceived *via* New Reproductive Technologies (NRT s)?

Olivia Schuman

Abstract

Sexual citizenship is a status entailing certain rights claims, some of which are sanctioned and recognized by the state. Specifically, it pertains to rights that are related to sex and sexuality, including conduct-based claims and identity-based claims. The claim to the legitimacy of same-sex marriage can be understood in terms of sexual rights and sexual citizenship. The exclusion from the ability to have a legally recognized marriage because of one's sexual orientation is often argued to be an exclusion from full sexual citizenship. When one's sexual rights are not recognized or supported by the state or society at large, then one's ability to enjoy the privileges of a fully-recognized sexual citizenship is impeded. Sometimes rights claims are not legitimate, or they cannot be upheld because they conflict with or violate the rights claims of others. One such argument, about the legitimacy of not upholding same-sex right's claims to marriage, is put forward by Ethicist Margaret Somerville. Somerville argues that same-sex marriage is unethical because it inevitably supports the 'unlinking' of the child-parent biological bond. This is because the formation of a family by a same-sex couple often requires the use of new reproductive technologies (NRTs), which can result in children lacking a full biological bond to their legal parents. This 'unlinking' of the child-parent biological bond results in harm to children, by violating what Somerville considers two of their fundamental human rights: their right to know their biological parents, and the right to be bonded with those biological parents. Therefore, she concludes, same-sex marriage should not be permitted. In this chapter, I show the weakness of her arguments by refuting that new reproductive technologies (NRT s) violate children's rights. I go on to prove that people do not have a right to unmodified biological origins nor a right to know their biological parents, fully rejecting Somerville's claim that same-sex marriage is unethical and should be banned.

 | DOI:10.1163/9789004392298_005

Keywords

new reproductive technologies – reproductive and sexual rights – sexual citizenship – children's rights – same-sex marriage – family making – bionormativity

1 Introduction

Sexual citizenship, as understood by Diane Richardson, is a status entailing certain rights claims, some of which are sanctioned and recognized by the state.[1] It refers particularly to rights that are related to sex and sexuality, including conduct-based claims (e.g. the right to have sex with a person of the same sex, without fear of criminal prosecution) and identity-based claims (i.e. the right to be a same-sex 'spouse' in civil union legislation).[2] The claim to the legitimacy of same-sex marriage is often understood in terms of sexual rights and sexual citizenship. The exclusion from the ability to have a legally recognized marriage, because of one's sexual orientation, is often argued to be an exclusion from full sexual citizenship.[3] When one's sexual rights are not recognized or supported by the state or society at large, then one's ability to enjoy the privileges of a fully-recognized sexual citizenship is impeded.

There may be good reasons for not upholding someone's claims to sexual rights. For example, their claims may not legitimately be a rights-claims (e.g. a claim to be able to have sex in public) or their rights might come in conflict with someone else's rights claims (e.g., a right not to be discriminated against on the basis of one's sexual orientation *vs.* a right to deny certain forms of religious membership to those of particular sexual orientations or genders). One such argument, about the legitimacy of not upholding same-sex right's claims to marriage, is put forward by Ethicist Margaret Somerville.[4] Margaret Somerville is one of Canada's eminent public intellectuals on bioethical and legal issues, including reproductive technologies, human rights in healthcare, and

1 Diane Richardson, 'Constructing Sexual Citizenship: Theorizing Sexual Rights', *Critical Social Policy* 20 (2000): 107.

2 Ibid.

3 Shane Phelan, *Sexual Strangers: Gays, Lesbians, and Dilemmas of Citizenship* (Temple University Press, 2001), 12–18.

4 Margaret Somerville, 'Children's Human Rights and Unlinking Child-Parent Biological Bonds with Adoption, Same-Sex Marriage and New Reproductive Technologies', *Journal of Family Studies* 13 (2007):179–201.

euthanasia. She is a full professor in both faculties of Law and Medicine at McGill University, and she is the founding director of the McGill Centre for Medicine, Ethics and Law.[5]

Somerville argues against same-sex marriage, claiming that it is unethical because it inevitably results in the unlinking of the child-parent biological bond. For Somerville the biological bond to the child *must originate from each parent.* Family formation by a same-sex couple might take place with the use of new reproductive technologies (NRTs), or it may not. To form a family through procreation, same-sex couples must resort to techniques that inevitably compromise the *double* biological bond of the parents to their child. For example, a lesbian couple may choose to get one partner impregnated by a family friend, or an unknown sperm donor; a gay couple might choose in vitro fertilization, using one of the partner's sperm to impregnate a surrogate mother. Alternatively, a same-sex couple may choose non-kin adoption as their means of family-formation, which would result in their child having no biological connections to his or her social parents. Regardless of the reproductive technique adopted, the children born from these relationships inevitably lack a *full* biological bond to both their social parents. When this unlinking occurs, Somerville argues, children are harmed, because two of their fundamental human rights are violated. These are: their right to know each biological parent, and the right to bond with both of them. Taking this line of argument to its furthest logical end, Somerville concludes that same-sex marriage should not be permitted.

Thus, Somerville is suggesting that the harm of this unlinking is significant enough to outweigh the goods which same-sex couples would access if they had full sexual citizenship status. For Somerville, the rights of procreation, sexuality and marriage are interdependent, such that if a person lacks a legitimate rights claim to one of these elements, their claims to the other elements must also be called into question. Other writers have written replies to Somerville's argument, but I hope to provide insight that gives greater focus on the sexual citizenship that is denied to same-sex couples on her account, particularly in light of the weak evidence she provides for the goods of parent-child genetic relatedness.[6]

5 McGill University, Faculty of Law Listings, viewed on 18 April, 2016, https://www.mcgill.ca/law/about/profs/somerville-margaret

6 Simon Woodcock, 'Five Reasons why Margaret Somerville is Wrong about Same-Sex Marriage and the Rights of Children', *Dialogue* 48 (2009): 867–887; Timothy F. Murphy, 'Same-Sex Marriage: Not a Threat to Marriage or Children', *Journal of Social Philosophy* 42.3 (2011): 288–304.

This chapter is organized into six sections. In the next section, I provide a brief description of Somerville's claims about the ways in which access to NRTs is both essential to same-sex marriage recognition and a tool that undermines basic 'biological origins rights.' In the third section of the chapter, I give a brief overview of Somerville's main thesis that same-sex marriage should not be allowed in virtue of the way that it undermines basic 'biological origins rights.' I will then discuss how she applies her view inconsistently for different couples, and I will point out some of the problematic outcomes of her thesis. The fourth section is divided into two subsections; the first discusses the author's claim that all children have a biological origins right to have 'unmodified biological origins.' I will argue that this claim is incoherent, and that children *do not* have this right. The second subsection discusses the author's second claim that all children have a biological origins right to know their biological parents. I will demonstrate that the implications of this right are much more limited than the author suggests. I conclude by providing a recapitulation of all arguments made in rejection to Somerville's assessment that same-sex marriage should not be allowed.

2 A Close Investigation of Somerville's Arguments

In this section, I provide a close analysis of the author's initial claims, which relate to marriage. She opens her discussion by considering its meaning and exploring its relationship to reproduction. If same-sex couples are permitted to marry, then same-sex couples should be given all the same rights that opposite-sex couples have that are essential to marriage. To deny them such rights once they marry would be to discriminate on the basis of sexual orientation, which Somerville thinks is unacceptable.[7] Marriage, according to the Universal Declaration of Human Rights, is a 'compound right.'[8] This means the right is composed of two parts: it is both the right to make a government sanctioned, public declaration of commitment to another person, and the right to form a family. The two rights are intertwined. Somerville considers these two rights to be *essential* to marriage.[9] That is, if one lacks rights that are *essential*

7 Margaret Somerville, 'The Ethical Imagination: Journeys of the Human Spirit', *Massey Lecture Series* (Toronto: House of Anansi Press, 2006).

8 UN General Assembly, *Universal Declaration of Human Rights*, 10 December, 1948, 217 A (III), Article 16.

9 Somerville, 'Children's Human Rights', 189.

to marriage, then one's right to marriage has not been fully recognized or is prevented from being fully exercised.[10]

Let us take a moment to explore an example, the right to vote, to clarify how compound rights function. If all citizens in a society were given the right to vote, but to be able to cast one's vote one had first to pay $100, then anyone who could not afford this fee would be prevented from exercising her right to vote. Then, it is *essential* to the right to vote that any physical and financial barriers to voting be removed. However, an *inessential* right vis-à-vis voting might be the right to a fair trial. Although this right would co-exist with the right to vote, it would not directly play a crucial role in whether one could exercise one's right to vote. Likewise, an *inessential* right vis-à-vis marriage might be the right to be free of arbitrary arrest. If this right is violated, it would not necessarily impact the recognition of one's marriage rights. Somerville focuses her argument on the latter *essential* right: the right to form a family.

The right to form a family gives members of a couple the right to have children that will be recognized by the state as belonging to them. According to Somerville, an essential component of this right is access to the means of having children, as having the right to form a family but being unable to exercise this right would make the right to form a family 'meaningless.'[11] However, since same-sex couples cannot conceive children 'naturally' (i.e., through gestation, following heterosexual insemination, without additional assistance), then it should follow that the state has an obligation to guarantee this opportunity to all couples, including same-sex couples, which is only possible through the use of NRT s.[12] If the state were to provide same-sex couples the right to marry, but not guarantee them the right to form a family through the use of NRT s, then the state would fail to uphold one of the necessary compound rights of marriage.

However, although the state could ensure that all these rights are upheld, the implications that arise from using NRT s are so harmful, according to Somerville, that they justify barring same-sex couples from marriage entirely. NRT s often involve the use of donated gametes (sperm and ova), techniques such as in vitro fertilization (IVF), artificial insemination by a donor (AID), or the

10 Woodcock takes issue with this, and denies that protecting the right to procreate is essential to marriage: 'with so many deviations from the standard of marriage serving a uniquely procreative function, it is not obvious that this function is an inherent feature of marriage;' see: Woodcock, 'Five Reasons Why', 871. I will, however, grant Somerville's assumption.

11 Somerville, 'Children's Human Rights', 189.

12 Ibid.

participation of a surrogate. Many companies offering NRT s strongly advocate anonymity for their donors for 'commercial reasons.'[13] Thus, the child emerging from these unions, which Somerville disparagingly terms 'experiments,' often does not know his or her biological origin.[14] Half or all of the child's genes might come from an anonymous donor, or from a donor that the child will not be raised by.

As the children born through NRT s grow older, Somerville argues, many of them begin to have difficulties with coming to terms with who they are, who their ancestors were, and who their 'real' parents are. Such uncertainty leads them to feel like 'genetic orphans' and to feel a great sense of loss at missing some of the pieces of what makes them who they are.[15]

The author contends that this situation is particularly problematic because the erasure of the knowledge of their biological origins is premeditated and intentional—it is not accidental. This situation is more serious than the case, for instance, in which a genetic mother is uncertain or knows little about the man who fathered her child. When NRT s are used to reproduce, the anonymity of the donor is not due to chance, but to deliberate choice. The consequence for the child then will be having unidentifiable and irretrievable biological origins.

These concerns arise in part, Somerville points out, because the advantages of NRT s tend to focus almost exclusively on the benefits which they bring to the individual or couple that desires children. The future harms or benefits to the conceived child are rarely contemplated or taken into account. Children resulting from NRT s have the additional challenge of lacking a course for complaint at having ended up without both of their 'real' parents. It is difficult to complain about the psychological stress of being a 'genetic orphan,' when necessarily the only alternative would have been not to have been born at all. Presumably, what a 'genetic orphan' would like to have is the impossible: to have been conceived 'naturally' by her social parents *and* to have existed.[16]

Somerville argues that not knowing one's biological origins constitutes a real harm to children, and legislation to prevent such harms from occurring should be introduced and enforced.[17] The basic human rights of children that

13 Ibid., 181.

14 Somerville uses very strong language to describe same-sex marriage, stating it is an 'unprecedented experiment on children, in general, in terms of the known and unknown risks it presents for them by unlinking children from their biological parents.' Ibid., 196.

15 Ibid., 186.

16 Ibid., 197.

17 Ibid., 188.

Somerville claims are violated by NRT s, which I will call 'biological origins rights,' are:

> 1.The right to be conceived with a natural biological heritage—that is, to have unmodified biological origins—in particular, to be conceived from a natural sperm from one identified living adult man and a natural ovum from one identified living adult woman. 2. The right to know the identity of one's biological parents.[18]

The justification for the first right should be evident from the psychological harm that presumably results from being a 'genetic orphan.' The justification for the second right, Somerville explains, is based on the fact that natural biological heritage is constitutive of a person's self-identity, and precedes citizenship. The 'natural right of biological identity and knowledge' cannot be denied someone for the sake of their parent/guardian's right to form a family. She writes, 'this right to found a family ... should be limited by children's right to have natural origins.'

The solution that Somerville proposes to mitigate the harm of NRT s is simply to prevent same-sex couples from marrying in the first place. Such draconian decision, in her mind, neatly circumvents the issue of discrimination on the basis of sexual orientation: same-sex couples would not have claims to the right to form a family on the basis of a state-sanctioned marriage. They would also be less likely, Somerville asserts, to want to have children if they are not able to access marriage; this, in turn, would reduce their demand to access NRT s.[19]

For her it would be more ethical to ban same-sex marriage outright, because otherwise the state would end up indirectly condoning the use and the right to access NRT s—which the state would have to do if it permits same-sex marriage—thus neglecting or failing to protect the rights of children, who are some of society's most vulnerable citizens. Somerville's concern for the rights and welfare of children is commendable. The psychological harms that may arise from being a child produced by NRT s are an issue that deserves more attention than it has hitherto received. However, I fundamentally disagree that same-sex marriage needs to be banned, because NRT s might potentially be psychologically harmful to the would-be children born from these unions. In the next section, I provide my arguments in support of this statement.

18 Ibid., 181.

19 Ibid.

3 Does Family Formation Come *First*? Questioning Somerville's Refusal to Extend Marriage Rights to Same-sex Couples

One of the major problems with Somerville's argument is inconsistency. In the first place, the reason Somerville gives for why a child's right to their biological identity cannot be overridden by their parent's right to form a family is that 'the right to found a family is a negative content right, that is, a right not to be interfered with in conceiving and bearing children naturally.'[20] The right to freedom of speech, for example, is a negative right because it merely requires the state to do nothing, to not prevent a person from communicating with others. That is, the right of two adults to form a family *does not* necessarily entail that they automatically gain the right to access NRT s, even if they are essentially incapable of conceiving a child naturally. On the other hand, the right to one's biological identity, she argues, is a positive right. The right to primary education, for example, is a positive right in that it requires the state to set up and fund schools to ensure the right to primary education is met. Having a positive right entails that the state has an obligation to do something to ensure that right, rather than merely refrain from acting. Positive rights outweigh negative rights, thus NRT use, which arises from a negative right violates children's positive rights.

However, this directly contradicts Somerville's earlier claim that the state would have an obligation to guarantee same-sex couples access to NRT s. She states: 'attributing the right [to procreate], as marriage necessarily does, without providing for its exercise would be meaningless.'[21] If the state has an obligation to do something for its citizens (rather than merely refrain from acting), then that right is a positive right. Thus, the author assumes that the right to form a family is a positive right. This means that Somerville here presents an inconsistent view, as she assumes that the right to form a family is *both* a positive right and a negative right. Moreover, if the right to natural biological origins and the right to form a family are both positive rights, then there is no immediate reason to think that one right should automatically outweigh the other. Somerville needs to give further arguments as to why that should be the case.

Moreover, if marriage provides only a negative right, and not a positive right to form a family, then same-sex couples can make no greater claim to the right to access NRT s than infertile opposite sex couples can. If this is the case, the

20 Ibid., 188.

21 Ibid., 189.

state should not be obligated to guarantee anyone the opportunities to procreate, but only guarantee non-interference. Thus, banning NRTs would not discriminate against same-sex couples on the basis of their sexual orientation, since the state would not be required to guarantee opportunities to procreate to any couple. In which case, there is no basis for preventing same-sex couples from marrying, if forming a family is a negative right.

Given the insight reached above, a second problem, the issue of harm, remains unresolved by Somerville's arguments. If NRT s ultimately harm children, then NRT s should simply be banned. There is no need to ban same-sex marriage in the process. Let us assume, as Somerville does, that children have rights to be conceived 'naturally' and to know their biological parents. Also, let us assume that this right takes precedence over another person's right to form a family.

That is, if there is a conflict between the right of an adult to have a child, and the right of an unborn child to have 'natural' origins and to know its biological origins (such as when an adult can only have a child through the assistance of NRT s), then the rights of the adult to have that child can legitimately be denied because in having him/her they are causing him/her potential harm. Even if that person or couple cannot have children without assistance, their rights to forming a family would still be secondary to the right of their potential child to not be conceived with modified biological origins because NRT s are always assumed to be harmful to that child. If this is the case, then Somerville should conclude simply that access to NRT s should be denied to all couples and individuals. Whether same-sex couples ought to have the right to marry is superfluous to this argument.

Moreover, as Somerville points out, marriage is a bundle of rights that goes beyond the right to form a family; it also entails the right to make one's commitment to another person public. By opposing same-sex marriage to prevent same-sex couples from accessing NRT s, same-sex couples are also denied the right to make their relational commitment public. For many couples, this right is the primary, if not the unique reason that they wish to marry. Many couples have no intention of having children, or already have children. Being able to publicly marry is a form of social recognition, a claim to legitimately call one's partner one's 'husband' or one's 'wife.' It is a means of accessing *marital status*.[22] This is a crucial step in gaining full sexual citizenship.

22 Katherine M. Franke, 'The Politics of Same-Sex Marriage Politics', *Colombia Journal of Gender and Law* 15 (2006): 240.

Aside from the compound rights that Somerville mentions, many same-sex couples wish to marry because they want access to the same legal and financial privileges that opposite sex married couples have (such as having visiting rights, getting tax breaks, sharing health insurance plans, etc.). No explanation is provided by Somerville to justify why claims to all other corresponding marriage rights must be denied to same-sex couples, once their right to have children cannot be guaranteed. Denying same-sex couples all rights and privileges that come with marriage because one right may not be able to be guaranteed is a considerably unjust approach to resolving the issue.

Finally, Somerville simply asserts that 'recognizing same-sex marriage could increase the use of these [NRT s].'[23] Having made this claim, she proceeds to build her arguments without providing evidence, except for asserting that gay couples are increasingly using these services. This claim does little to support the argument that allowing same-sex couples to marry will inevitably increase the use of NRT s in a significant way. It does not show that *marriage* is the determining factor in the increased use of NRT s. Of course, it is possible that being married may provide some extra incentive for same-sex couples to have children, since marriage can provide a sense of enduring stability, or because tradition encourages it.

However, preventing same-sex couples from being married does not prevent them from using NRT s, given that unmarried couples and individuals can access these services. Moreover, if marriage *does* somehow benefit children, by providing them with more stability, then marriage ought to be encouraged for those same-sex couples who would like to have children, or who already have them. If the use of NRT s causes harm to children, the issue will not be mitigated by denying same-sex couples the right to marry. These are just some initial inconsistencies and problems in Somerville's arguments, supposing that we accept her assumptions regarding children's biological heritage rights, and her assumption that these rights take precedence over the rights of a person to form a family. In the next section, I will question these assumptions.

4 Questioning Somerville's Assumptions on the Rights of Children

Let us now return to Somerville's two basic assumptions: first, that a person has a right to unmodified biological origins, i.e., to be conceived 'naturally;' and second, that a person has the right to know both his/her biological parents.

23 Somerville, 'Children's Human Rights', 181.

I will address each of these assumptions, ARGUING that, contrary to Somerville's intimation, these are not basic human rights. I will conclude by showing that, in regards to NRT use, there is actually no conflict between the rights of parents to choose to reproduce, and the rights of children to being conceived in particular manner. These arguments will allow me to convincingly conclude that same-sex marriages are legitimate and beneficial unions that deserve the full recognition of the state and should continue to be safeguarded.

4.1 *Do Children Have a Right to 'Unmodified' Biological Origins?*

Somerville's discussion does not clearly describe what it would mean to have a right to 'natural,' unmodified biological origins. She digressively alludes that this issue did not arise in the past (before the introduction of NRT s) because biological origins could only mean 'the natural union of a man's sperm and a woman's ovum.'[24] What Somerville likely means by this, is that this is the right to be conceived the 'traditional' way; the way our ancestors were conceived, i.e., only through the penetration of a penis into a vagina.

Somerville would most likely approve of all sorts of aids to help with conception, including taking vitamins and hormones, using a phone application to calculate ovulation, making use of erotica to stimulate desire and even applying lubricants. And yet, any intervention *outside* the mother's body, by having the parents' gametes manipulated by any NRT technique, would, on Somerville's account, violate the child's right to 'natural biological origins.' I question the 'moral' difference between having the sperm and ovum joined inside a woman's body, or introduced in other ways, is difficult to see. As such aids appear to be morally neutral, the decision to condemn modifications that take place outside the body rather than inside the body need greater justification than merely that they 'modify' a traditional way of conceiving a child.

Generally, individuals end up knowing very little about the circumstances and precise details of their conception. For instance, it does not usually matter to people if their conception took place in a bed, or on a boat, or in a laboratory. Rarely anyone has any insight into the mood, attitude or atmosphere that presided during the moment of intercourse, or the actual moment the gametes joined to form the zygote (which might have taken place hours or even days after coitus). These are details that few of us dwell on, and that matter very little to the manner in which we perceive ourselves, our value, or our place within the human web.[25]

24 Ibid., 188.

25 An exception, of course, is rape. It does seem to matter and affect people's self-worth to discover that they were conceived as the result of rape. But the harm in being conceived

Since we cannot be present to witness our own conception, and we generally construe our origins based only on what we are told, it is quite difficult to infer how important such matters are for the construction of our sense of self. The knowledge that one was conceived through the use of NRT s, and outside the body of the biological mother, does not, on its own, constitute harm to the child, any more than knowing other details about the circumstances or the manner of one's conception. It is even less plausible that one should have the right to *demand* specific circumstances of one's conception if they do not directly or greatly affect them. Therefore, for this to be a right, something else must make it morally significant.

A possible explanation could be that the consequences of conceiving a child outside a woman's body results in a more complex, and possibly very complicated origin. Once conception is allowed to happen outside the body, the possibility to manipulate, select, or alter the conception and gestation can take on great complexity. When conception can only happen in the woman's body, the couple's ability to conceive a particular child is limited to fate and the couples' innate capacities. But once conception can occur outside the body, identifying one 'mother' and one 'father' of the child might become less straightforward: is a surrogate a 'mother'? Are two lesbians conceiving a baby through a sperm donor *both* the 'mother'? Is their sperm donor the 'father'? This pushes us to question the meaningfulness and dominant discourse of having one 'parent' of each sex.[26]

And the moral questions become more complex: is it problematic that a couple wants their baby to look a certain way, and chooses a sperm donor based on physical characteristics? Is it problematic for an egg donor to be given compensation? Is it better for the donor to be anonymous, or is it better if he/she is known to the intended parents? These questions do not arise if conception is reserved to the narrow range of possibilities that Somerville has in mind. Somerville goes on to argue 'the danger is that moving away from a norm of naturally conceived children ... opens up precedents that carry serious risks and harms for all children.'[27] Modified biological origins are a departure from a long-standing precedent, but then again, so is eating refrigerated food or giving

this way seems to be of a very different sort: namely that its intention is associated with violence, lack of consent, and powerlessness. Whereas NRTs are usually the opposite: the intention is a non-violent, fully consenting desire for a child. If 'non-traditional' conception is harmful, the harm does not lie in the same kind of intention as rape.

26 Sarah Hannan, Samantha Brennan and Richard Vernon, eds., *Permissible Progeny?: The Morality of Procreation and Parenting* (New York: Oxford University Press, 2015).

27 Somerville, 'Children's Human Rights', 182.

women the right to vote. It will not suffice as justification *ipso facto*. It is, thus, not self-evident how having a more 'complex' origin is harmful to the resulting child. It just requires making our notion of what constitutes a 'family' or a 'parent' more flexible, pluralistic, and adaptive to today's possibilities.

It seems, however, that changing the notion of 'family' may precisely be the basis for Somerville's concern. David J. Velleman echoes this worry, asking: 'first comes love, then comes marriage, and then the proverbial baby carriage. Well, it's not such a ridiculous way of doing things, is it?'[28] Somerville agrees: [same-sex marriage] radically changes the primary basis of parenthood to legal (and social parenthood) ... consequently, [it] has a major impact on the societal norms, symbols and values associated with parenthood.[29] This change, she believes, is not for the best.

But, if the only 'harm' that arises from children being brought into same-sex (or opposite-sex) marriages through modified biological means is that these children were conceived differently than other children, the problem is, once again, not apparent. Perhaps the worry is that people will ask the child how they were conceived, or other children will question them about who their 'real' parents are. But, in the past, children have had to face much greater stigma because of their parents' decisions, without those decisions being legally challenged because they were 'different.' For example, some parents have chosen to live in Orthodox enclaves within a city, or live segregated from society in a religious sect that resists the use of technology. Despite eschewing mainstream ways of raising children, the decisions of these parents were legitimate. The decisions of parents to raise children with modified biological origins should likewise be recognized as a legitimate way for parents to create families that are in line with their own values and needs.

Somerville does not explain why these harms are more legitimate than the harm of having modified origins. Certainly, she provides no reason why modified origins could justify state intervention into the decisions of parents. After all, an intervention would not be condoned for any of the instances mentioned above. Difference cannot justifiably be equated with harm if there is no relevant negative effect occurring from this difference, especially since the benefits of modified biological origins tend to be a very good thing (i.e., the ability to procreate for a couple that cannot otherwise have a child).

If the 'atmosphere' of the conception, the resulting complexities, and the mere difference in the method of conception are not morally relevant, then

28 David J. Velleman, 'Family History', *Philosophical Papers* 34 (2005): 370.

29 Somerville, 'Children's Human Rights', 181.

the only remaining possibility is that having natural biological origins is somehow important in virtue of Somerville's second assumption: people have a right to know their biological parents. If people have modified natural biological origins, then there is a higher likelihood that they will not know or not be raised by their biological progenitors. However, this answer seems unsatisfactory as well.

First of all, not all cases of 'modified' biological origins result in the child not knowing her biological heritage. For example, a child could be raised by both her biological parents, but her aunt could have been used as a surrogate, meaning that the child had modified biological origins and yet fully knows her complex biological origins. Thus, knowing one's biological parents and having modified origins can be dichotomous. Even if most cases of modified biological origins did result in children lacking knowledge of their biological genesis that still does not explain what makes a modified conception, *qua* modification, wrong.

Second of all, even if it *were* the case that having modified biological origins were wrong in virtue only of the modification, it would make no difference to the veracity or falsity of whether a person has a right to know her biological parents. The negative connotation attached to biological modifications is superfluous. Whether a child ought to have a right to know her biological origins can be a separate issue from the methods used to conceive her. An adopted child, for example, has non-modified biological origins, and yet could lack any knowledge of his biological progenitors. These two assumptions are in no way contingent on one another.

However, even if Somerville were to resist this explanation and argue that the right to unmodified biological origins is actually contingent on the fact that one has a right to know one's parents, such conclusions would also be moot. I will illustrate in the discussion below that 'knowing' one's biological parents is *not* a right. The weakness of this assumption makes it an inadequate basis for justifying the right to unmodified biological origins. Given that neither assumption holds up to scrutiny, they cannot provide any basis for Somerville's conclusions that the harm of NRTs invalidates the legitimacy of same-sex marriage.

4.2 *Do Children Have a Right to Know Their Biological Parents?*

Much of the force of the argument will depend on how we conceptualize the meaning of the verb *to know*. Two relevant possibilities are propositional knowledge ('to know that') or knowledge by acquaintance. To have propositional knowledge about one's biological parents, one would know, for example, their dates of birth, their medical history, their height, what they studied in college, their favourite activities, their ethnicity, etc. Much of this information can be gathered from questionnaires which even anonymous gamete donors fill out (and much more can be gathered from non-anonymous donors).[30]

Such information is understandably important: it can give advance warning of health conditions one may have inherited, it might indicate certain natural predispositions one has, and it can help an individual construct a more coherent sense of where she 'comes from' (what events may have shaped the trajectory of time that led to her coming into existence). Legislating mandatory and more in-depth questionnaires, which do not necessarily identify the donor, could greatly help in satisfying a person's right to know propositional facts about her biological parents.

If *to know* is to be interpreted as acquaintance knowledge, then the demands could be much higher. To *know* one's biological parents in this sense means to have contact with them, to be familiar with them, to develop a relationship of some kind with this person. Thus, to satisfy this right, the biological offspring of gamete donors would have to have identifying information (name, address, occupation, etc.) about their biological parents, in case they want to contact or meet them, and the biological parent or parents would have to be willing to meet and spend time getting to know their biological offspring. This is a more difficult demand.

Many donors may be less willing to donate if they know that they must be open to contact with any resulting children.[31] If a young man in his 20s donates sperm, and then later goes on to have a wife and his own biological children, he may feel uneasy at the thought of a stranger one day appearing on his doorstep looking for his 'father.' This could have an upsetting effect on his children (who might not know they have a genetic half-sibling), on his wife (who might not have been aware of the gamete donation), and even on the child seeking contact with her biological father (who might have had a very different picture in her mind of what her biological father is like). Moreover, if a young man donates sperm once or several times in his life, he might have dozens of children in the world that are his biological offspring.[32] Having obligations of contact

30 Alexina McWhinnie, 'Gamete Donation and Anonymity: Should Offspring from Donated Gametes Continue to be Denied Knowledge of their Origins and Antecedents?', *Human Reproduction* 16 (2001): 808.

31 Ken Daniels, 'Donor Gametes: Anonymous or Identified?', *Best Practice & Research Clinical Obstetrics & Gynaecology* 21.1 (2007): 113–128.

32 In Canada for example, the restrictions permit 25 pregnancies for a population of 800,000. Canwest News Service, 'Women Shopping for Super Sperm', 10 December 2005. Viewed on 1 March, 2016, http://www.canada.com/vancouversun/story.html?id=52e43aa6-b15c-423f-a845-13a845143e70&k=9062

toward all these children may be impractical, and something the donor might not wish for.

Velleman interprets this 'knowing' as the latter, as a form of familiarity, or of deep acquaintance. He believes that knowing one's biological parents is crucial for developing a healthy self-knowledge, a personal identity, and to be able to situate oneself within a narrative. He argues that children ought to be raised in families where the legal parent(s) and the biological progenitor(s) are the same (he makes an exception for adoption). He writes:

> What is most troubling about gamete donation is that it purposely severs a connection of the sort that normally informs a person's sense of identity, which is composed of elements that must bear emotional meaning, as only symbols and stories can.[33]

These symbols and stories are important aspects of the human psyche. It is important for people to be able to build stories about their origins, and locate where they fit in within these narratives. For example, knowing that your grandmother survived a bitter winter on only 'a sack of potatoes' (regardless of whether this is true or only a myth) might be inspirational to a young person who is going through a difficult time herself. It may give her a reason to persevere, because she knows it's 'in her genes' or because she 'owes it' to her ancestor who did not give up.

Additionally, Velleman argues that it is only when we are raised by those we are biologically related to that they are available to us as mirrors of ourselves: we can 'recognize' ourselves in them. Many things about family resemblance cannot be analysed or articulated, but still they can inform our self-knowledge, about, for example, our personalities, our limits, or our manners, if we have extended interaction with them. They help us cultivate and shape ourselves, and provide mediums of self-reflection by giving us a 'third-person' reference of ourselves. Without an acquaintance with people to whom we bear a literal resemblance, having a grasp of a sense of identity might be much more difficult. This kind of knowledge of one's biological parents, i.e., knowledge by acquaintance, is likely the same kind of knowledge that Somerville has in mind.

A problematic issue for Velleman with NRTs is the deliberate severance of biological ties from at least one of the parents. He believes bringing children into the world whose biological ties have been deliberately severed, makes

33 Velleman, 'Family History', 363.

them 'disadvantaged by the lack of a basic good [i.e., knowledge of one's biological parents and origins].'[34] Therefore, most uses of NRTs are inherently wrong: people 'should not deliberately create children who they already know will be disadvantaged.'[35] It is not a matter of whether such children who have already been produced through NRTs ought to be alive or ought to be celebrated, but rather, it is a matter of whether a couple ought to have chosen to use NRTs in the first place.[36] For Velleman, it would be morally wrong for that couple to choose to have that child, knowing that it will be denied the opportunity to know its biological parents, since lacking that knowledge will greatly disadvantage that child in terms of self-knowledge and identity formation.

Sally Haslanger takes issue with this. She thinks it is wrong to portray a lack of contact with one's biological ties as a serious disadvantage. She cites studies on adoption to make her point:

> I believe that even in non-kin adoption where children have no contact with biological relatives, adopted children have families and adoptive parents have children in a sense that is at least good enough and actually equal to the relations between biological parents and children.[37]

The child-parent relationships are at least as good, she argues, because the ability to form a full self and a healthy identity do not require contact with, or particular knowledge of, biological relatives. A person can gain self-understanding and self-development from many sources, including close relatives or significant others, friends, or even inspiring characters in films and literature. These 'social mirrors' do not have to come only from our own biological parents. She therefore disagrees that lacking knowledge of one's biological origins is so great of a disadvantage, if even a disadvantage at all and rightly points out that 'Velleman's emphasis on biological parents and heritage is highly exaggerated.'[38]

---

34 Ibid., 364.

35 Ibid.

36 Velleman explains that people often conflate the disapproval of the event of bringing the child into the world with disapproval of the child. We can have the former without the latter and *vice versa*. For example, you can disapprove of a poor family having more children than they can afford, but still celebrate the lives of each of the children and be thankful for their existence.

37 Susan Haslanger, 'Family, Ancestry and Self: What is the Moral Significance of Biological Ties?', *Alliance for the Study of Adoption and Culture* 2 (2009): 2.

38 Haslanger, 'Family, Ancestry and Self', 14.

Haslanger goes on to argue that the main reason that biological families are seen to be important for the formation of narratives is because of a 'bionormative' view of the family, which has been given primacy and is dominant in Western society today. She points out that adopted children who are taught that biological connections are important fare worse than adopted children who are taught that biological connections are *not* important.[39] This suggests that the harms of being raised by genetically unrelated parents depend on the value one places on genetic relatedness. And, as even Velleman admits, it is not the truth of narratives and family myths that is important in formation of a self, but just the belief or acceptance of them.[40]

In other words, narratives of our origins, their significance, how far back they have to reach, and in what ways we ought to be connected with others, are themselves social constructions that can be changed and challenged. If a person is stigmatized for lacking a bionormative narrative structure, then the problem at the heart of the matter is this normative injunction. Rather than preventing people from choosing families that would have a non-bionormative narrative structure, we ought to reject and overturn the bio-centric norm. If children can and do flourish in families without a fully biological relation to their parents, then we ought to remove the stigma that surrounds these families, not prevent those families from forming.[41]

Moreover, the kind of information that is supposed to provide self-knowledge tends to be quite limited, even in biologically-related families. For example, information about our extended families, such as knowledge about our grandparents and great grandparents, which are supposed to figure into our bionormative narratives, are often less abundant than even the information provided on questionnaires filled out by anonymous gamete donors. Moreover, these relations are far enough removed that they can rarely be met or fully apprehended.

If useful narratives can be created out of the little and disjointed information people tend to have of their biological ancestors, then it should also be possible to forge useful narratives from the data provided by gamete donors.[42] The importance given to knowing our biological parents, in both the 'propositional sense' and as a form of familiarity—or of deep acquaintance—will mostly be a function of how much value society places on these kinds of knowledges.

39 Ibid., 26.

40 Velleman, 'Family History', 377.

41 Haslanger, 'Family, Ancestry and Self', 27.

42 Ibid., 25.

Haslanger maintains that it is best for children to be raised by their biological progenitors. We would not, for example, all things being equal, prefer to take children born to parents who want them and, instead, redistribute the children among couples that might make even better parents. Little good would come of such a situation. But often things aren't 'equal.' The situation of same-sex or opposite-sex couples who seek out NRT s because they are unable to conceive on their own, or a family unable or unwilling to care for their biological offspring, are precisely the kind of non-standard occurrences that would merit permitting and supporting parents to raise children they are not genetically related to.

I would argue the claim that people have a right to know their biological parents is too strong, if knowing is understood in terms of acquaintance and close interpersonal contact. There are definitely some advantages, such as knowing propositional facts about them, which are medically relevant or which might satisfy a curiosity Nevertheless, one cannot go as far as to claim that this is a 'right.'

In our cultural context, that gives great value to a bionormative narrative, it may be easier to be acquainted with one's biological parents. But, as Haslanger points out, often little more than a glimpse at one's biological parents is needed or desired.[43] Many adopted children who meet their biological relations report no great advantages in the construction of their identity formation, and even those who establish good relationships with their birth mothers, rarely privilege that relationship over that of their adoptive mothers.[44] Healthy self-knowledge and coherent identities can emerge non-problematically as long as children receive relevant support from their social parents and families.

It is clear that knowing one's biological parents can be helpful for narrative formation and it will be difficult to replace the value of being acquainted with one's biological parents. Nevertheless, lacking this advantage is not a justified reason for morally condemning or banning NRT s. For example, it would be justifiable for a woman to decide to raise a child by herself, even if she knows that because of this, her child may endure *some* loss relative to children who have two parents. Likewise, parents using NRT s are aware that their child may endure *some* loss compared to other children who are raised by both of their biological parents. However, similarly to the situation of single parenting, the hardships faced need not be insurmountable.

---

43 Ibid., 18.

44 Ibid., 17.

Counselling, family therapy, and simply the fact that raising non-biologically related children is becoming more common, and therefore more 'normal,' should counterbalance any disadvantages such a decision presents.[45] Moreover, there is an abundance of other relationships from which a child can gain self-knowledge, including her social parents and grandparents, siblings, significant others such as care-givers, teachers, friends, and inspirational figures, real or literary. Many of the benefits of self-knowledge that can purportedly be gained from knowing a genetic parent can be fulfilled via other means.

On the whole, however, it seems that children and their parents will benefit from the ability to use NRT s, even if that means severing the child's knowledge of their full biological origins. Thus, there is not sufficient justification for the claim that children have a right to know their biological parents, because they can still healthfully develop self-knowledge, personal identity, and new kinds of narratives without such knowledge.

We, therefore, only have a right to 'know' our biological parents in the propositional sense, since this kind of knowledge can be medically relevant and crucial for practical reasons. In the context of NRT s, this can be satisfied by in-depth, fact-checked (non-identifying) questionnaires that donors would be required by law to provide. If that is the extent of that right, then the first supposed right, which is to have non-modified biological origins, cannot rely on the second right—the right to know a genetic parent—for its justification. One can have modified biological origins and still have the means of knowing a biological parent in the ways that matter.

In similar terms, one can know propositional facts about one's biological parents and have either modified or non-modified biological origins. In short, Somerville's first claim does not stand up to scrutiny, and her second claim can only be adopted if interpreted in its weakest form. A result of this conclusion is that the issue of competing rights claims between parents and children does not arise. A person's right to found a family, even if only through NRT s, does not infringe on the rights of potential unborn children to be conceived through biologically unmodified means (because they do not have this right) nor does it infringe on their right to 'know' their biological parents (because this right is satisfied, so long as we mandate sufficiently in-depth questionnaires).

---

45 Woodcock, 'Five Reasons Why', 885.

5 Conclusion

In this chapter, I have presented my arguments in rebuttal to Somerville's rejection of same-sex marriage. I opened my discussion with a brief description of Somerville's claims about the ways in which access to NRT s is both essential to same-sex marriage recognition and a tool that undermines basic 'biological origins rights.' I refuted her thesis by teasing out the inconsistencies in her arguments and by taking some of her statements to their logical conclusions. I found fallacy in the author's claim that all children have a right to 'unmodified biological origins,' and a right to know their biological parents.

I have conclusively argued that all the points made by Somerville to reject the legitimacy of same-sex marriage do not hold up to scrutiny and, therefore, her motivations for its condemnation dissolve. As she considers herself a supporter of same-sex marriage, were it not for conflicting rights claims, if she were to accept my arguments, then she ought to find no reason to reject the claims of same-sex couples to full participation in marriage and full recognition of their sexual citizenship.

Bibliography

Daniels, Ken. "Donor Gametes: Anonymous or Identified?" *Best Practice & Research Clinical Obstetrics & Gynaecology* 21.1 (2007): 113–128.

Canwest News Service. "Women Shopping for Super Sperm." December 10, 2005. Viewed 1 March, 2016. http://www.canada.com/vancouversun/story.html?id=52e43aa6-b15c-423f-a845-13a845143e70&k=9062

Franke, Katherine M. "The Politics of Same-Sex Marriage Politics." *Colombia Journal of Gender and Law* 15 (2006): 236–248.

Hannan, Sarah, Samantha Brennan, and Richard Vernon, eds. *Permissible Progeny? The Morality of Procreation and Parenting*. New York: Oxford University Press, 2015.

Haslanger, Susan. "Family, Ancestry and Self: What is the Moral Significance of Biological Ties?" *Alliance for the Study of Adoption and Culture* 2 (2009): 1–40.

McWhinnie, Alexina. "Gamete Donation and Anonymity: Should Offspring from Donated Gametes Continue to be Denied Knowledge of their Origins and Antecedents?" *Human Reproduction* 16 (2001): 808–817.

Murphy, Timothy F. "Same-Sex Marriage: Not a Threat to Marriage or Children." *Journal of Social Philosophy* 42.3 (2011): 288–304.

Phelan, Shane. *Sexual Strangers: Gays, Lesbians, and Dilemmas of Citizenship*. Temple University Press, 2001.

Richardson, Diane. "Constructing Sexual Citizenship: Theorizing Sexual Rights." *Critical Social Policy* 20 (2000):105–135.

Somerville, Margaret. "The Ethical Imagination: Journeys of the Human Spirit." *Massey Lecture Series*. Toronto: House of Anansi Press, 2006.

Somerville, Margaret. "Children's Human Rights and Unlinking Child-Parent Biological Bonds with Adoption, Same-Sex Marriage and New Reproductive Technologies." *Journal of Family Studies* 13 (2007):179–201.

UN General Assembly. *Universal Declaration of Human Rights*, 1948.

Velleman, J. David. "Family History." *Philosophical Papers* 34 (2005): 357–378.

Woodcock, Simon. "Five Reasons why Margaret Somerville is Wrong about Same-Sex Marriage and the Rights of Children." Dialogue 48 (2009): 867–887.

CHAPTER 4

Gender Procreative Roles in the First Codes of Law

René Hirsch

Abstract

This chapter aims at showing how the procreative knowledge that characterized a specific period of our history influenced the approach legislative institutions had on gender. As a probable consequence of animal and plant domestication, the procreative vision that dominated Antiquity attributed the creation of the child to men's seed, while women's function was reduced to nurturing the seed planted in them. As Aeschylus put it, 'The mother of her so-called child is not parent, but nurse of the young life sown in her. The male is parent: she, but a stranger to him, keeps safe his growing plant, unless fate blight it.'[1] The first books of law that appear in the Levant between the 3rd and the 1st millennium BCE[2] all confirm the state of subordination imposed on women. However, focusing more particularly on the way sexual offences were regulated reveals how the lawmakers distributed gender roles according to the procreative vision that prevailed at the time.

Keywords

procreation – knowledge – antiquity – codes of law – gender – sexual offences – rape – adultery – incest – Hammurabi – Old Testament – paternity – patriarchy – Levant

1 Introduction

The period that stretches from the chiefdoms to the late empires of Antiquity (between the second half of the 6th and the 1st millennium BCE)[3] established the hierarchical domination of the masculine in all facets of society. Not only

1 Aeschylus, *The Oresteia*, trans. R.C. Trevelyan (Cambridge: Bowes & Bowes, 1920), 146.

2 All dates mentioned in this text are BCE ("before contemporary era").

3 Kent Flannery, 'The Cultural Evolution of Civilizations,' *Annual Review of Ecology and Systematics* 3 (1972): 403.

 | DOI:10.1163/9789004392298_006

men occupied all positions of authority, but they also filled the ranks of the castes on which the economy of the urban society thrived, principally the two castes on which the power rested: the caste of soldiers and the caste of priests. However, women still enjoyed prestige and privileges, and took an active part in the economy. They possessed lands and slaves, lent and borrowed money, and were involved in commercial activities, whether those of their spouses or their own. In palaces and temples of the third millennium BCE, many women had titles of nobility and occupied high positions. They were also scribes, musicians, or practiced an independent profession, such as weaver or goldsmith. But women were also objectified, left as a pledge for debts contracted by their fathers, their brothers or their husbands, or offered as a tribute. In addition, they practiced prostitution. As a matter of fact, various testimonies indicate their complete dependency on men: 'I am a daughter, I am a daughter-in-law, I am a spouse, I am a house-keeper,'[4] asserted a hymn dedicated to the popular Babylonian goddess Gula. The tables of laws that were written at that time confirm the state of subordination imposed on women.

It has generally been established that one of the main purposes of the law was to pass the family estate along the male line, from the deceased to his legitimate sons, or to his male collaterals if there was no son.[5] In some cases, however, daughters could also inherit – if they were unmarried, for example, – and in some cases, they were even considered as equal heirs as their brothers.[6] But the law was also meant to implement norms that were not fully integrated in the mores of the populations under its rule:

> In general, it may be said that legislation does not precede the conditions of life with which it is intended to deal, but arises out of actually existing conditions and situations which it seeks to guide and control.[7]

This article particularly focuses on how the first codes of law that appear during the second and first millennia BCE in the Middle East were influenced by the

---

4 Saana Teppo, *Women and Their Agency in the Neo-Assyrian Empire* (Helsinki: University of Helsinki, 2005), 29.

5 *Laws of Lipit-Ishtar* (LL) 31–33; *Laws of Hammurabi* (LH) 168–169. See also Hans Jochen Boecker, *Law and the Administration of Justice in the Old Testament and Ancient East* (Augsburg: Augsburg Publishing House, 1980), 114; Gerda Lerner, *The Creation of Patriarchy* (Oxford: Oxford University Press, 1986), 106; Raymond Westbrook, *A History of Ancient Near-Eastern Law* (Leiden, Brill, 2003), 57.

6 LL b, 22; LH 178, 181–182; Boecker, *Law Administration*, 50.

7 J. M. Powis Smith, *The Origin and History of Hebrew Law* (Chicago, 2006), 3.

way procreation was understood. Analysing the way these codes regulated sexual offences reveals that the legislator aimed at distributing and reinforcing gender roles according to the understanding of procreation that prevailed at the time.

I first briefly examine how procreation was understood during Antiquity, and how procreative functions were distributed between men and women. I move on to review how the different Levantine codes of law approached and regulated sexual offences, and how they defined gender relationships. I lastly analyse the correlation existing between procreative knowledge and gender roles as they were envisioned by the law.

2 The Patriarchal Procreative Understanding

Although the sources on how the procreative roles of men and women were understood during the last two millennia BCE are scarce, several literary texts of the time refer to women as *fertile fields*, and to men as those who have to 'plough these fields' in order to 'sow their seed.' 'Farmer, plough my field' was a commonly used metaphor to invite someone for sexual intercourse. 'My field, for lack of ploughing, is like a woman without a husband,' lamented a Phoenician king engaged in continuous warfare.[8] Ninurta was the Babylonian god of ploughing and possessed great creative powers.[9] An incantation from the end of the second millennium summarized the dichotomy between the procreative function of men and women in the following terms: 'My father begot me, my mother bore me.'[10] In 458 BCE, Aeschylus could still write:

> The mother of her so-called child is not parent, but nurse of the young life sown in her. The male is parent: she, but a stranger to him, keeps safe his growing plant, unless fate blight it.[11]

As a matter of fact, this understanding of procreation was a direct application of the agricultural know-how to the human reproductive process, and rested

8 Marten Stol, *Birth in Babylonia and the Bible: Its Mediterranean Setting* (Groningen: Styx Brill, 2000), 1.

9 Amar Annus, *The God Ninurta: in The Mythology and Royal Ideology of Ancient Mesopotamia* (Helsinki: Neo-Assyrian Text Corpus Project, 2002), 70–71.

10 Benjamin Foster, *Before the Muses: An Anthology of Akkadian Literature* (Bethesda: CDL Press, 1996), II, 549.

11 Aeschylus, *The Oresteia,* 146.

on two basic principles: first, the seed that is sown in the ground determines the properties of the plant that will grow; second, the soil in which the seed is planted has no influence whatsoever on the characteristics of the plant it nurtures, only on its growth.

Applying this knowledge to human procreation brought the conclusion that it was the seed of the man that determined the nature of the child to be born, while the role of the woman was limited to that of a soil, providing a nurturing environment that could influence the development of the seed planted in her, but not its nature. Men were thus believed to be the 'creators' of their offspring, whereas women were relegated to play a secondary and foremost replaceable role: having no distinctive bearing on her progeny, any woman could perform the nurturing task.

Finding probably its roots in the wake of plant and animal domestication during the Neolithic,[12] this understanding of procreation has dominated gender roles and relationships for many thousand years. In the fifth century, Hippocrates challenged this vision with his 'two-seed theory' that held that both men and women emitted sperm and that the foetus was created by mixing male and female sperm together. He further postulated that each seed contained both male and female germs.[13] A few years later, however, Aristotle contradicted this theory, saying that the embryo was created by the action of the masculine sperm on menstrual blood. In his view, female contribution was limited to supplying 'material for the semen to work upon.' Aristotle thus reaffirmed the traditional one-sex model in which 'effective' and 'active' males engendered, while 'passive' females merely provided the nurturing environment for the male's seed.[14]

12 Lerner, *Creation Patriarchy*, 149.

13 Hippocrates and Galen, *The Writings* (Philadelphia: Lindsay and Blakiston, 1846), 160; Philip Grace, 'Aspects of Fatherhood in Thirteenth-Century Encyclopedias,' *Journal of Family History* 31 (2006): 221.

14 Aristotle, 'De Generatione Animalium', trans. Arthur Platt, in *The Works* (Oxford: Clarendon Press, 1912) V, 1, 20, 729a. These two theories will divide the intellectual world until the discovery of the fertilization process in 1874 CE. See Jacques Gonzalès, *Histoire Naturelle et Articificielle de la Procréation* (Paris: Bordas, 1996); René Hirsch, 'Procreative Knowledge, Gender Roles, and Beliefs: Past and Present Parallels' (paper, presented at the World History Theory and Practice: Gender, Technology, Culture conference, New York, St John's University, May 2, 2015).

3 The Codes of Law

Except for the *Code of Ur-nammu* (LU) that dates from around 2,100, the oldest codes of our history date from the second millennium: the *Code of Lipit-Ishtar* (LL) from around 1930, the *Code of Eshnunna* (LE) from around 1770, and the famous *Babylonian Code of Hammurabi* from around 1750 (LH). Later, the *Hittite Laws* (HL) appeared around 1,500 and the *Middle Assyrian Laws from Assur* around 1076 (MAL). Finally, the codes of law that we find in the Hebrew Bible and the Old Testament are estimated to have been written between the eighth and the fifth century.[15]

In this text, I will exclusively consider the laws dealing with sexual offences, which the *Code of Hammurabi*, the *Middle Assyrian Laws* and the *Book of Leviticus* particularly cover. Although no evidence indicates that these laws were ever intended to be applied,[16] they certainly structured the norms and values of the kingdoms and empires of the Middle East during that era. They also give an accurate picture of the way gender roles were distributed in the society. It is interesting to observe that, though these codes were written many centuries apart, the way they regulated sexual offences, and, as a result, and to a certain extent, the way they approached gender roles, did not differ much from one to the other. The fact that some of these texts, like the *Code of Hammurabi*, were still in use more than a thousand years after their first appearance further shows the scope of their influence in the region.[17] In addition, the many similitudes found between the former codes and their more recent biblical counterpart confirm the persistence of this influence. They also indicate that the norms implemented by the law had kept their value through time, but that they had not, up to that point been integrated in the mores of those populations.[18]

15 Martha Roth, *Law Collections from Mesopotamia and Asia Minor* (Atlanta: Scholar Press, 1995), xiv; Westbrook, *History Law*, 8–9.

16 Westbrook, *History Law*, 19; G. R. Driver and John C. Miles, *The Babylonian Laws*, edited with Translation and Commentary (Oxford: Oxford University Press, 1952), I, 45.

17 Bernard M. Levinson, *Legal Revision and Religious Renewal in Ancient Israel* (Cambridge: Cambridge University Press, 2008), 24.

18 Lerner, *Creation Patriarchy*, 102–103.

4 Sexual Offences and Gender Roles

Three types of sexual infractions are systematically dealt with by the books of law: rape, adultery, and sexual intercourse with close relatives.

4.1 *Rape*

In the case of rape, the sentence depended on whether the rape had occurred in the city or in the countryside. In the city, the girl or woman who was raped but did not shout – or shouted but was not heard – shared the fate of her rapist, death. In the countryside, however, she might have shouted, but not have been heard. In that case, only the man was condemned to death.[19] The *Hittite Code* further condemned to death the woman who was raped in her house, presupposing that the man could not enter without her consent. Regardless of the location of the rape, if the husband caught the rapist in the act, he could kill him in that instant and his own wife as well.[20]

The earlier codes adapted their sentence according to the marital status of the victim: although the rape of a married woman mostly carried the death penalty for the rapist and his victim, the rape of a virgin woman who was promised to a man entailed the death of the rapist, while the woman incurred no blame.[21] In the case of the rape of a virgin woman not engaged to be married, the rapist had simply to compensate the girl's father by giving him a sum of money and by marrying his daughter. The marriage was indissoluble. If the rapist was already married, the *Middle Assyrian Laws* applied 'vicarious talion': the father of the victim was authorised to have the wife of the rapist raped – the law did not mention by whom. She would then join his household as a servant, and the rapist would marry his victim. As for the rape of a female slave, it was considered a lesser offence and was handled as damage to property, the owner of the slave having to be compensated according to her value.[22]

4.2 *Adultery*

Adultery was, at the time, defined as 'consensual sexual intercourse by a married woman with a man other than her husband,'[23] and was considered to be a very serious crime that required the death sentence. In the *Code of Ur-nammu*

19 LH 130; *Hittite Laws* (HL) 197; *Middle Assyrian Laws* (MAL) A12; Deut. 22:23–27 (*Holy Bible*, English Standard Version, 2001 (ESV)).

20 HL 197.

21 *Laws of Ur-Nammu* (LU) 6; LH 130.

22 LU 8; MAL A55; Deut. 22:28–29 (ESV); Westbrook, *History Law*, 82.

23 Ibid., 80.

and in the *Middle Assyrian Laws*, the woman who followed a man to have sex with him was condemned to death. To avoid the same fate, the man had to prove that he did not know the woman was married and could go free. In the *Code of Hammurabi*, both the woman and her lover were condemned to be bound and drowned. The *Assyrian Code* further authorised the husband who caught his wife with her lover in 'flagrante delicto' to kill both with impunity. But if he decided to forgive his wife, or if he wished to punish her less harshly, her paramour was to share the same fortune. However, no forgiveness was to be found in the *Old Testament*: the lovers had to die.[24]

If a woman was accused of adultery by her husband, but was not caught in the act, it was sufficient for her to take an exculpatory oath, and she could return to her house. But if she was incriminated by a third person, even though she had not done anything wrong, she had to drown herself for the sake of her husband.[25]

Hammurabi presented the case of a woman whose husband has been absent for a long time and has left her with nothing to eat in the house. In such circumstances, the law allowed her to leave him for another man. But if she left her husband while there was enough food to feed her, she was committing adultery and had to perish by drowning.[26]

In *Deuteronomy*, the case of a man who accused the woman he had just married not to have been a virgin at the time of the wedding is discussed. The old Babylonian custom of 'claiming at the house of the father-in-law,' a custom that was still practiced by the Assyrians and the Israelites, entitled the groom, once full payment of the bride price had been made, to come and claim his bride at her father's house.[27] Her parents would then keep the sheets that had been tainted with the blood of her first sexual intercourse, in case they would have to prove that she had not *fornicated* before her marriage: to this effect, they would bring forth the 'tokens of the damsel's virginity unto the elders of the city,'[28] and the husband would be condemned to pay a fine to the father of the woman. She could remain his wife for as long as she lived. But if her virginity could not be proved, she was condemned to be stoned to death in front of her father's house.[29]

24 LU 7; LH 129; HL 198; MAL A13-16; Lev. 20:10 (ESV); Deut. 22:22 (ESV).

25 LU 14; LH 131–132.

26 LH 133–134.

27 MAL A38; Deut. 22:14–21 (ESV); Westbrook, *History Law*, 587.

28 Deut. 22:14–21 (*Holy Bible*, King James Version, 1987 (KJV)).

29 Westbrook, *History Law*, 387.

Generally, the adulterous woman was almost always guilty, and if she was not condemned to death, her husband could divorce her without paying any compensation[30] and keep her dowry.[31] On the other hand, the issue of a man committing adultery is not discussed in any text. As a matter of fact, a man could have multiple sexual relationships, as long as he obeyed certain fundamental rules, as we will see below. Nevertheless, a deceived wife could ask for divorce, but she had to prove that she had been a good housewife and that her 'decency' was without reproach. If that was the case, she might recover her dowry and return to her father's house. However, 'if she is not innocent, but leaves her husband, and ruins her house, neglecting her husband, this woman shall be cast into the water.'[32]

4.3 *Sexual Intercourse with Close Relatives*

Among the laws addressing sexual relationships, those regulating what we nowadays call incest deserve special scrutiny. Defined as 'sexual intercourse between persons so closely related that they are forbidden by law to marry,'[33] the word 'incest' had apparently no equivalent before its introduction in Latin.[34] It is also worth mentioning that the laws concerning sexual intercourse with close relatives were not set apart from those addressing adultery. The punishments they required were also modelled on those applied for adultery, pointing towards a different understanding of these sexual relationships from the way we conceive them today.

In the *Code of Hammurabi*, only five of the laws regulating heterosexual relationships are not directly related to rape or to adultery. One involved sexual intercourse between a father and his daughter, offence for which the father was banished. Two of them addressed the sexual relationship between a father and his daughter-in-law: the father was here condemned to death if the marriage had been consummated; if that was not the case, he only had to pay a fine. As

30 Only a first-ranking wife was eligible for a divorce settlement: LU 9–11; LL 30; LH 138–139.

31 LH 141. Middle Assyrian law (MAL A37) went straight to the point: 'If a man intends to divorce his wife, if it is his wish, he shall give her something; if that is not his wish, he shall not give her anything, and she shall leave empty-handed' (Roth, *Law Collections*, 166–167). Westbrook, *History Law*, 49.

32 LH 142–143.

33 *Merriam-Webster's Dictionary of Law*. Merriam-Webster, Inc., Viewed February 24, 2015, <http://dictionary.reference.com/browse/incest>.

34 See Andrew Roy Dyck, *A Commentary on Cicero, De Legibus* (Ann Arbor: University of Michigan Press, 2004), 317.

for the last two laws, one addressed the sexual relationship of a son with his mother, and the other, that of a son with his stepmother, both occurring after the death of the father. In the first case, both mother and son were condemned to be burned at the stake. In the second case, the son was disinherited.[35]

Much closer to our understanding of incestuous relationships, the *Hittite Code* denounced as 'unpermitted sexual pairing' the relationship of a man with his mother, with his daughter, or with his son.[36] Surprisingly, punishment was not stipulated. The law further stated that sexual intercourse between a man and his stepmother was not an offence, except if the father was still alive. The same applied to the relationship with one's sister-in-law, which was authorized if her husband was dead.[37] Other 'unpermitted sexual pairings' were the relationship of a man with his stepdaughter, with his mother-in-law, or with his sister-in-law. In reality, all these relationships entailed adulterous activities from the part of the man.[38]

The same book of law considered the relationship between a man, a woman and her daughter(s) to be an offence if they all lived in the same locality. However, if the women were slaves, there was no offence, no matter where they resided. The law also stipulated that brothers might have intercourse with a free woman, and that a father and a son could sleep with the same slave or with the same prostitute.[39]

Most of the Hittite laws dealing with sexual offences were directly related to a context of adultery. Even the separated article prohibiting sexual pairing between a father and his daughter (or his son), and a mother and her son, could be understood as implicating adultery, be it on behalf of the father or on that of the mother.

Finally, it is worthwhile to dedicate some attention to the laws addressing sexual relationships between humans and those sanctioning sexual activity between a person and an animal in the *Hittite Code*.[40] Cases of bestiality involving a cow, a sheep, a pig or a dog – each of them sacrificial animals – commanded the death of the perpetrator and were dealt with by the royal court of justice presided by the king. On the other hand, having sex with a horse or a mule was not considered to be an offence.[41] Let us remember that the only

---

35 If the father was still alive, the rules governing adultery were then applied. LH 154–158.

36 HL 189; Roth, *Law Collections*, 236.

37 HL 190, 192, 193.

38 HL 195; Roth, *Law Collections*, 237.

39 HL 191, 194.

40 HL 187-200a.

41 HL 187, 200a.

sexual relationship between a man and a woman punishable by death was when a woman was raped in her house. The punishment for all other sexual offences was not specified.[42]

Chapters 18 and 20 of the *Book of Leviticus* described with great detail the familial prohibitions for sexual relationships. A man could not have intercourse with his mother or stepmother, his sister or stepsister, his granddaughter, his aunt or step aunt, his daughter-in-law, and his sister-in-law. Similarly, to the *Hittite Code*, having a relationship with a woman and her daughter (or granddaughter) was condemned, or with a woman and her sister. Also forbidden was sex with a woman having her period, sex between two men, and sex with an animal.[43]

In five of these cases, the death penalty was required: 1) for both the man and his mother or stepmother; 2) for both the man and his daughter-in-law; 3) for the man, his wife and her daughter in case of parallel sexual relationships; 4) for both men involved in a homosexual relationship; 5) for the man or the woman who practiced bestiality, the animal being also condemned to die. Other cases were punished with banishment – as in the case of a man having sex with his sister (or stepsister),[44] or with a menstruating woman. Finally, the man and his aunt having sexual intercourse were cursed and condemned to die childless.[45]

The last three cases did not entail an adulterous relationship, which can explain why they commanded a milder sentence.[46] All the other cases, aside from those concerning homosexuality and bestiality, involved adultery and required the death penalty. In fact, according to the letter of the law, the interdiction to commit adultery preceded all other sexual offences and served as a benchmark to them.[47]

Although the various books of law were consistent in the way they approached adultery and sexual relationships with close relatives, there remained a few exceptions. We find the first one in the death sentence required by the *Code of Hammurabi* for the man who had sex with his mother after the death of his father, although it did not involve an adulterous relationship. If we compare this law to the one that condemns the man who had sex with his

42 HL 187-200a; Westbrook, *History Law*, 649.

43 Lev. 18:6–23 (ESV).

44 See, for example, the story of Tamar and Amnon (2 Sam. 13:11–14).

45 Lev. 20:20 (ESV).

46 Everyone concerned was supposedly unmarried or a widow/widower, otherwise the law governing adultery would apply.

47 Lev. 20:10–21 (ESV); see also Deut. 22:30 (ESV).

stepmother after the death of his father and had to be disinherited, we can conclude that the incestuous content of the first offence aggravated its sentence. This conclusion, however, does not fit the case of the father who had sexual intercourse with his daughter – offence combining incest with adultery – an act that only required banishment.[48]

A second exception to the application of the death penalty in an adulterous relationship is found in the *Book of Leviticus* that condemned the man that had a sexual relationship with his sister-in-law to die childless. As is the case in the articles 192 and 193 of the *Hittite Code*, the law might here have presupposed that the sister-in-law was a widow: in the absence of adultery, no death penalty was required. Another noticeable anomaly found in this text is that no mention was made of the case of a father having had a sexual relationship with his daughter.

It is not clear whether the different books of law covering this period tried to convey any notion of incest in their text.[49] First, the cases discussed which entailed an incestuous relationships did not specifically address the incestuous aspect of these relationships, with the exception of article 189 of the *Hittite Code*. Let us not forget that many incestuous relationships were simply omitted in the law. Furthermore, the sentences stipulated in the law took almost exclusively the adulterous aspect of the relationship into account, not the incest. However, most noticeably, while women played a central role in the laws directly related to adultery, those dealing with sexual intercourse between close relatives essentially recognised men as the main perpetrators. This leads us to conclude that, by regulating those specific instances that mostly took place within the household, the lawmaker made sure that the control of patriarchal sexual behaviour was kept within the realm of his legislative authority.

48 LH 154–158.

49 Sasanian law, inspired by Zoroastrianism, imposed, besides the obligation to procreate, the acceptance and promotion of incestuous alliances as one of its most important requisite. These alliances were also very commonly found among the Israelites, with Abraham, Isaac, Jacob, Judah, Moses, David having all married close relatives. 'Judicial and Legal System. iii. Sasanian Legal System.' In *Encyclopaedia Iranica* XV, 2, 181–196, Viewed March 15, 2015,<www.iranicaonline.org/articles/judicial-and-legal-systems-iii-sasanian-legal-system>

5 Women as Property

For the entirety of their lives, most women were dependent on a man: first on their father, then on their father-in-law, then on their husband. And although their status differed from that of a slave,[50] they were still considered to be the property of the man on which they depended.[51]

A father had a right of life and death on his wife and children. He could pledge them for debts incurred by him, and if he failed to pay these debts back, wife and children could be enslaved.[52] A father could give his daughter in marriage at a very young age in exchange for a bride price. He could also consecrate her to the service of the temple, or sell her as debt bondage or as a prostitute.[53] This implies that incestuous relationships between father and daughter were probably common. Except for the very rare instances in which such a case came before the law, the father incurred no punishment (*Leviticus* does not even mention it). One reason for this is that it almost always happened when the girl still lived with her father, when she still was his 'property,' and when no other man could claim sexual rights on her. The story of Tamar and Amnon gives a good example of this paternal proprietary monopoly. The fact that Amnon rapes his sister condemns him (and her) because he has infringed upon the rights of her father:

50 Westbrook, *History Law*, 47, 504. Unlike female slaves, a wife was not totally excluded from 'the goods of citizenship, she could own property and have heirs. What is more, the rape of a slave did not raise procreative issues. Susanne Scholz, '"Back Then It Was Legal." The Epistemological Imbalance in Readings of Biblical and Ancient Near Eastern Rape Legislation', in *The Bible and Critical Theory* 1, 4 (2005): 1–22, 10. See also LU 8; Lev. 19:20 (ESV).

51 A few women could escape this domination by becoming *naditu*, for example, women who lived in relative seclusion and were not allowed to bear children, but could marry – they had to provide their husband with a second wife to father progeny – and were free to administer their dowry. Norman Yoffee, *Myths of the Archaic State Evolution of the Earliest Cities, States, and Civilizations* (Cambridge: Cambridge University Press, 2004), 117; Gwendolyn Leick, *Historical Dictionary of Mesopotamia* (Lanham: Scarecrow Press, 2003), 85.

52 LH 117; Lerner, *Creation Patriarchy*, 89.

53 As the Babylonian *naditu* coming from the upper segment of the society, who were women who could not get married; as *qadištu*, women who had a cultic function who could marry and procreate; as *kezertu* of *harimtu*, women with a cultic function that may have included sexual activities. See Lerner, *Creation Patriarchy*, 127–132; Westbrook, *History Law*, 172, 199, 424; Teppo, *Women Agency*, 94–95. See also Gen. 19:8; Lev. 19:29; Judg. 19:24 (ESV).

> … he grabbed her and said, "Come to bed with me!" She answered, "No! Please don't force me! This sort of thing isn't done in Israel. It's too disgusting! Think of me. I'll be disgraced forever! And think of yourself. Everyone in Israel will say you're nothing but trash! Just ask the king, and he will let you marry me." But Amnon would not listen to what she said. He was stronger than she was, so he overpowered her and raped her.[54]

From the moment a girl got married, all the rights possessed by her father were transmitted to her husband. Marriage gave him exclusive sexual access to her. However, many brides passed first through the hands of their father-in-law: as the above mentioned hymn to the goddess Gula asserts, a woman was first a daughter-in law before being a wife. It was customary for the bride to join the household of her father-in-law,[55] and undoubtedly, he might have exercised certain rights on the woman joining his domesticity. A woman was, therefore, a daughter-in-law before becoming a wife. Moreover, if her husband passed away and she had no son, her father-in-law could marry her to one of his sons, or marry her himself.[56] In the *Hittite Code*, if her brothers-in-law and her father-in-law were all deceased, the woman was married to her uncle-in-law.[57] By marrying, a woman became the property of her in-laws.

A husband had some obligations toward his wife. He had also to provide his household with food. As discussed earlier, a woman whose husband had been absent for a long time – taken prisoner of war, for example – was allowed to leave him for another man if there was nothing to eat at her house. But if she left him while there was enough food to feed her, she was considered to be adulterous and had to perish by drowning.[58]

Just like fathers could sell their daughters, so husbands could prostitute their wives. In case of 'emergency,' the rules concerning adultery could be suspended. This explains why most codes gave the final word to the husband as to the punishment of his adulterous wife, and why the sentence for the paramour could never exceed that given to the woman.[59]

54 2 Sam. 13:11–14 (*Holy Bible*, Contemporary English Version, American Bible Society, 1995 (CEV)).

55 Westbrook, *History Law*, 45.

56 MAL A33, A45; HL 193; G. Driver & John Miles, *The Assyrian Laws* (Oxford, Clarendon Press, 1935), 166; Westbrook, *History Law*, 538.

57 HL 193.

58 LH 133–136.

59 Gen. 12:11–15, 20:2–14, 26:7; Judg. 19:24 (ESV). Westbrook, *History Law*, 1010.

6 A Procreative Monopoly

Besides confirming women's dependent status by establishing the proprietary rights men had on them, one common value to these laws is that they systematically outlined the procreative functions along gender lines.

Although the rape of a non-betrothed virgin infringed the proprietary rights of her father, its punishment was much milder than the death sentence that was required in the case of the rape of a promised or of a married woman, which infringed upon the procreative monopoly of the prospective or actual husband. Actually, the *damage* caused by the rape of a non-betrothed girl could easily be repaired by obliging the rapist to marry his victim.

An identical line of reasoning can be applied to the case of a man who has a sexual relationship with his daughter-in-law. Punishment varied according to whether either the proprietary rights or of the procreative rights[60] of the husband had been infringed upon: in the first situation, the marriage was not consumed, and a symbolic fine had to be paid; but in the second one, the marriage had been consumed, and the death penalty was required.

Both cases undoubtedly show that the law sought to protect men's procreative activity. Furthermore, the case of the father-in-law reveals that the protection of the patriarchal authority came second to that of the procreative monopoly: although the father had a right of life and death on his children, he could himself be condemned to death if he infringed upon the procreative territory of his son.

The laws dealing with adultery point in the same direction. A man was not punished for having a sexual relationship with another woman than his wife, as long as this woman did not belong to another man.[61] The law did not intend to limit men's sexual activity, but aimed at delimiting and protecting paternal territory. For that reason, a married woman involved in an adulterous relationship was, as a principle, always guilty because she inevitably breached the procreative monopoly of her husband. Her lover, on the other hand, could never get a harsher sentence than she did. He could even be absolved if he could prove that he did not know the woman was married.

Finally, the very harsh punishment detailed in *Deuteronomy* that was inflicted on a woman who could not prove she was a virgin at the moment of her

---

60 Roth, *Law Collections*, 35.

61 Westbrook mentions the case of a man who brought a woman to court for having caused his brother to leave his wife. The woman not being married, she had not committed adultery and was not punished in any way. The married man was also freed from any charges. Westbrook, *History Law*, 516.

wedding confirms the importance of guaranteeing to the would-be husband that he would not only acquire proprietary rights on his wife to be, but that this propriety was unspoiled.[62]

The establishment of the masculine procreative monopoly reduced the feminine to a functional status: the woman becoming the 'receptacle'[63] of the seed of the man to whom she was subordinated, no other man could make use of her reproductive capacities. In contrast to the rigid sexual constraints imposed on her, the law offered much more leeway to the man: whereas she was defined as the procreative territory of one man, his procreative territory could be extended to several wives, to concubines, to slaves, to prostitutes, and to any other woman he might want to possess, as long as his sexual activities did not infringe upon the procreative monopoly of another man:

> ... adultery is possible only on the side of the wife, because she is the property of the husband, but not on the part of the husband... the wife owes faithfulness to her own marriage; the husband owes faithfulness to another man's marriage.[64]

The pre-eminence of procreative rights on proprietary ones is also apparent in the case of a man who wanted to divorce his wife, the law according a better treatment to the woman who had borne him children.[65] The law even specified

62 This does not mean, however, that girls who had lost their virginity while still living at their father's house could not get married, and that they were forced to become concubines, prostitutes, or employees of a temple. In Babylon, the marriage contract used different terms to describe the status of the bride. However, whether she was a virgin or not was a significant factor in determining the bride price. *Exodus* relates the case of a man who wanted to acquire a wife without the consent of her father by sleeping with her. He was condemned to pay the "virgin" bride-price. The father could further decide whether the man could marry his daughter or not (Exod. 22:16–17 (ESV). Additionally, widows could marry again. Finally, it is important to note that, before *Deuteronomy*, none of the books of law make mention of the fact that a woman had to be a virgin at the time of her wedding. See Leick, *Historical Dictionary Mesopotamia*, 79; Jerrold Cooper, 'Virginity in Ancient Mesopotamia', in *Sex and Gender in the Ancient Near East*, Proceedings of the 47th Rencontre Assyriologique Internationale (Helsinki: Helsinki University Press, 2002), 91–112, 101; Westbrook, *History Law*, 323, 389, 536, 933.

63 Donald Zeyl, 'Plato's Timaeus', in *The Stanford Encyclopaedia of Philosophy* (Spring 2014 Edition), Edward N. Zalta (ed.), Viewed March 29, 2015, <http://plato.stanford.edu/archives/spr2014/entries/plato-timaeus/>.

64 Louis Epstein, *Sex Laws and Customs in Judaism* (New York: Bloch, 1948), 194.

65 *Laws of Eshnunna* (LE) 59; LH 137–138.

the inheritance rights of a child born of a prostitute, and applied 'vicarious talion' to the person who struck a prostitute and caused her to abort her foetus.[66] Lastly, Middle Assyrian law considered a self-inflicted abortion to be a most serious infringement of the paternal procreative rights and condemned the guilty woman to be impaled and to be denied burial.[67]

7 Conclusion

According to the 'agricultural' understanding of procreation that prevailed at the time,[68] the man was considered to be the creator of the child, and the law granted him exclusive procreative rights. The woman, for her part, was regarded as the soil in which the man plants his seed. In order to demarcate paternal pro-creative activity with the utmost certainty, the law sought to impose on women's sexual activities the necessary boundaries to prevent them from engaging in any promiscuous relationships. Hence, the books of law stipulated gender roles according to how the procreative functions of each sex were perceived, thus defining, rooting and consecrating the normative foundations of the patriarchal family. A document of the *Urukagina Reform* confirms this idea. Dating from around 2,400, it forbids the practice of polyandry, a seemingly accepted tradition in Sumer until then:

> The women of former days used to take two husbands, (but) the women of today (if they attempted this) were stoned with stones (upon which was inscribed their evil) intent.[69]

The particularly high number of laws regulating sexual offences found in the first codes in the Levant allows us to think that the norms they enforced were not totally shared and accepted, especially if we consider the idea that the enactment of a law signals an underlying necessity in the society in which the

---

66 LL 27; LH 209–210; MAL A52; Westbrook, *History Law*, 558. Most codes specified the price one had to pay if he or she caused a woman to lose her foetus (LL c, f; LH 209–211, 213; MAL A21, A50-53; HL 17–18). The Middle Assyrian Laws adapted the sentence to the sex of the foetus: if it was female, the assailant was fined; if it was male, the assailant had to die (MAL A50).

67 MAL A53; Lerner, *Creation Patriarchy*, 120.

68 Hirsch, 'Procreative Knowledge', 2015.

69 Samuel Kramer, *The Sumerians: Their History, Culture, and Character* (Chicago: University of Chicago Press, 1963), 322.

law is to be applied. What is more, the fact that the laws found in the *Old Testament*, while comparable to those found in the older codes, were more extensive and restrictive than the laws preceding them, could indicate a hardening of the norms regulating sexual interaction between men and women.[70] However, this regulatory intensification might also have had to do with the population for whom these laws were intended. While the older codes were meant to regulate sexual behaviour in the first kingdoms and empires of Antiquity, the laws found in the *Old Testament* were written for a pastoral people who lived at the margins of the 'urban revolution,'[71] and whose sexual heritage might have been less 'normalised' and regulated than that of their urban contemporaries.[72] A further study of the parallels existing between the various sexual mores of the last millennium BCE around the East Mediterranean area might shed more light on this aspect.

Bibliography

Aeschylus, *The Oresteia.* Translated by R.C. Trevelyan. Cambridge: Bowes & Bowes, 1920.

Aristotle. 'De Generatione Animalium'. In *The Works.* Translated by Arthur Platt. Oxford: Clarendon Press, 1912.

Annus, Amar. *The God Ninurta: in The Mythology and Royal Ideology of AncientMesopotamia.* Helsinki: Neo-Assyrian Text Corpus Project, 2002.

Boecker, Hans Jochen. *Law and the Administration of Justice in the Old Testament and Ancient East.* Augsburg: Augsburg Publishing House, 1980.

Boyarin, Daniel. ' "This We Know to Be the Carnal Israel": Circumcision and the Erotic Life of God and Israel'. *Critical Inquiry* 18, 3 (1992): 474–505.

---

70 Segregation along the gender lines is already present in the Middle Assyrian laws, which were the first to require women to veil themselves (MAL A40).

71 Gordon Childe, 'The Urban Revolution', *The Town Planning Review* 21, 1 (1950): 3–17.

72 Daniel Boyarin, ' "This We Know to Be the Carnal Israel": Circumcision and the Erotic Life of God and Israel', *Critical Inquiry* 18, 3 (1992): 474–505. Today, we witness a similar conflicting discrepancy between societies that introduce laws aiming at "normalising" our contemporary understanding of procreative functions and sexual identities (new family structures, sexual fluidity, etc.) and those that still promote the traditional distribution of gender roles, as Nick Mulé shows in Chapter 1 in this collection. See also *Brief of Historians of Marriage and the American Historical Association as Amici Curiae in Support of Petitioners*. The Supreme Court of the United States, Nos. 14–556, 14–562, 14–571 and 14–574.

Brief of Historians of Marriage and the American Historical Association as Amici Curiae in Support of Petitioners. The Supreme Court of the United States, Nos. 14–556, 14–562, 14–571 and 14–574, March 6, 2015.

Childe, Gordon. 'The Urban Revolution'. *The Town Planning Review* 21, 1 (1950): 3–17.

Cooper, Jerrold. 'Virginity in Ancient Mesopotamia'. In *Sex and Gender in the Ancient Near-East*. Proceedings of the 47th Rencontre Assyriologique Internationale, 91–112. Helsinki: Helsinki University Press, 2002.

Driver, G., and John Miles. *The Assyrian Laws*. Oxford, Clarendon Press, 1935.

Driver, G., and John Miles. *The Babylonian Laws*, edited with Translation and Commentary. Oxford, 1952–1955.

Dyck, Andrew Roy. *A Commentary on Cicero, De Legibus*. Ann Arbor: University of Michigan Press, 2004.

Encyclopaedia Iranica XV,2. 'Judicial and Legal System. iii. Sasanian Legal System.' 181–196. Accessed March 15, 2015.<www.iranicaonline.org/articles/judicial-and-legal-systems-iii-sasanian-legal-system.>

Epstein, Louis. *Sex Laws and Customs in Judaism*. New York, Bloch: 1948.

Flannery, Kent. 'The Cultural Evolution of Civilizations'. *Annual Review of Ecology and Systematics* 3 (1972): 399–426.

Foster, Benjamin. *Before the Muses: An Anthology of Akkadian Literature*. Bethesda: CDL Press, 1996.

Gonzalès, Jacques. *Histoire Naturelle et Articificielle de la Procréation*. Paris: Bordas, 1996.

Grace, Philip. 'Aspects of Fatherhood in Thirteenth-Century Encyclopedias'. *Journal of Family History* 31 (2006): 211–236.

Hammurabi's Code of Laws. Translated by L.W. King. Ancient History Sourcebook. Accessed April 10, 2015.<www.fordham.edu/halsall/ancient/hamcode.html.>

Hippocrates and Galen. *The Writings*. Philadelphia: Lindsay and Blakiston, 1846.

Hirsch, René. 'Procreative Knowledge, Gender Roles, and Beliefs: Past and Present Parallels.' Paper presented at the World History Theory and Practice: Gender, Technology, Culture conference, St John's University, New York, May 2015.

Holy Bible (The), Contemporary English Version. American Bible Society, 1995. Accessed June 21, 2015.<https://www.biblegateway.com/>.

Holy Bible (The), English Standard Version. Crossway Bibles, 2001. Accessed June 21, 2015<https://www.biblegateway.com/>.

Holy Bible (The), King James Version. Bible Gateway, 1987. Accessed June 21, 2015.<https://www.biblegateway.com/>.

Kramer, Samuel. *The Sumerians: Their History, Culture, and Character*. Chicago: University of Chicago Press, 1963.

Leick, Gwendolyn. *Historical Dictionary of Mesopotamia*. Lanham: Scarecrow Press, 2003.

Lerner, Gerda. *The Creation of Patriarchy*. Oxford: Oxford University Press, 1986.

Levinson, Bernard. *Legal Revision and Religious Renewal in Ancient Israel*. Cambridge: Cambridge University Press, 2008.

Levinson, Bernard. 'Middle Assyrian Laws'. In *Law Collections from Mesopotamia and Asia Minor* by Martha Roth, 153–194. Atlanta: Scholar Press, 1995.

Merriam-Webster's Dictionary of Law, s.v. "incest"http://dictionary.reference.com/browse/incest (accessed: February 24, 2015).

Powis Smith, J. M. *The Origin and History of Hebrew Law*. Chicago, 2006.

Roth, Martha. 'Hittite Laws'. In *Law Collections from Mesopotamia and Asia Minor. SBL Writings from the Ancient World*. Atlanta: Scholar Press, 1995, 213–247.

Roth, Martha. 'Laws of Hammurabi'. In *Law Collections from Mesopotamia and Asia Minor. SBL Writings from the Ancient World*. Atlanta: Scholar Press, 1995, 71–142.

Roth, Martha. 'Laws of Lipit-Ishtar'. In *Law Collections from Mesopotamia and Asia Minor. SBL Writings from the Ancient World*. Atlanta: Scholar Press, 1995, 23–35.

Roth, Martha. 'Laws of Ur-Nammu'. In *Law Collections from Mesopotamia and Asia Minor. SBL Writings from the Ancient World*. Atlanta: Scholar Press, 1995, 13–22.

Scholz, Susanne. '"Back Then It Was Legal." The Epistemological Imbalance in Readings of Biblical and Ancient Near Eastern Rape Legislation', in *The Bible and Critical Theory* 1, 4 (2005): 1–22.

Steele, Francis. *The Code of Lipit-Ishtar*. Philadelphia: The University Museum, 1948.

Stol, Marten. *Birth in Babylonia and the Bible: Its Mediterranean Setting*. Groningen: Styx Brill, 2000.

Teppo, Saana. 'Women and Their Agency in the Neo-Assyrian Empire'. PhD diss., University of Helsinki, 2005.

The Code of Nesilim, c. 1650-1500 BCE. Ancient History Sourcebook. Accessed April 10, 2015.<http://legacy.fordham.edu/halsall/ancient/1650nesilim.asp>.

Westbrook, Raymond, ed. *A History of Ancient Near-Eastern Law*. Leiden: Brill, 2003.

Yoffee, Norman. *Myths of the Archaic State Evolution of the Earliest Cities, States, and Civilizations*. Cambridge: Cambridge University Press, 2004.

Zeyl, Donald. 'Plato's Timaeus', in *The Stanford Encyclopaedia of Philosophy* (Spring 2014 Edition), Edward N. Zalta (ed.).Accessed March 29, 2015.<http://plato.stanford.edu/archives/spr2014/entries/plato-timaeus/>.

CHAPTER 5

Micromanaging the Massage Parlour: How Municipal Bylaws Organize and Shape the Lives of Asian Sex Workers

Elene Lam

Abstract

Debates on sex work in Canada have focused on its criminal aspects, its harms, and the 'nuisance' it posits for communities. Not much attention has been devoted to more subtle forms of regulation that take place in other juridical spaces, such as the legal apparatus of municipalities. A growing number of cities are restricting sex work and using micro-regulation to police, constrain and control the activities and lives sex workers.[1] Municipal bylaws are used by local governments to suppress sex work and prosecute sex workers. By 'micro-regulation' I mean the devious introduction of a myriad of rules that strictly constrain the range of activities that can take place in massage parlours, effectively creating barriers to sex work, even though municipalities do not have the power to prohibit the offering of sexual services. This paper aims to alleviate a lacuna in the research and literature on sex work in the juridical space of the municipality. I wish to bring attention specifically to the plight of Asian sex workers employed in massage parlours in the city of Toronto, whose voices and struggles are ignored and go unnoticed.[2] My data was collected during a practice-based research study conducted in Toronto in 2014. My findings will show that municipal bylaws create barriers to the practice of sex work in the context of holistic centres, barriers that push sex work underground, endangering sex workers and exacerbating their stigmatization and exploitation.

Keywords

sex work – migrant sex workers – massage parlours – micro-regulation – municipal regulation and bylaws – ethnography

---

1 Jacqueline Lewis, Eleanor Maticka-Tyndale, Frances, Shaver, and Heather Schramm. 'Managing Risk and Safety on The Job: The Experiences of Canadian Sex Workers,' *Journal of Psychology and Human Sexuality* 17. 1/2 (2005), 147–167.

2 Elene Lam, *Chinese Sex Workers in Toronto,* unpublished report prepared for *Butterfly*, the Asian and Migration Sex Workers Support Network, 2014.

 | DOI:10.1163/9789004392298_007

1 Introduction

The debate surrounding reform of federal criminal laws regarding sex work has been raging for many years in Canada. Sex workers, their allies in the legal and medical profession, policy experts, politicians and academics continue to lend their voices to the debates, and have been the catalysts of significant changes in the last two years in the country's policies and its criminal legal apparatus. Sex workers and sex work rights activists have successfully challenged some criminal prohibitions, bringing them to the attention of the Federal Supreme Court of Canada for constitutional examination. Some criminal prohibitions have been struck down, and new laws been introduced, significantly changing the juridical landscape of the country.

The majority of these debates have focused on the criminal aspects of sex work, its harms, and the 'nuisance' it posits for communities. Not much attention has been devoted to more subtle forms of regulation that take place in other juridical spaces, such as the legal apparatus of municipalities. A growing number of cities are restricting sex work and using micro-regulation and bylaws to police, constrain and control the activities and lives sex workers.[3] By 'micro-regulation' I mean the devious introduction of a myriad of rules that strictly constrain the range of activities that can take place in massage parlours, effectively creating barriers to sex work, even though municipalities do not have the power to prohibit the offering of sexual services. These municipal regulations and bylaws are seldom made part of larger policy debates and discussions on criminalization, virtually passing unnoticed by sex work theorists, activists and policy makers alike.

This paper aims to alleviate a lacuna in the research and literature on sex work in the juridical space of the municipality. I wish to bring attention specifically to the plight of Asian sex workers employed in massage parlours in the city of Toronto, whose voices and struggles are ignored and go unnoticed.[4] My data was collected during a practice-based research study conducted in Toronto in 2014. My findings will shed light on the ways in which municipal regulations control and police sexual services, and the impact they have on the lived experiences of Asian women who work in massage parlours.

My work will show that there is an important incongruence in ideology between the latest Federal regulations on sex work and their municipal

3 Lewis, Maticka-Tyndale, Shaver, and Schramm, 'Managing Risk and Safety on The Job,' 155.

4 Lam, *Chinese Sex Workers in Toronto.*

counterparts. On one hand, Federal criminal law makes the act of selling sex a licit practice, given that Canada has now adopted what is known as the 'Nordic Model' for regulating sex work: clients and third party profiteers are criminalized, while sex workers are permitted to sell sex, *supposedly* without fear of criminal prosecution. Fundamentally, the Canadian system sees sex workers as 'victims' in need of protection, making 'johns,' the purchasers of sex, and 'pimps' and 'madams,' the profiteers of its sale, the criminal elements.[5]

On the other hand, municipal micro-regulation continues to conceive sex work as a 'nuisance' and sex workers as a 'criminal element.' Municipal regulation assumes that the exchange of money for sex is illicit, and conflates the culpability and criminality of the recipient of sex services and the sex worker providing them. It creates barriers to the practice of sex work in the context of the massage parlour, barriers that ultimately endanger, stigmatize and push sex work underground, generating conditions of greater and more severe exploitation for the sex workers involved, a situation that the State is *supposedly attempting to mitigate* with its new iteration of Federal Criminal Law.

This chapter is organized into seven sections. In the next section, I provide a brief description of the research project and its methodology. In the third section of the chapter, I give a brief overview of the evolution of the criminal regulation of sex work in Canada. The fourth section discusses the ways sex work has been regulated in the context of the city, providing a review of current research on its impacts on the lives of those who work in this sector. In the fifth section, I provide a detailed analysis of the evolution of municipal legislation in the city of Toronto. I illustrate how the regulation of sex work has been specifically carried out in insidious ways, in the business space of the massage parlour. In the sixth section, I report on the lives and lived experiences of Asian sex workers in Toronto, analysing the findings of this research project, and discuss how the licencing and policies institutionalized by the city are used to regulate, control, and police their lives. I conclude by providing some thoughts on the recent collaborative efforts between municipalities and the Canada Border Services Agency to curb human trafficking, arguing that such efforts further exacerbate the potential exploitation and abuse of one of the most vulnerable groups in our society, migrant workers, especially those without legal status.

5 Jaqueline Davies 'The Criminalization of Sexual Commerce in Canada: Context and Concepts for Critical Analysis,' *The Canadian Journal of Human Sexuality* 24.2 (2015), 78.

2 Methodology

This paper is based on research conducted in Toronto in 2014 to explore how municipal bylaws control and regulate sexual services in massage parlours, in which ways they affect the experiences and lives of the women who work therein. I have been involved in the sex work, migrant and labour rights movement for more than 15 years. While enrolled in a Masters of Social Work, I carried out a placement in a community centre that supports Asian sex workers in Toronto. My working experiences there allowed me entry and acceptance in the community, which enabled me to carry out this research project.

This research project has been informed by the methodology of Institutional Ethnography[6] and delved into the daily practices of Asian sex workers in Toronto, showing how they are constrained and regulated in massage parlours. Mixed research methods were adopted to map how the everyday lives of sex workers are organized by institutional processes. The experiences of sex workers became the point of entry into a broader investigation which examined how Municipal codes were activated and became an integral form of regulation in their lives. My research specifically illustrates how texts become instrumental in coordinating ruling relations.[7]

I conducted this work in 2014 as a practice-based research paper for my Master of Social Work. The research was funded and supported by the Community Support Project for Chinese Sex Workers in Toronto. It was multi-faceted and involved mixed research methods. I interviewed two owners of massage parlours, five employees, as well as three health professionals who serve sex workers. Additionally, I carried out field work[8] in a courtroom setting, observing a trial of a sex worker who was charged with breaching Toronto's *Municipal Code* in relation to the licensing of holistic

6 Dorothy Smith. *Institutional Ethnography. A Sociology for People* (Lanham: Rowan & Littlefield Publishers Inc., 2005).

7 Ibid., 19.

8 Michael Quinn Patton. *Qualitative Research* (London: John Wiley and Sons, 2005), 236. I conducted field work in 2014 at the Ontario Court of Justice, observing the trial of sex worker, who will be kept anonymous, charged with breaching the *Toronto Municipal Code* related to the licensing of holistic practitioners. I observed the court proceedings, which included dialogue between the informant, and a prosecutor, and a translator, and the statement given by a police officer and an informant during the trial, and the judgement given by a judge.

practitioners.[9] Finally, I carried out textual analyses of municipal bylaws and committee reports of the City of Toronto.

All of the participants were recruited through the 'snowball' method[10] and found through my network and during outreach activities with Butterfly, the Asian and Migration Sex Workers Support Network. A semi-structured, open-ended, in-depth qualitative research approach was used for all of the interviews. Open-ended questions allowed the interviewees to take control of the interview process, deciding the type of questions they were willing to answer, and choosing the depth of disclosure.

Interviews spanned from 1 hour, to 2 hours and 15 minutes, with the average interview lasting 1 hour and 30 minutes. During initial contact, I gave details on the purpose of the research, I went over the consent form, explained the type of questions that would be asked, and covered any confidentiality issues and ethical considerations that would be involved. I informed participants that the interviews would be recorded, if they consented. I also stressed that participation would be completely voluntary, and that, at any time, individuals could refuse to answer any question, or stop and withdraw from the study with no negative consequences to themselves.

I arranged times and locations for the interviews once the individuals had agreed to participate in the study. The location for interviews was chosen by the participants, and included massage parlours, offices, restaurants, and food courts. A monetary honorarium was given to sex workers and owners of massage parlours as a thank you for their time and participation in the research. In addition, participants were given a list of community resources in case they required support and/or services after the interviews. Data collected during the interviews (including the consent forms, interview notes, and audio-tapes) was destroyed immediately after the research was finished.

3 The Evolution of Federal Criminal Law on Sex Work in Canada

In this section, I will provide a brief history of the evolution of the criminal regulation of sex work in Canada. Canadian criminal law has changed its

9 Any reference to this court case has been purposely omitted from this text, to guarantee and safeguard the anonymity of the person prosecuted.

10 Biernacki, Patrick, and Dan Waldorf, 'Snowball Sampling: Problems and Techniques of Chain Referral Sampling' *Sociological Methods and Research* 10 (1981) 147.

approach to regulating sex work over the last hundred and fifty years, moving from the outright criminalization of selling sex, to ceasing to criminalize sex work altogether, and criminalizing the purchase of sex and third party profiteering instead, shifting to what is known as the 'Nordic Model.'[11]

Debates over sex work in the past few years in Canada have been polarized into two positions: on one hand prostitution has been seen as a nuisance, a moral turpitude carried out by a deviant element, polluting neighbourhoods; on the other it has been framed as an exploitative practice, from which victims must be rescued.[12] The public debates have been further complicated since the 1970s by the mobilization and engagement of sex workers and their allies into public debates, who have countered the tropes of moral degeneration/victimization and abuse with the 'language of work and commerce.'[13] I align myself with this last political positioning and consider myself a political ally of the sex workers, legal professionals and activists who see sex work *as labour*. Of great importance here is the issue of agency, because fundamentally *a worker is an agent*: she may or may not face mistreatment but, as a worker, she is engaged in action and has a stake at controlling her own destiny. I advocate for the decriminalization of sex work. It would be an essential step towards legitimating this profession and erasing the stigma that currently mars it, constituting:

> ...a shift from the status quo, where sex workers are subject to extreme levels of violence and social marginalization, to a society where sex workers are empowered to create safe and dignified working conditions.[14]

In the 19th Century, sex work related activities were targeted and criminalized by *The Contagious Disease Act* and *The Vagrancy Act*.[15] The first *Criminal Code*

11 Davies, 'The Criminalization of Sexual Commerce in Canada,' 78.

12 Ibid., 79.

13 Ibid.

14 Pivot Legal Society, *Beyond Decriminalization: Sex Work, Human Rights and a New Framework for Law Reform* (Vancouver: Pivot, 2009), 9; viewed 21 August, 2015,www.pivotlegal.org/pivot-points/publications/beyond-decriminalization.

15 Constance Backhouse, 'Nineteenth-Century Canadian Prostitution Law: Reflection of a Discriminatory Society,' *Histoire Sociale/Social History* 18 (1986): 389; Emily van der Meulen and Mariana Valverde, 'Beyond the Criminal Code: Municipal Licensing and Zoning Bylaws,' in *Selling Sex: Experience, Advocacy, and Research on Sex Work in Canada*, ed. Emily van der Meulen, Elya Durisin, and Victoria Love (UBC Press: Vancouver, Toronto, 2013) 319.

was ratified in 1892 and it included a wide range of provisions against sex workers, including bawdy-house offences, which criminalized brothel owners and women working therein, and prohibited outright procuring sex for money.[16] Over the course of the next century the code underwent significant permutations: some provisions were struck down, modified or re-introduced; generally the *Criminal Code of Canada* continued to criminalize most of the activities related to sex work.

The 1985 iteration of the *Criminal Code* did not criminalize the sale of sex for money *per se*, but it continued to create significant barriers to the sale of sex and, in the process, caused significant problems for the safety of the sex workers engaged in this sector. For example, prohibitions criminalized the act of keeping and being found in a 'bawdy-house,' as well as 'living on the avails of prostitution,' and 'communicating in public for the purpose of prostitution,' forcing sex workers to often work in dangerous conditions.[17]

The 1970s and 1980s saw the organization of sex workers and their allies into a powerful lobby, which began advocating for human and labour rights, challenging criminal laws prohibiting and criminalizing sex work. Sex workers adopted a jargon that stressed the importance of work, the right to sell one's sexual labour as a form of legitimate commerce,[18] and define themselves in terms of labour politics, adopting a stance that gave them agency as workers, against the State's efforts to define them instead as either 'victims' in need of salvations, or 'corrupt criminals' in need of reformation.[19] Once the focus was shifted to a definition of sex work as a form of labour, it became possible to show that criminal laws forced sex workers 'to live and work in conditions where they experience[d] systemic discrimination, exploitation and violence.'[20] Activists pointed out that the law kept sex workers from enjoying and accessing their labour and sexual rights.[21]

The case of *Hutt v R*[22] of 1978 was an emblematic example of the success this line of political mobilization could have in transforming the framework of criminal law on sex work. In this seminal court case, Debra Hutt, a sex worker, was brought to justice on 'soliciting' charges: she had engaged an undercover police officer for the purposes of selling sex by smiling at him, and this

16 Ibid.

17 *Criminal Code,* RSC 1985, c C-46 s 745, s 210, s 212.1 (i), and s 213.1.

18 Davies, 'The Criminalization of Sexual Commerce in Canada,' 79.

19 Ibid.

20 Pivot Legal Society, *Beyond Decriminalization,* 8.

21 van der Meulen & Valverde, 'Beyond the Criminal Code,' 320.

22 *R. v. Hutt,* [1978] 2 S.C.R. 476.

exchange was taken to demonstrate that she had been available for prostitution. Yet, the nature of the exchange was deemed insufficient for a conviction for solicitation, which was quashed. The Supreme Court ruled that the conduct of soliciting had to be 'importuning,' or 'pressing or persisting;' this ruling, from this moment forward, ensured that a charge of soliciting could only apply if there had been significantly more communication between parties than just 'a mere indication.' The Supreme Court decision temporarily decreased the number of police arrests, until the federal government introduced new stringent laws in 1985 to criminalize communicating in a public place for the purpose of prostitution.

It would take another three decades for sex workers to achieve another victory, albeit a short lived one, in those chambers. In December 2013, the Supreme Court of Canada made a landmark decision in the case of *Canada v. Bedford*[23] and struck down a number of laws regulating sex work. Three sex workers, Terri-Jean Bedford, Amy Lebovitch and Valerie Scott brought forth the challenge, arguing that Canadian criminal laws relating to sex work deprived sex workers of the basic human right to safety, and should be struck down because unconstitutional.

The court ruled that three provisions of Canada's *Criminal Code* were unconstitutional and must be struck down,[24] because they violated the right to security of the person, protected by s. 7 of the *Charter of Rights and Freedoms*.[25] These were s. 210, 'keeping or being found in a bawdy-house,' which prevented sex workers from working at a fixed location; s. 212(1) (j), 'living on the avails of prostitution,' which punished everyone without distinguishing among those who exploited sex workers and those who assured their security and safety; and s. 213(1) (c), 'communicating in public for the purpose of prostitution,' which prevented sex workers from screening clients and having safer sex in a safer environment. The court gave the government one year to modify the parts of the *Criminal Code* that were unconstitutional or introduce new legislation. On June 4th, 2014 the Federal government introduced Bill 36-C, *The Protection of Communities and Exploited Persons Act.* It received Royal Assent on November 6th, 2014 and went into force on December 6, 2014.[26]

---

23 *Canada (Attorney General) v. Bedford*, [2013] SCC 72.

24 *Criminal Code*, RSC 1985, c C-46 s 745, s 210, s 212.1 (i), and s 213.1.

25 *Canadian Charter of Rights and Freedoms*, s. 2, Part I of the *Constitution Act, 1982*, being Schedule B to the *Canada Act 1982* (UK), 1982, c 11.

26 Government of Canada. Department of Justice. 'Technical Paper: *Bill C-36, Protection of Communities and Exploited Persons Act*,' 1, viewed 25 January, 2015,http://www.justice.gc.ca/eng/rp-pr/other-autre/protect/p1.html.

The new law was a complete paradigm shift from the previous approach to regulating sex work. It was not a coincidence that this piece of legislation no longer used the term 'prostitution' to describe the exchange of sexual favours for money. This discoursive shift was very significant because it denoted a change in the 'interpretation' of the act's moral character from a 'nuisance,' to an 'exploitative practice' that harmed women, children and society itself:

> Bill C-36 reflects a significant paradigm shift away from the treatment of prostitution as a "nuisance," as found by the Supreme Court of Canada in *Bedford*, toward treatment of prostitution as a form of sexual exploitation that disproportionately and negatively impacts on women and girls.[27]

It effectively brought Canada into alignment with Scandinavian countries which were the first to introduce what is known as the 'Nordic model.'[28]

Davies has argued that in this model the culpability for the offence moves away from the *seller* of sex, to the *purchaser* of sex:

> The law is supposed to replace unfair blaming of those who are paid for their sexual services with a new focus on the criminal exploitation they suffer. The legislation constructs the payment itself as an instance of criminally culpable exploitation.[29]

The new legislation assumes that the victims of sex work are 'manifold:' they include 'individuals who sell their own sexual services,' 'children who are exposed to prostitution' and 'society' itself.[30] It is intended to curb the 'public nuisances' associated with this practice and the exploitation of individuals who engage in sex work.[31] It assumes that those who make use of sex workers are always abusive exploiters: they de-humanize the sex worker while at the same time continue to create a demand for sex work. Similarly, those who 'capitalize

27 Ibid.

28 Davies 'The Criminalization of Sexual Commerce in Canada,' 78.

29 Ibid.

30 Government of Canada, 'Technical Paper,' 4.

31 Lyne Casavant and Dominique Valiquet, *Legislative Summary of Bill C-36: An Act to Amend the Criminal Code in Response to the Supreme Court of Canada Decision in Attorney General of Canada v. Bedford and to Make Consequential Amendments to Other Acts*, Publication no. 41-2-C36-E, (Legal and Social Affairs Division, Library of Parliament: Ottawa, Canada, 2014), viewed 15 August, 2015,http://www.lop.parl.gc.ca/About/Parliament/LegislativeSummaries/bills_ls.asp?ls=c36&Parl=41&Ses=2.

on that demand' – any third party that makes a profit from these monetary exchanges – are culpable of both causing and perpetrating sex work's 'harms.'[32]

Although the Supreme Court struck down 'living on avails of prostitution' in *Bedford*, two new provisions in the *Criminal Code*, s. 286(2) and s. 286(3), continue to criminalize those who 'procure' or 'gain material benefits from sex work.' Even though the law states that it does not apply to those in 'legitimate living arrangements' or those with 'legal or moral obligations' to sex workers, it criminalizes third parties who provide services and support to sex workers.[33]

S. 213(1), additionally, criminalizes sex workers who communicate in public for the purpose of selling sexual services, which 'still prohibits communications in most public places.' With s. 286(1), the State aims to decrease the demand for sex work by criminalizing the act of communicating or obtaining sex services, by a client at any time, and in any place. Finally s. 286(4) of the code makes it an offence for any third parties to advertise sexual services; any organization that hosts or publishes a sex worker's advertisement is caught by this prohibition.[34]

As President of Butterfly, I penned a brief to the Senate's Standing Committee on Legal and Constitutional Affairs regarding Bill C-36, in October 2014, articulating the numerous dangers that this new piece of legislation continues to pose for sex workers. I quote the paragraph that summarises them:

> We urge the Committee to recognize the constitutional and human rights of sex workers by rejecting Bill C-36, because, to implement this proposed act as it has been drafted would force this work to go underground. In so doing, it would further restrict and stigmatize all sex workers, in general, and the Asian and migrant sex workers, in particular. It would not only increase the isolation and exclusion of all sex workers, it would have an especially negative impact on racialized and migrant sex workers, and this would affect the sex workers' health, equity, dignity, safety and human rights.[35]

---

32 Government of Canada, 'Technical Paper, ' 4.

33 *Criminal Code*, RSC 1985, c C-46 s 745, s 210, s 212.1 (i), and s 213.1.

34 Power & Pivot Legal Society *Sex workers and Bill C-36: Analysis based on Social Science Evidence* (Power & Pivot, 2014), 2, viewed 21 August, 2015,http://www.powerottawa.ca/Briefing_Note_C-36_Social_Science_Evidence.pdf

35 Elene Lam, *Brief to the Senate Standing Committee on Legal and Constitutional Affairs Regarding Bill C-36 (Protection of Communities and Exploited Persons Act)*, (Butterfly, the Asian and Migrant Sex Workers Support Network, October 2014), viewed 15 January, 2015,https://www.google.ca/?gws_rd=ssl#q=Brief+to+the+Senate+Standing+Committee+on+Legal+and+Contitutional+Affairs+Regarding+Bill+C-36+%28Protection+of+Communities+and+Exploited+Persons+Act%29++by+Elene+Lam

I am sure that discussion of and advocacy for legal reform of the *Criminal Code* will continue. Sex workers and activists are already mobilizing, preparing to challenge criminal laws again and advocating for the reform of the *Criminal Code*.[36]

4 Regulating Sex Work in the City

Although numerous research studies have been conducted on how sex workers are affected by the criminalization of sex work,[37] there have been only a

36 Antonella Artuso, 'Sex Workers Urge Premiers Not to Enforce New Prostitution Law,' *Toronto Sun,* 17 December, 2014, viewed 21 August, 2015,http://torontosun.com/2014/12/17/sex-workers-says-bill-c-36-leaves-them-vulnerable.

37 See, for example, D. Sansfaçon, Prostitution in Canada: A Research Review Report, Working Paper (Ottawa: Department of Justice Canada, 1984); John Lowman et al, eds. Regulating Sex: An Anthology of Commentaries on the Findings and Recommendations of the Badgley and Fraser Reports (Burnaby, BC: Simon Fraser University, 1984); F. Shaver, 'Feminist Defense of the Decriminalization of Prostitution,' Resources for Feminist Research,14.4 (1985), 38–39; Cecilia Benoit and Alison Millar. Dispelling Myths and Understanding Realities: Working Conditions, Health Status, and Exiting Experiences of Sex Workers (Vancouver: Peers, 2001); Sharry Allinott, et al, Voices for Dignity: Call to End the Harms Caused by Canada's Sex Trade Laws. Research Report (Vancouver: Pivot Legal Society, 2004); Canadian HIV/AIDS Legal Network. Sex, Work, Rights: Changing Canada's Criminal Laws to Protect Sex Workers' Health and Human Rights (Toronto: The Network, 2005), viewed 21 August, 2014,www.aidslaw.ca/publications/publicationsdocEN.php?ref=197; Lewis, Maticka-Tyndale, Shaver, and Schramm, 'Managing Risk and Safety on The Job;' John Maloney, *The Challenge of Change: A Study of Canada's Criminal Prostitution Laws. Research Report.* (Ottawa: Communication-Canada, Publishing, 2006), viewed 21 August, 2015,http://www.parl.gc.ca/Content/HOC/Committee/391/SSLR/Reports/RP2610157/391_JUST_Rpt06.pdf/; Pivot Legal Society, Beyond Decriminalization: Sex Work, Human Rights and a New Framework of Law Reform, viewed 21 August, 2015,www.pivotlegal.org/pivot-points/publications/beyond-decriminalization; Laura Barnett and Lyne Casavant, *Prostitution: A Review of Legislation in Selected Countries*, Publication No. 2011-115-E, 3 (Ottawa: Library of Parliament, 3 November 2011, Revised 21 July, 2014), viewed 21 August, 2015, http://www.parl.gc.ca/Content/LOP/ResearchPublications/2011-115-e.pdf; Tamara O'Doherty, 'Victimization in Off-Street Sex Industry Work,' *Violence Against Women* 20. 10, 2011, 944–963; viewed 21 August, 2015.http://www.vaw.sagepub.com/content/early/2011/26/03/1077801211412917;

few studies about the impact of municipal laws.[38] Canadian criminal laws are under federal jurisdiction, and as such, municipalities cannot prohibit sex work. However, 'municipalities have independent power to control prostitution through municipal bylaws and other local measures.'[39]

Emily van der Meulen and Elya Maria Durisin argue that current Canadian municipal and federal regulations 'violate sex workers' basic labour rights and contribute to physical and economic vulnerability.'[40] In Canada, provincial governments delegate control of local matters to municipal governments. Municipalities have been free to institute a series of bylaws, that pertain zoning and licensing, that are aimed at controlling and limiting local sex industries: 'the full extent of these regulations varies by province and according to local pressure and desires.'[41] Municipalities then, have the power to regulate space and activities by drafting bylaws, granting and revoking business licenses, and controlling the numbers of licenses issued. They have the right to inspect the premises of businesses with the purpose to ensure that health and safety regulations are being followed, for consumer protection as well as nuisance control. The extent of the enforcement of municipal power can differ from city to city, and can have a significant impact on the lives of sex workers, their safety, health and psychological wellbeing.[42]

In the 1980s a number of cities, including some of the largest urban centres (Montreal, Winnipeg, Vancouver and Calgary), enacted bylaws that increased individual municipalities' power to forbid sex workers from using streets and other public areas to engage in sex work. Some introduced legislation against obstructive solicitation, anti-jaywalking and loitering, that allowed law enforcement to give fines to sex workers, to stop street based sex work.[43]

---

38 See, for example, Jacqueline Lewis and Eleanor Maticka-Tyndale, 'Licensing Sex Work: Public Policy and Women's Lives,' *Canadian Public Policy* 26.4 (2000): 437–449; John Lowman. *Identifying Research Gaps in the Prostitution Literature*. RR 2002-9e (Government of Canada, Department of Justice, Research and Statistics Division, 2001), viewed 14, July, 2014,http://www.justice.gc.ca/eng/rp-pr/csj-sjc/jsp-sjp/rr02_9/rr02_9.pdf; Christine Bruckert and Stacey Hannem, 'Re-Configuring the Margins: Tracing the Regulatory Context of Ottawa Strip Clubs, 1974–2000,' *Canadian Journal of Law and Society* 17. 1 (2002), 69–87; Emily van der Meulen and Elya Durisin, 'Why Decriminalization? How Canada's Municipal and Federal Regulations Increase Sex Workers' Vulnerability,' *Canadian Journal of Women and the Law* 20.2 (2008), 289–312; van der Meulen and Valverde, 'Beyond the Criminal Code, '314–322.

39 Barnett and Casavant, *Prostitution*, 15.

40 van der Meulen and Durisin, 'Why Decriminalization?,' 310.

41 van der Meulen and Valverde, 'Beyond the Criminal Code,' 316.

42 Ibid., 315.

43 Barnett and Casavant, *Prostitution*, 15.

A number of these municipal laws were challenged, especially those that prohibited and regulated sex services, including the *International Escort Services Inc. v Vancouver (City); Kovinic v. Niagara Falls (City); Pimenova v. Brampton (City)* and *Vaughan (City) v. Tsui.*

However, in 2003 the Supreme Court, in *Siemens v. Manitoba (Attorney General)* stipulated that even though criminal jurisdiction was the exclusive domain of federal law, provinces retained the right to regulate over matters that had a moral connotation (in this particular case, gambling): 'the presence of moral considerations does not *per se* render a law *ultra vires* the provincial legislature.'[44] This decision gave provinces the ability to introduce provincial and municipal legislation that affected sex work, allowing municipalities to continue to use bylaws to regulate the sale of sex services.[45]

Since most of the activities that involve managing, gaining material benefits, procuring sex services or providing sexual services in a business space are criminalized by the *Criminal Code*, it is almost impossible to run and manage an establishment that offers the direct sale of sexual services.[46] Businesses have to be run on the grounds that they do not involve any exchange of money for sexual services.

Research conducted by Pivot Legal Society has shown that there are more than tens of thousands of people who work in businesses that are registered as legitimate establishments across Canada, such as escort agencies, bawdyhouses, body-rub parlours, massage parlours, strip clubs and dating services.[47] Several research studies have been conducted about the municipal regulatory impact on escort companies, body rub centres and strip clubs in Canada. However, the Canadian public has very limited understanding on how sex work is regulated by municipal law. The next sections of this paper address this issue and provide a detailed discussion and analysis of the governance of sex work in the city of Toronto, and its impact on sex workers.

---

44 *Siemens v. Manitoba (Attorney General)* [2003] SCC 3, para 30.

45 See, for example, City of Toronto, Bylaw No. 514–2002, Chapter 545, *Licensing* (20 June 2002); City of Vancouver, Bylaw No. 4450, *License By-Law* (23 September 1969); City of Calgary, Bylaw No. 48-M (2006), *Dating and Escort Service Bylaw* (17 October 2006); City of Edmonton, Bylaw No. 12452, *Escort Licensing Bylaw* (1 December 2009); van der Meulen and Valverde, 'Beyond the Criminal Code,' 321–322.

46 Pivot Legal Society, *Beyond Decriminalization*, 9.

47 Ibid.

5 Micromanaging the Massage Parlour in Toronto

Due to public and political pressure, numerous new bylaws aimed at curbing the proliferation of massage parlours and the suppression of other sex-related businesses were developed beginning in 1970s in the city of Toronto.[48] Two types of licenses currently regulate massage parlours: 'body-rub' licenses and 'holistic' licenses. Since only twenty five body-rub centres are allowed to operate in the city and the cost of obtaining a license is high, the majority of businesses apply for a holistic license to operate in the city.[49] Despite the fact that they are not allowed to have sexual contact with clients, many holistic centres provide body rubs as well as a selection of sexual services. Research studies on holistic licenses in Toronto have yet to be conducted.

Statistics provided by the City of Toronto in 2015 show that there are 427 holistic centres operating in this municipality, with 2,279 people are licensed as holistic practitioners.[50] Research findings show a dramatic increase in the number of migrants in all sectors of the sex industry in Canada.[51] Further, service providers and sex workers' organizations in Toronto assert that the number of Asian female sex workers has increased in recent years, particularly in massage parlours.[52]

I will now provide a detailed analysis of the evolution of bylaws that impact sex work in massage parlours. Article XI of Chapter 545 of the City of Toronto *Municipal Code*,[53] which pertains to 'licensing,' was introduced in 1998 as a bylaw to regulate holistic businesses. The new licensing categories for 'holistic centre' owners and 'holistic practitioners' were developed to regulate the 'modalities used for therapeutic and wellness purposes that involve touching or massaging.'[54]

48 Lewis and Maticka-Tyndale, 'Licensing Sex Work,'439.

49 City of Toronto, Municipal Licensing & Standard Statistics, Number of Holistic Centers and Practitioners, email, 15 March, 2015.

50 Ibid.

51 Natalya Timoshkina and Lynn McDonald. *Building Partnerships for Service Provision to Migrant Sex Workers* (University of Toronto, Institute for Life Course and Aging. 2009), viewed 21 August, 2015,http://www.wellesleyinstitute.com/wp-content/uploads/2011/11/Building-Partnerships-for-Service-Provision-to-Migrant-Sex-Workers.pdf.

52 Lam, *Chinese Sex Workers in Toronto*.

53 City of Toronto *Municipal Code, Licensing*, Article XI, Chapter 545, 158–186.

54 Toronto City Council, *Emergency and Protective Services Committee Report* No. 11 Clause No. 2, Bylaw No. 806 (1998), accessed 21 August, 2015,http://www.toronto.ca/legdocs/minutes/council/appa/cc981028/ep11rpt.htm.

It is important to dedicate some attention to the specific language of these regulations, as they make evident the ideological basis and the intent for their introduction. The bylaw for holistic licenses appears, at first glance, to be protective in nature, and to exist for the purposes of ensuring the health and safety of practitioners, as well as that of consumers. However, its true aim was articulated in *The Emergency and Protective Services Committee Report* of the Toronto City Council, which clearly stated that the purpose of the bylaw was 'to control the body rub parlours without having an impact on the complementary therapy disciplines,' and 'to screen out the illegitimate operators.'[55] To obtain licensees, proprietors were required to file proof of training for their employees. Additionally, proof of employees' age of majority was necessary, and needed to be filed alongside their proof of training. The conduct of service providers was strictly regulated as well: they are to 'remain fully clothed,' and 'provide services only to clients who are clothed or appropriately draped.'[56]

Municipal regulation, in alignment with the federal orientation of criminal law of the period, interpreted sex work as a 'nuisance' that 'polluted' neighbourhoods, and thus needed to be repressed and eventually eradicated. It is important to note however, that its regulatory measures, differently from the federal Criminal law which made the act of selling sex licit, were organized in a manner that impacted sex workers and parlours owners alike, essentially making each of them 'culpable' and therefore deserving of punishment. It is important to flag such an important regulatory inconsistency between the federal and the municipal legal apparatus to the regulation of sex work, one that *continues to persist in the present*, which is particularly incongruous now that Canadian criminal law has switched to the 'Nordic model'!

The offering of sexual services continued to remain a major concern for the process of licensing of holistic centres and practitioners, one that was revisited in the coming years. After the enactment of the bylaw in 1998, the Toronto City Council found that the regulations governing holistic centres 'did not adequately address the problem of holistic centres conducting business as unlicensed and illegal body rub parlours or protect consumers and promote health and safety and/or nuisance control.'[57] The bylaw was amended in 2004 and 2005, imposing additional regulations to control holistic centres and practitioners, with the aim of preventing sexual services from being offered or obtained.

55 Ibid.

56 Ibid.

57 Toronto City Council, *Policy and Finance Committee Report No. 5*, Clause No.11, Bylaw No. 656 (22 July, 2004).

Ten additional sections were added to clause 545 of Toronto's *Municipal Code,* greatly tightening the controls over these spaces and the activities that could take place therein. S. 160 introduced a stipulation that owners be aware of the type of business that was run on their premises (by having to provide a letter in support of the business). S. 158 & s. 161 respectively introduced the need to have obligatory and continuous proof of good standing from the business' professional holistic association. S. 163 & s. 164 stipulated that each business needed to file proof of major age for all holistic practitioners employed. S. 173 made mandatory the keeping of patients' records, while s. 177 regulated the way the space was built and equipped, in any manner that would hinder or prevent the enforcement of other regulations. S. 183 limited hours of operation from 8 AM to 9 PM, ensuring business could not offer services at night, a time in which sex work was *assumed* to thrive. S. 185 strictly specified standards for appearance and behaviour for the owner and practitioners. Finally s.186 greatly restricted the standards of comportment with clients, specifying with great care the ways in which bodies could be touched, and the ways in which special areas of the body (parts related to sexual activity, the genitals, the buttocks and the breasts) had to be kept covered at all times.[58]

The City of Toronto has increasingly made regulations on massage parlours and sex work more draconian and, in 2005, it proceeded to strengthen its executive powers as well, making inspections and prosecutions better coordinated, more systematic and thorough. The Municipal Licensing and Standards Division is the entity generally responsible for the enforcement of bylaws, through the mechanisms of inspection and investigation. The Toronto Police also has the power to carry out inspections and investigations of holistic centres. The activities of the regulatory body and its executive counterpart were coordinated by the introduction of clause No. 6 of Bylaw No. 719 of the *Planning and Transportation Committee Report* of 2005, which required the Toronto Police to 'establish a formal protocol to co-ordinate operations and share information with Municipal bylaw enforcement to control the sex trade.'[59]

A holistic centre as well as a practitioner may be fined if found in breach of municipal regulations. The Municipal Licensing and Standards Division has the power to refuse to issue or renew a license of a holistic centre, its owner or a practitioner if they have accumulated a certain amount of demerit points or have been convicted of breaching a particular code. In 2012 the City of Toronto

58 City of Toronto *Municipal Code,* Licensing, Article XI, Chapter 545, s. 158, s. 160, s. 161, s. 163, s. 164, s. 173, s. 177, s. 183, s. 185 and s. 186 (26 July, 2005).

59 Toronto City Council, *Planning and Transportation Committee Report No. 6,* Clause No. 6, Bylaw No. 719 (26 July, 2005).

further expanded the power of the Municipal Licensing and Standards Division and the police. Bylaw s. 169 gives power to the Chief of Police to negate an application or renewal of a license. Municipal bylaws continue to be used against sex workers in massage parlours. The Consideration of Licensing and Standard Committee of the Toronto City Council in 2012 requested that staff to 'explore pro-active enforcement at locations that have become fronts for prostitution and human trafficking...'[60]

In 2013, Toronto City Council once again moved to strengthen its executive reach, developing legislation and forging inter-institutional collaborations to address human trafficking.[61] At this juncture, a simple suspicion of potential human trafficking became a legitimate reason to justify raids, enforce municipal bylaws, and prosecute people who worked and provided sexual services in massage parlours. Enforcement power was greatly increased by forging collaborations between police trafficking teams and the Canada Border Services Agency.

Staff of the Municipal Licensing and Standards was directed 'to develop and deliver training specific to the needs of Municipal Licensing and Standards front-line and management staff,'[62] and to conduct a 'review of licensing bylaws concerning trades and businesses that are known to be destinations for human trafficking.'[63] The council decided to request the City Manager, the City Solicitor, and Deputy City Managers to create strategies to more vigorously prosecute charges related to municipal by-law infractions by the adult entertainment industry, body rub and holistic license classes.[64] It is important to note that the city council document did not clarify in any way how trafficking was related to the business of holistic license centres.

I have illustrated how municipal regulatory measures have been organized, over the last fifty years, in a manner that has impacted sex workers and parlours owners alike, essentially making each of them 'culpable' and therefore deserving of punishment. I point out once again that this approach is ideologically misaligned with the approach currently taken by federal criminal law, which has switched to the 'Nordic model,' that gives sex workers the freedom to sell their services, and only prosecutes those who purchase sex and third party profiteers. In the coming sections I will show the ways in which municipal law

60 Toronto City Council, *Licensing and Standard Committee Consideration* (28 June, 2012).

61 Toronto City Council, *Initiatives to Address Human Trafficking, City Council Consideration* (16 December, 2013).

62 Ibid, para 12.

63 Ibid, para 2.

64 Ibid, para 10.

discussed in this section intrudes in the lives of holistic centres' owners and sex workers alike, similarly harassing them, fining them and suspending their licenses to work. I will demonstrate that these interventions do not create safer conditions for sex work, and end up marginalizing, victimizing, and exacerbating potential dangers for those who are already at risk for exploitation.

6 The 'Real Life' Effects of Micromanaging the Massage Parlour

The regulations of the licensing of holistic centres and holistic practitioners by Toronto's *Municipal Code* are organized in four major areas: the first area stipulates the process for application for licenses; the second has to do with recording and reporting the activities that take place in the holistic centre; the third specifically targets the minutiae of the operation of the business of the holistic centre; finally, the fourth regulates the appearance and the behaviour of practitioners during service. The repressive effects that each area has on the lives of sex workers will be discussed in detail.

6.1 *Licencing and Registration*

Chapter 545 of the Toronto *Municipal Code* on 'Licensing' requires each holistic centre and practitioner to obtain a license.[65] A holistic practitioner must be a member *in good standing* of a professional holistic association, which in turn must be registered and listed with the Municipal Licensing and Standards Division.[66] My investigation of Asian women working in massage parlours in Toronto indicate that the majority of them were aware of and followed the complex regulations to operate in the city. They obtained training in massage skills and relevant conduct requirements to meet licensing standards.

The owners of the massage parlour for which they worked provided significant guidance and help in applying for a holistic practitioner license. These women often had limited language skills and were not able to complete the application process by themselves. Employers also helped them in carrying out criminal background checks for their immigration applications. Such heavy involvement created a significant power imbalance between workers and owners, essentially placing these women in a position of indebtedness.

Many of the women I interviewed reported that as they were undertaking training, registration and criminal checks, they were told repeatedly that

65 City of Toronto *Municipal Code, Licensing*, Article XI, Chapter 545, s.158 (2004).

66 Ibid., s.161.

engaging in sex work was prohibited while working in massage parlours. Owners passed along similar messages, indicating that practitioners were not allowed to engage in sex work while on their business premises. One of the interviewees said that an officer in the licensing office had told her that she was not allowed to offer sexual services when she obtained her holistic practitioner license. The prohibition of offering sexual service in holistic centres was an important message passed on the holistic practitioners, by trainers, licencing officers and owners alike.

Strong policing and discouragement from practicing sex work on the part of owners has the inevitable effect of making sex workers feel more vulnerable. Strong discouragement from training agencies and licencing offices can inadvertently push the practice sex work further underground. Some of the holistic practitioners not only hide sexual services from enforcement authorities, but also from co-workers and owners, which further marginalizes them. For instance, one of my interviewees recounted an incident in which, during service, she had been sexually assaulted by a client, and been unable to seek help because she was not supposed to have engaged in any act of a sexual nature at work. She felt she could not tell her co-workers and boss, nor report the incident to the police, because she feared that it would be revealed to them that she offered sexual services, and this would mean immediate termination.

Other practitioners expressed similar concerns that a situation might get out of hand, and escalate to include sexual acts that they were not comfortable performing, such as oral sex or unprotected sex. These real lived experiences show that a climate of strong prohibition against sex work can exacerbate problems. Additionally, the precarious immigration status of many of these women can make disclosure of abuse to authorities impossible, as it might bring to light that the workers do not have the required work permit or citizenship status.

6.2 *Recording and Reporting*

Municipal legislation leverages professional holistic associations to regulate and control the care standards of their members, by demanding adherence to extremely detailed codes of ethics, and strictly governing the process that must be followed to file complaints, and the disciplinary processes that follow. Such prolix legislation is specific to the holistic centre *only*, and not typical for other types of businesses, proving that its intent is the repression of sex work, ideologically informed by moral condemnation.

Owners of massage parlours must submit information on business partnerships, corporations and disclose all shareholders. They have to file incorporating documents and annual returns.[67] Owners are required to submit lists with all the names of holistic practitioners operating on the premises.[68] Additionally, the *Municipal Code* requires that owners keep detailed patient records. The people that I interviewed, owners and practitioners alike, had great concerns about the requirement of keeping patient records: they pointed out that often clients refused to provide personal information, and that such information was very difficult to compel. Yet owners were held accountable and could be fined if they were unable to produce records during inspections by police and bylaw officers.

My interviewees indicated that municipal bylaw enforcement officers and Toronto Police officers sometimes use this bylaw well beyond its scope, effectively to 'punish' any massage parlour operator or practitioner for any form of non-compliance, if they refused to go along with requests, admit to infractions, or plead guilty in court. Any resistance on their part can be met with draconian retaliation, and officers are able to harass massage parlour operators and practitioners by checking their records extremely frequently, with the clear intent of disrupting business.

6.3 *Operation*

Toronto's *Municipal Code* provides very strict guidelines for the operation of holistic centres on the issue of health, to ensure the 'sanitary' operation of the space. These regulations span from shaping the geography of the parlour (indicating, for example, the number of toilets and washroom facilities that must be present on the premises), to maintenance and cleanliness of the space. All areas can be inspected to ascertain sanitary conditions, from any space or rooms (change rooms and private treatment rooms), to any tools used for the trade (massage tables, mats, and towels used for draping).[69] The women I interviewed told of situations in which these bylaws were used to suspend a holistic centre's operation, if there was suspicion that sex work was taking place on the premises. Owners or practitioners would be fined with a ticket, if found in breach of these standards. If tickets were not paid, practitioners could have their license suspended and not be allowed to work, and the holistic center shut down. Thus bylaw officers and the police were often able to use these regulations in punitive ways, to repress even 'imagined' sex work.

67 Ibid., s.164, s. 165, and s. 167.

68 Ibid., s. 166.

69 Ibid., s. 177.

The management of time was also used in ways to curb potentially worrisome activities on the holistic centre: the City of Toronto assumes – possibly erroneously – that sex work thrives at night. Holistic centres are forced to operate during the day and stay open no later than the early evening, from 8 AM to 9 PM, with bylaw s.183. The strict regulation of operation hours is clearly aimed at curbing sex services from being offered at night.

Municipal law further shapes the space of the massage parlour, legislating the ways in which treatment rooms are set up, and walls and partitions located, in a manner that greatly exceeds the regulation of the geography of any other business space. Holistic centres must be built and equipped in a manner that does not create a 'hindrance' to the 'application' of any governing bylaws, allowing enforcement officers a clear view for investigation and unobstructed entrance into each and every treatment space.[70] It is important to note that this requirement is unique to holistic centres and not applicable in any other businesses space.

The management of space is related to the surveillance practices carried out by municipal bylaw enforcement and the Toronto police. These entities were given greater power to investigate suspected cases of sex work in holistic centres in 2005, then again in 2012 and 2013.[71] The people I interviewed stated that investigations were aimed at finding sex work *primarily*: health and practitioners' conduct inspections were not carried out of a concern for the healthcare of clients: monitoring cleanliness was an excuse to 'ferret out' frowned upon sexual practices and used as a tactic to ascertain where sexual services were sold.

The people I interviewed stated that it was common for municipal bylaw enforcement and police officers to enter holistic centres and barge into treatment rooms, to surprise and interrupt practitioners and clients, with the hope of finding them 'in the act.' The owners and holistic practitioners did not feel they could resist such incursions. They felt obligated to let officers in to carry out whatever check they wished, even if they thought this was disrespectful behaviour, infringing on the privacy rights of their customers, also potentially robbing them of return business.

Resistance to such raids was strongly discouraged by the officers, as mentioned earlier. In one instance, an owner chose to challenge a bylaw

70 Ibid., s. 177 (h).

71 Toronto City Council, *Planning and Transportation Committee Report No. 6,* Clause No.6, Bylaw No. 719 (26 July, 2005); Toronto City Council, *Licensing and Standard Committee Consideration* (28 June, 2012); Toronto City Council, *Initiatives to Address Human Trafficking, City Council Consideration* (16 December, 2013).

enforcement official, and this had very negative consequences. The officer proceeded to use his/her power to enforce bylaws in punitive ways, carrying out four inspections in one month, and fining the owner for a breach on s. 173 (failure to keep clients' records). The owner felt pressured to comply to any request or whim on the part of the enforcement official, even when overboard or unreasonable.

6.4 *Services, Appearance and Behaviour*

All owners and holistic practitioners interviewed reiterated that inspections on breach of service, appearance or behaviour were covers to actually prosecute the sale of sexual services. This makes evident an important incongruence in ideology between the latest Federal regulations on sex work and their municipal counterparts: sex workers should be permitted to sell sex, without fear of criminal prosecution!

And yet, municipal bylaw conceives sellers of sex servicers, owners of massage parlours, and purchases of sex services as one singular 'nuisance,' and harasses them and fines them with equal enthusiasm. As such, it operates in a way that creates barriers to the practice of sex work that ultimately makes it more dangerous, heightens its stigma, and pushes it underground, creating conditions of greater and more severe exploitation for the sex workers involved. The irony of this is that current criminal federal laws assume that sex workers are 'victims' and their primary goal is to specifically *mitigate exploitation in sex work.*

Toronto's bylaw officers and police officers have the right to carry out inspections at any time, and can interrupt treatment, barging into massage rooms as holistic practitioners are providing service to their clients. As we have seen, although the privacy rights of both service provider and client are violated, they seldom resist and are forced to keep silence, for fear of retaliation. The Toronto *Municipal Code* for holistic licensing does not prohibit sexual services explicitly, but s. 166 regulates 'services being offered,' giving inspectors the ability to enter a treatment space to ensure that the treatment that is being provided aligns with the permitted list of activities stipulated by the license. Given that holistic centres are required to file the services they offer and the fees they charge,[72] and given that sexual services are not permitted and cannot be listed as treatment options, in every instance an officer finds that a sex act is taking place, owners and practitioners can be charged with the offence of 'offering unlisted services,'[73] fined and placed on a probation list. Repeated breaches

72 City of Toronto *Municipal Code, Licensing*, Article XI, Chapter 545, s. 181 (a), (2004).

73 Ibid., s. 181(c).

of this section of the code will mean a suspended license to practice, or even closure of the centre.

Once in the treatment room, bylaw and police officers have wide and unchecked discretion and have the right inspect not only the acts that are taking place, but the appearance of the practitioner and the client as well. The appearance and behaviour of holistic practitioners is regulated by s. 185. This section of the code requires them to dress in a 'professional' manner, and this language is vague and can be applied in highly subjective ways. Enforcement personnel interpret them is sexualized ways, and take them to mean that practitioners should not wear provocative clothes, and must conceal those parts of their bodies that might elicit an erotic response, such as the cleavage and the legs.

One of the holistic practitioners I interviewed received a warning by an enforcement officer who warned her not to wear a dress and high heel shoes. She was also asked to remove her manicure in order to look 'less sexy.' The women I interviewed stated that they had never been prosecuted for being found in breach of this regulation, and yet they reported they felt 'policed' by enforcement officials' attitudes and expressed frustration towards such blatant attempts to regulate and control their behaviour and bodies.

The ways clients' bodies have to be covered and touched is strictly regulated by the *Municipal Code*, by s. 186.[74] Any area of the body that might 'charge' the character of the exchange erotically, and thus transform it into a sexual service for money, is deemed taboo. S. 185-A outlines the body areas that are imbued with dangerous connotations: these are the breasts in the case of owners or practitioners; the areolae in the case of clients; and the genitals and the anus for all involved.[75] My interviewees stated that owners monitored closely the service provided and discussed in detail how to properly drape and acceptably touch the bodies of clients with their holistic practitioners.

The people I interviewed explained that during a surprise inspection, officers were specifically watchful of instances of 'erotic transgression,' and looked for 'signs' that the service being provided had taken on a sexual tone. Any inappropriate exposure of the client's body, or any form of touching that 'transgressed' into forbidden erogenous zones on the bodies of either client or practitioner, was assumed to mean that sex work was taking place, shifting the act from a 'licit' health service, to an 'illicit' sex act.

74 Ibid., s. 186.

75 Ibid., s. 181 (a).

It did not matter that no law in Canada made the practitioner's offering of sexual service *technically a legal and permitted act* – enforcement officers could rely on an arsenal of more subtle micro-regulations to suppress such sex work, punishing owners, practitioners and clients by issuing warnings, fines and suspending licences and, as a last resort, shutting down holistic centres. My interviewees also indicated that Toronto police officers sometimes used entrapment, pretending to be clients and initiating the exchange of sexual services, actually to collect evidence; they proceeded to prosecute owners and practitioners for offering the unlisted services.

The sex workers I interviewed were aware that they did not necessarily run the risk of being charged under criminal law for providing sexual services; nevertheless, they found that the incursions and investigations conducted by municipal enforcement officials and the Toronto police were a tremendous source of stress, in terms of their personal and mental health. They also posed a threat to their economic well-being, disrupting practitioner-client relationships, placing their job security in jeopardy, and often resulting in fines being levied against them.

The health professionals I spoke to expressed great concern that these practices were placing Asian sex workers at risk. Most holistic practitioners and owners were reluctant to receive condoms from community workers and health promoters, because having them on the premises would give municipal bylaw enforcement and police officers evidence that sex work was occurring, giving them a reason to prosecute them or charge them with fines.

6.5 *Federal and Municipal Collaborations on Human Trafficking*

As discussed in section four, municipal bylaw officials can now work in collaboration with Canada Border Services Agency and investigate any holistic centre that is suspected of human trafficking by potentially harbouring workers who are not present in the country legally. A simple suspicion that this is taking place is sufficient to justify raids, enforce municipal bylaws, and prosecute sex workers. An emblematic example of such collaborations, and the devastating effects they can have on the lives of precarious migrant sex workers, took place in Ottawa, another municipality found in the Province of Ontario. On April 27, 2015, the Ottawa Police Service Human Trafficking Unit, the Canada Border Services Agency and Ottawa Bylaw Services conducted a three-day series of raids in massage parlours and body rub facilities.

Eleven bylaw fines for improper licensing were delivered and eleven women of illicit migrant status working in massage parlours were arrested and detained. Officials stated that their action was taken in response to public complaints, based on nuisance, of '30 to 40 cars in and out of the driveway next door.'[76] In this case, the excuse of 'anti-trafficking action' was used as the justification to investigate and arrest the women who worked in massage parlours. The police reported that they would be deported, even though no instances of human trafficking were found to have occurred.[77]

This is a significant detail: even though criminal law decriminalizes the sale of sexual services in Canada, in instances of this kind illegal migrant workers are not afforded any protections, because they are not recognized as citizens of the country, and thus deemed 'undeserving' of any safeguards. The refusal to extend any human rights to migrant sex workers is particularly devastating, compromising their ability to forge a life in a new country and having terrible effects on their health, equity, dignity, and safety. It remains to be seen if similar raids will be carried out in the city of Toronto.

7 Conclusion

In this chapter, I have argued that municipal micro-regulation is used by local governments to suppress sex work and prosecute sex workers, even though municipalities do not have the power to prohibit the offering of sexual services. Federal initiatives against human trafficking have allowed municipalities to further extend their powers, imposing stricter regulations for conducting surveillance in holistic centres, and joining forces with local police, the Canada Border Services Agency and the Royal Canadian Mounted Police. I have shown that Asian sex workers employed in massage parlours in the city of Toronto, bear the brunt of these repressive strategies, are victimized and marginalized.

Even though Federal criminal law makes the act of selling sex legal, municipal micro-regulation refuses to acknowledge this recent development and continues to approach sex work as a nuisance that needs to be repressed. Municipal regulation conflates the culpability and criminality of the recipient of sex services, the sex worker providing them, and the massage parlour owner that facilitates the exchange. It creates barriers to the practice of sex work in the context of the massage parlour, barriers that ultimately endanger, stigmatize and push sex work further underground, creating conditions of greater and more severe exploitation for the sex workers involved.

76 Doug Hempstead, '11 Women Face Possible Deportation After Massage Parlour Raids,' *Ottawa Sun*, 8 May, 2015, viewed June 20, 2015,http://www.ottawasun.com/2015/05/08/11-women-face-possible-deportation-after-massage-parlour-raids.

77 Ibid.

Bibliography

Allinott, Shari, Judith Boer, Naomi Brunemeyer, Rielle Capler, Cristen Gleason, Kerry Jacox, Kat Kinch, Carol Liao, Karen Mirsky, Katrina Pacey, Laurie Pelletier, Julie Shugarman, Elin Sigurdson, Oridine Snowdon, Kim Walton, Lisa Weich, and Debra Woelke. *Voices for Dignity: Call to End the Harms Caused by Canada's Sex Trade Laws.* Vancouver, B.C.; Pivot Legal Society, 2004.

Artuso, Antonella. "Sex Workers Urge Premiers not to Enforce New Prostitution Law." *Toronto Sun*, December 17, 2014. Viewed 21 August, 2015.http://torontosun.com/2014/12/17/sex-workers-says-bill-c-36-leaves-them-vulnerable.

Backhouse, Constance. "Nineteenth-Century Canadian Prostitution Law: Reflection of a Discriminatory Society." *Histoire Sociale/Social History* 18 (1986): 387–423.

Barnett, Laura, and Lyne Casa vant. *Prostitution: A Review of Legislation in Selected Countries*, Publication No. 2011-115-E, 3 (Ottawa: Library of Parliament, 3 November 2011, Revised 21 July, 2014). Viewed 21 August, 2015. http://www.parl.gc.ca/Content/LOP/ResearchPublications/2011-115-e.pdf.

Biernacki, Patrick, and Dan Waldorf. "Snowball Sampling: Problems and Techniques of Chain Referral Sampling." *Sociological Methods and Research* 10 (1981): 141–163.

Benoit, Cecilia, and Alison Millar. "Dispelling Myths and Understanding Realities: Working Conditions, Health Status, and Exiting Experiences of Sex Workers." Victoria, BC: Prostitutes Empowerment, Education and Resource Society (PEERS), October 2001.

Bruckert, Christine, and Stacey Hannem. "Re-Configuring the Margins: Tracing the Regulatory Context of Ottawa Strip Clubs, 1974–2000." *Canadian Journal of Law and Society* 17.1 (2002): 69–87.

Canadian Charter of Rights and Freedoms, s 2, Part I of the *Constitution Act, 1982*, being Schedule B to the *Canada Act 1982* (UK), 1982, c 11.

Casavant, Lyne and Dominique Valiquet. *Legislative Summary of Bill C-36: An Act to Amend the Criminal Code in Response to the Supreme Court of Canada Decision in Attorney General of Canada v. Bedford and to Make Consequential Amendments to Other Acts*, Publication no. 41-2-c36-E, (Legal and Social Affairs Division, Library of Parliament: Ottawa, Canada, 2014). Viewed 15 August, 2015.http://www.lop.parl.gc.ca/About/Parliament/LegislativeSummaries/bills_ls.asp?ls=c36&Parl=41&Ses=2.

City of Toronto, *Municipal Code, Licensing*, Article XI, Chapter 545, 2004.

Criminal Code of Canada, RSC 1985, c C-46 s 745.

Canada (Attorney General) v. Bedford, 2013 SCC 72.

Canadian HIV/AIDS Legal Network. *Sex, Work, Rights: Changing Canada's Criminal Laws to Protect Sex Workers' Health and Human Rights.* Toronto: The Network, 2005. Viewed 21 August, 2014.www.aidslaw.ca/publications/publicationsdocEN.php?ref=197

Casavant, Lyne, and Dominique Valiquet. "Legislative Summary of Bill C-36: An Act to Amend the Criminal Code in Response to the Supreme Court of Canada Decision in Attorney General of Canada v. Bedford and to Make Consequential Amendments to other Acts." *Library of Parliament*: Publication No. 41-2-C36-E, 2014. Viewed 15 August, 2015.http://www.lop.parl.gc.ca/About/Parliament/LegislativeSummaries/bills_ls.asp?ls=c36&Parl=41&Ses=2

Davies, Jaqueline. "The Criminalization of Sexual Commerce in Canada: Context and Concepts for Critical Analysis." *The Canadian Journal of Human Sexuality*, 24. 2 (2015), 78–91.

Government of Canada. Department of Justice. "Technical Paper: Bill C-36, *Protection of Communities and Exploited Persons Act*." 1. Viewed 25 January, 2015.http://www.justice.gc.ca/eng/rp-pr/other-autre/protect/p1.html.

Hempstead, Doug. "11 Women Face Possible Deportation After Massage Parlour Raids." *OttawaSun*, 8 May 2015. Viewed June 20, 2015.http://www.ottawasun.com/2015/05/08/11-women-face-possible-deportation-after-massage-parlour-raids.

Hutt v. The Queen, [1978] 2 S.C.R. 476.

Lam, Elene. *Chinese Sex Workers in Toronto*, unpublished report prepared for Butterfly, the Asian and Migration Sex Workers Support Network, 2014.

Lam, Elene. *Brief to the Senate Standing Committee on Legal and Constitutional Affairs Regarding Bill C-36 (Protection of Communities and Exploited Persons Act)*. Butterfly, the Asian and Migrant Sex Workers Support Network, October 2014. Viewed 15 January, 2015.https://www.google.ca/?gws_rd=ssl#q=Brief+to+the+Senate+Standing+-Committee+on+Legal+and+Contitutional+Affairs+Regarding+Bill+C-36+%28Protection+of+Communities+and+Exploited+Persons+Act%29++by+Elene+Lam

Lewis, Jacqueline, Eleanor Maticka-Tyndale, Frances Shaver, and Heather Schramm. "Managing risk and safety on the job: The experiences of Canadian sex workers." *Journal of Psychology and Human Sexuality* 17, 1–2 (2005): 147–167.

Lewis, Jacqueline, and Eleanor Maticka-Tyndale. "Licensing Sex Work: Public Policy andWomen's Lives." *Canadian Public Policy* 26.4 (2000): 437–449.

Lowman, John, Margaret Jackson, Ted Palys, Shelley Gavigan, eds. *Regulating Sex: An Anthology of Commentaries on the Findings and Recommendations of the Badgley and Fraser Reports.* Burnaby: Simon Fraser University, 1984.

Lowman, John. *Identifying Research Gaps in the Prostitution Literature. RR 2002-9e* (Government of Canada, Department of Justice, Research and Statistics Division, 2001). Viewed 14 July, 2014.http://www.justice.gc.ca/eng/rp-pr/csj-sjc/jsp-sjp/rr02_9/rr02_9.pdf.

Maloney, John. *The Challenge of Change: A Study of Canada's Criminal Prostitution Laws*. Ottawa: Communication Canada-Publishing, December 2006. Viewed 21 August, 2015.http://www.parl.gc.ca/Content/HOC/Committee/391/SSLR/Reports/RP2610157/391_JUST_Rpt06.pdf/

O'Doherty, Tamara. "Victimization in Off-Street Sex Industry Work." *Violence Against Women 10* (2011). Viewed 21 August, 2015.http://www.vaw.sagepub.com/content/early/2011/26/03/1077801211412917.

Pivot Legal Society. *Beyond Decriminalization: Sex Work, Human Rights and a New Framework for Law Reform.* (Vancouver: Pivot, 2009). Viewed 21 August, 2015.www.pivotlegal.org/pivot-points/publications/beyond-decriminalization.

Power & Pivot Legal Society. *Sex workers and Bill C-36: Analysis based on Social Science Evidence.* Power & Pivot, 2014. Viewed 21 August, 2015. http://www.powerottawa.ca/Briefing_Note_C-36_Social_Science_Evidence.pdf.

Patton, Michael Quinn. *Qualitative Research.* London: John Wiley and Sons, 2005.

R. v. Hutt, [1978] 2 S.C.R. 476

Sansfaçon, D. *Prostitution in Canada: A Research Review Report.* Ottawa: Department of Justice, 1985.

Shaver, Frances. "Feminist Defense of the Decriminalization of Prostitution." *Resources for Feminist Research* 14.4 (1985), 38–39.

Shaver, Frances. "A Critique of the Feminist Charges against Prostitution." *Atlantis* 14.1 (1988): 82–89.

Siemens v. Manitoba (Attorney General) [2003] SCC 3.

Smith, Dorothy. *Institutional Ethnography. A Sociology for People.* Lanham: Rowan & Littlefield Publishers Inc., 2005.

Timoshkina, Natalya and Lynn McDonald. *Building Partnerships for Service Provision to Migrant Sex Workers.* Toronto: University of Toronto, Institute for Life Course and Aging, 2009. Viewed 21 August, 2015.http://www.wellesleyinstitute.com/wp-content/uploads/2011/11/Building-Partnerships-for-Service-Provision-to-Migrant-Sex-Workers.pdf.

Toronto City Council, *Emergency and Protective Services Committee Report* No. 11 Clause No. 2, Bylaw No. 806, 1998. Viewed 21 August, 2015.http://www.toronto.ca/legdocs/minutes/council/appa/cc981028/ep11rpt.htm.

Toronto City Council, *Policy and Finance Committee Report No. 5, Clause No.11*, Bylaw No. 656, 2004.

Toronto City Council, *Planning and Transportation Committee Report, No.* 6, Clause No.6, Bylaw No. 719–2005, 26 July, 2005.

Toronto City Council, *Licensing and Standard Committee Consideration*, Toronto City Council, 26 July, 2005.

Toronto City Council, 'Initiatives to Address Human Trafficking,' City Council Consideration, 16 December, 2013.

van der Meulen, Emily, and Elya Maria Durisin. "Why Decriminalization? How Canada's Municipal and Federal Regulations Increase Sex Workers' Vulnerability." *Canadian Journal of Women and the Law* 20, 2 (2008): 289–311.

van der Meulen, Emily, Elya Durisin, and Victoria Love, eds. *Selling Sex: Experience, Advocacy, and Research on Sex Work in Canada*. Vancouver: UBC Press, 2013.

van der Meulen, Emily, and Mariana Valverde. "Beyond the Criminal Code: Municipal Licensing and Zoning Bylaws." In *Selling Sex: Experience, Advocacy, and Research on Sex Work in Canada*, edited by Emily van der Meulen, Elya M. Durisin, and Victoria Love. Vancouver: UBC Press, 2013, 314–322.

CHAPTER 6

Kink and the DSM-5: Pathologisation, Regulation, Stigmatisation

Nick J. Mulé

Abstract

This chapter will provide a queer liberationist, socio-political analysis of the American Psychiatric Association's (APA) *Diagnostic and Statistical Manual of Mental Disorders* (DSM), fifth edition. Specifically the section on the Paraphilias in the manual will be discussed. Utilizing a queer liberationist lens that resists heteronormative and cisgender notions of sexuality and gender identity and expression, the subsection on the Paraphilias will be interrogated based on social constructions of dominant notions of 'normal' race, sexuality, gender and class. Hence, the paraphilias, which encompass fetishistic sex, warranting to some extent diagnostic status for being what is perceived to be outside of normative sexual activities are questioned. The lack of scientific evidence to substantiate the inclusion of a number of paraphilia-based desires and diagnoses and the resulting negative implications of labelling individuals as pathological will be addressed. Also, reviewed are the disagreements both internal within the APA and external, both during the review of the DSM-5 and ongoing. I argue that the mere inclusion of such fetishistic paraphilias with conditions potentially leading to diagnostic labels contribute to oppressive forms of hegemonic discourse via pathologisation. Such inclusions also contribute to the regulation of sexual desire that serve to further marginalize kinksters and LGBTQ populations therein, in particular through systemic forms of stigmatisation. I ultimately argue that the APA should end its conflation of BDSM with pathology by removing all forms of paraphilic and fetishistic behaviours from the DSM as the inappropriate use of such is already addressed by the law.

Keywords

BDSM – DSM-5 – fetish – kink – LGBTQ – neoliberalism – paraphilias – pathology – regulation – stigmatisation – surveillance

 | DOI:10.1163/9789004392298_008

1 Introduction

Sexual behaviours and practices are a natural part of human existence, yet one that is not free from being socially surveilled and regulated in various ways. One such body that engages in social surveillance and regulatory practices, in the health sector and beyond, is the American Psychiatric Association (APA) via their Diagnostic and Statistical Manual of Mental Disorders (DSM). This diagnostic tool is utilized by psychiatrists in their interventions with patients living with mental illness. It has been over a decade since the last version was published; the release of the new DSM-5 took place in 2013.[1] Of the numerous disorders and issues addressed in the DSM-5, this chapter will focus specifically on the paraphilias, forms of sexual activities and practices that fall outside of what the APA deems conventional conceptions of sexual behavioural norms.

In this chapter, background information on the DSM is provided; its far reaching influence in the field of psychiatry, medicine, mental health, the law and beyond, is discussed. The paraphilias are historically defined and politicized, due to the varying perspectives on their place in the DSM and how they are deployed via diagnostic judgement. I then apply a critical queer analytical lens, in which I deconstruct the role the paraphilias play in the DSM and its implications on those diagnosed with them, queer communities that have a sexual outlaw history and the tainting effect on society's views of fetishistic sex such diagnoses have.

Changes between the last version (DSM-IV TR) and the current (DSM-5) are discussed, and I show the minimal progress that has taken place between them, also pointing out those aspects that remain relatively the same. Given the far-reaching implications of a DSM-paraphilic diagnosis, I argue that there is a cost to incremental vs. progressive change. Exposed is that the controversy of having the paraphilias in the DSM is also being taken up within psychiatry itself with internal deep divides on the issue. In the discussion I challenge the existence of the paraphilias in the DSM with a series of questions formulated based on extensive evidence. I conclude the chapter by arguing that the paraphilias should be removed altogether from the DSM. To begin, let us learn of the historical background of the DSM and how it came to become so influential.

1 American Psychiatric Association, DSM-5 (Washington, DC: American Psychiatric Association, 2013a). Abbreviated in the endnotes moving forward as: APA, DSM-5, 2013a.

2 The Diagnostic and Statistical Manual (DSM)

First published in 1952, the DSM, is a document issued by the American Psychiatric Association (APA), that features descriptions, symptoms, and other criteria that assist in the diagnosing of mental disorders. It has since been revised five times with the most recent revision being the DSM-5, which emerged after a lengthy 14-year revision process of the previous edition, the DSM-IV-TR (text revision).[2] The purpose of the DSM is to provide clinicians who treat patients with mental illnesses, with an agreed upon and shared language for accurate and consistent diagnosis. Also, it includes criteria for diagnosis that guide research on psychiatric disorders. It should be specified that the DSM's focus is on diagnosis only: it does not provide recommendations for treatment, the intent being that appropriate treatment will follow accurate diagnosis. Based in the United States, the DSM is a powerful psychiatric taxonomy recognized in numerous countries by clinicians, researchers, psychiatric drug regulation agencies, health insurance companies, pharmaceutical companies and policy makers. The DSM has a pronounced influence in the fields of mental health, medicine and law, which speaks to its hegemonic authority and impact.

3 The Paraphilias

In the 19th century the medical sciences pathologised what had been previously considered 'sins' (acts that up to then had been the purview of Religious authorities), or 'crimes' (up to then the purview of the Judiciary and the Criminal Justice system), as perversions. They were categorized henceforth as 'paraphilias, first coined by Wilhelm Stekel in the 1920s.[3] John Money further popularized the paraphilias as a means of categorizing and diagnosing unusual sexual interests that were are not aligned with hegemonic norms.[4]

---

2 Ibid.; American Psychiatric Association, DSM-IV-TR (American Psychiatric Association, 2000); American Psychiatric Association, DSM-5. 'Highlights of Changes from DSM-IV-TR to DSM-5.' (American Psychiatric Publishing, 2013b), Abbreviated moving forward as: APA, DSM-5, 2013b.

3 Vern L. Bullough and Bonnie Bullough, *Sin, Sickness, and Sanity.* (New York: New American Library, 1977); Wilhelm Stekel, *Sexual Aberrations: The Phenomenon of Fetishism in Relation to Sex,* translated from the 1922 original German edition by S. Parker. (Liveright Publishing, 1930).

4 John Money, *Gay, Straight, and In-Between: The Sexology of Erotic Orientation.* (Oxford, UK: Oxford University Press, 1990); Susan McCammon, David Knox, and Caroline, Schacht,

Medical science framed such norms in white, middle class and heterosexist ways creating an ideology of what it considers acceptable sexual behaviours. Such ideological norms are views that some continue to support today.[5] Others take a more critical stance that challenges rigid notions of sexuality alternatively promoting an approach that is tolerant of sexual diversity.[6] Moser and Kleinplatz, for example, have provided an extensive review of the diagnoses carried out by practitioners, and found that there is no diagnostic proof that the paraphilic assertions in the DSM are accurate.[7]

As a matter of fact, these authors found several studies that contradict the statements made in the DSM. Lacking is empirical data supporting the classification of paraphilias as mental disorders. Moser and Kleinplatz have argued that clinical evaluations are subjective, as consensus does not exist in the scientific literature, and this precludes any objective interpretations by experienced clinicians.[8] They have called for the removal of the section on paraphilias from the DSM: the criteria for diagnosis of unusual sexual interests as pathological are based on assumptions both unproven and untested, and this may lead therapists to misuse them and cause harm.

Choices in Sexuality (Mason, Ohio: Atomic Dog Publishing, 2004); Michael Weiderman, 'Paraphilia and Fetishism.' *The Family Journal* 11.3 (2003): 315–32.

5 Ray Blanchard. 'The DSM Diagnostic Criteria for Pedophilia.' *Archives of Sexual Behavior* 39.4 (2009a): 304–316; Ray Blanchard. 'The DSM Diagnostic Criteria for Transvestic Fetishism.' *Archives of Sexual Behavior* 34 (2009b): 439–446; Robert Spitzer, 'Sexual and Gender Identity Disorders: Discussion of Questions for DSM-V,' in *Sexual and Gender Diagnoses of the Diagnostic and Statistical Manual (DSM): A Reevaluation,* eds. Dan Karasic and Jack Drescher, (New York: Haworth Press, 2005), 111–116; Ken Zucker, 'Reports from the DSM-V Work Group on Sexual and Gender Identity Disorders.' *Archives of Sexual Behavior* 39.2 (2010): 217–220.

6 Glen Gabbard, Charles Moser, and Peggy Kleinplatz, 'DSM-IV-TR and the Paraphilias: An Argument for Removal,' *Sexual and Gender Diagnoses of the Diagnostic and Statistical Manual (DSM): A Reevaluation*, eds. Dan Karasic and Jack Drescher (New York: Haworth Press, 2005), 91–109.

7 Charles Moser, and Peggy Kleinplatz, 'DSM-IV-TR and the Paraphilias: An Argument for Removal,' *Sexual and Gender Diagnoses of the Diagnostic and Statistical Manual (DSM): A Reevaluation*, eds. Dan Karasic and Jack Drescher, (New York: Haworth Press, 2005), 91–109.

8 Ibid.

4 Critical Queer Analysis

The following analyses of the DSM-5's categorization of the Paraphilias, including their diagnoses, are guided by a critical queer framework.[9] A critical queer analysis challenges the notion of essential, fixed and binary categories of sex, gender and sexuality; it instead proposes that these are fluid and unstable, and are discursively produced cultural constructs[10] Most importantly, a critical queer perspective recognizes that hegemonic notions of sex, gender and sexuality reflect the norms and values of the dominant groups. They are heteronormative, reflecting the values of the white, heterosexual, middle-class majority, and are seamlessly reproduced and reconstituted in social institutions.[11] In essence this analysis celebrates diversity and rejects binary concepts of normality and abnormality, particularly in the realm of the psy sciences, which tend to frame them in the context of pathologisation.

Given the history and significance of the DSM in psychiatric, mental health, legal/criminal and social sectors, and paraphilias traditionally being and continuing to be, albeit conditionally, one of the diagnostic categories therein, this chapter examines how the paraphilias are framed in the DSM-5 versus the DSM IV-TR. Utilizing a queer liberationist lens which rejects heteronormative and cisgender notions of sexuality and gender identity, I will interrogate how the paraphilias are positioned in relation to social constructions of dominant notions of 'normality' in relation to race, sexuality, gender and class. Hence, I will question the inclusion of fetishistic sex in the DSM as a paraphilic disorder simply for being outside what are perceived to be 'normal' sexual activities. I will address the insufficient scientific evidence to substantiate the inclusion of a number of paraphilia-based diagnoses, as well as question the negative implications of that individual's experience for being labelled as such.

Additionally, I will expose the internal disagreements within psychiatry that emerged during the revision process and after the publication of the new DSM-5 manual. I argue that the mere inclusion of fetishism into the paraphilias may contribute to diagnostically label these activities as 'abnormal' and 'unhealthy,' thus contributing to sexual oppression through authoritative psychiatric discourses of pathologisation.

---

9 Andrea Daley and Nick J. Mulé, 'LGBTQs and the DSM-5: A Critical Queer Response.' *Journal of Homosexuality* 61, 9 (2014): 1288 – 1312.

10 Judith Butler, *Gender Trouble: Feminism and the Subversion of Identity.* (New York: Routledge, 1999).

11 Johnathan Metzl, *The Protest Psychosis: How Schizophrenia Became a Black Disease* (Boston, MA: Beacon Press. 2009).

Such inclusions also contribute to the regulation of sexual desire that serve to further marginalize kinksters and, in particular, the LGBTQ populations therein through systemic forms of stigmatisation. I conclude that the APA need end its conflation of BDSM with pathology, and must remove all forms of paraphilic and fetishistic behaviours from the DSM. This is warranted by the understanding that any inappropriate BDSM behaviours, such as engaging in unsafe and/or non-consensual practices, can be better regulated and governed in another realm, that of the Law.

5 Changes in the Paraphilias: DSM-IV-TR to DSM-5

There were a few significant changes to the diagnostic category of the paraphilias from the DSM-IV-TR to the current DSM-5. An implemented revision to the DSM-5 included structural changes that eliminated the supra category 'Sexual and Gender Identity Disorders,' instead introducing the Paraphilias as a separate diagnostic category.[12] Before discussing a number of significant changes that have occurred in the DSM-5, outlined here are the eight paraphilic conditions that have remained unchanged from the previous diagnostic manual, the DSM-IV-TR:

- Exhibitionistic Disorder (exposing the genitals);
- Fetishistic Disorder (using nonliving objects or having a highly specific focus on non-genital body parts);
- Frotteuristic Disorder (touching or rubbing against a non-consenting individual);
- Pedophilic Disorder (sexual focus on children);
- Sexual Masochism Disorder (undergoing humiliation, bondage, or suffering);
- Sexual Sadism Disorder (inflicting humiliation, bondage, or suffering);
- Transvestic Disorder (engaging in sexually arousing cross-dressing);
- Voyeuristic Disorder (spying on others in private activities).'[13]

As a colleague and I have previously argued, listing these eight conditions out of context, as standalones – as was the case in previous manual editions – is highly problematic as these are merely expressions of sexual desires and/or behaviours that provide sexual stimulation for individuals engaging in them.[14]

12 American Psychiatric Association (APA). *Diagnostic and Statistical Manual of Mental Disorders (DSM-IV)*. (Washington DC: APA, 1994); APA, DSM-5, *Paraphilic Disorders*, 2013a.

13 APA, DSM-5, 2013a.

14 Andrea Daley and Nick J. Mulé, 'LGBTQs and the DSM-5: A Critical Queer Response.' *Journal of Homosexuality* 61, 9 (2014): 1288 – 1312.

Therefore, a significant point of progress in the DSM-5 is the distinction made between paraphilias and paraphilic disorders.[15]

Whereas the former pathologised the mere presence of paraphilic desires and a manifestation of behaviours, the latter makes pathological only the feelings of distress about having a paraphilic disorder: the element of judgement, which Daley and I have argued to be problematic elsewhere,[16] has been removed. The manual now specifies: 'or have a sexual desire or behaviour that involves another person's psychological distress, injury, or death, or a desire for sexual behaviors involving unwilling persons or persons unable to give legal consent.'[17] In essence, the DSM-5 sees paraphilias as non-psychopathological, whereas paraphilic disorders are categorized as psychopathological.[18]

Further to the characteristics of paraphilic disorders are their specifiers, which bracket behaviour and context in specific ways. In the DSM-5 two new specifiers have been implemented, which are 'in a controlled environment' and 'in remission,' addressing an individual's status regarding the presence of a paraphilic disorder.[19] The former speaks to 'controlled environments' in which individuals have no opportunity to act on their paraphilic urges, making assessment particularly difficult; the latter speaks to a paraphilic disorder being 'in remission,' even if not in complete remit or if the paraphilic interest continues to exist.[20]

Of significant importance to the process of diagnoses is the structure of the diagnostic criteria for all paraphilias, which has remained unchanged since the DSM-III-TR. Criterion A identifies the qualitative nature of the paraphilia, much as the paraphilias are described earlier in this section. Criterion B identifies the negative consequences of the paraphilia, such as 'distress, impairment, or harm – or risk of harm – to others.'[21] New to the DSM-5 is that individuals

15 American Psychiatric Association (APA). 'Paraphilic Disorders.' *American Psychiatric Publishing*, last modified 2013c; (abbreviated in the endnotes moving forward as: APA, DSM-5, 2013c), Viewed September 14, 2014, <http://www.dsm5.org/Documents/Paraphilic%20Disorders%20Fact%20Sheet.pdf>.

16 Daley and Mulé, 'LGBTQs and the DSM-5,' 1295.

17 APA, DSM-5, 2013c.

18 APA, DSM-5, 2013c.

19 APA, DSM-5, 2013a; Abbreviated in the endnotes moving forward as: APA, DSM-5, 2013b, 18.

20 American Psychiatric Association (APA). "Highlights of Changes from DSM-IV-TR to DSM-5." *American Psychiatric Publishing*, 2013b, Viewed September 14, 2014<http://www.dsm5.org/Documents/changes%20from%20dsm-iv-tr%20to%20dsm-5.pdf>

21 Ibid., 18.

can be diagnosed with having a paraphilic disorder if they possess *both* Criterions A and B, but not if they only exhibit Criterion A.[22]

Two additional changes are paraphilic-disorder specific.[23] The first, related to transvestic disorder, used to be limited to heterosexual males in DSM-IV, whereas in the DSM-5 it now applies to anyone.[24] Again, a diagnosis of transvestic disorder would require the criterion of 'significant stress or impairment.'[25] The second change relates to pedophilic disorder, which is now the term used to describe 'pedophilia;' the diagnostic criteria are unchanged and are the same as in DSM-IV-TR.[26]

6 Consequences of Incrementalism vs. Progressive Change

As with most large bureaucratic institutions, change tends to happen incrementally, in slow, measured stages. The history of the APA's work on the DSM is no different. An example of such incrementalism is the evolving conceptualization of homosexuality and its gradual reclassification before removal. Homosexuality was first classified as a 'sociopathic personality disturbance' in the inaugural DSM-I publication in 1952, then reclassified to 'sexual deviation' in 1968's DSM-II publication.

Due to lesbian and gay activists' pressure, the APA removed homosexuality in 1973 but replaced it with 'sexual orientation disturbance' in the 1974 printing of the DSM-II. This in turn was replaced by 'egodystonic homosexuality' in the DSM-III, further replaced with 'sexual disorder, not otherwise specified (NOS)' in the revised edition of the DSM-III in 1987. This latter diagnosis remained in the DSM-IV-TR version.[27] What is noteworthy in reviewing this 50 plus year historical trajectory is that although homosexuality was declassified as a mental disorder, APA continued to introduce a series of other and often ambiguous

22 Ibid.

23 Ibid.

24 American Psychiatric Association (APA). *Diagnostic and Statistical Manual of Mental Disorders* (*DSM-IV-TR*). (Washington DC: APA, 2000).

25 American Psychiatric Association (APA). 'Paraphilic Disorders.' *American Psychiatric Publishing*, last modified 2013c, Viewed September 14, 2014: <http://www.dsm5.org/Documents/Paraphilic%20Disorders%20Fact%20Sheet.pdf>, 1–2.

26 Ibid.

27 Drescher, J. 'Queer Diagnoses: Parallels and Contrasts in the History of Homosexuality, Gender Variance, and the Diagnostic and Statistical Manual.' *Archives of Sexual Behavior*, 39, 2 (2010): 427–60.

disorders that permitted psychiatrists to perpetuate an ongoing pathology of homosexuality.[28]

Made evident by the evolution of homosexuality in the DSM is the issue of whether incrementalism can actually be considered 'progressive' change. Clearly change did happen, due in part to shifting societal perspectives on homosexuality and also due to the gay liberation movement's staunch refusals to accept such diagnoses. In retrospect, what exactly was psychiatry's contribution to such 'change'?

Over the years the APA had contributed with increasing influence to the cultural discourse on matters related to the diagnoses featured in its DSM. The fact that the APA opted for an incremental approach in how it addressed homosexuality, demonstrates an institutional stubbornness and a lack of flexibility to progress beyond its moralizing and heterosexist notions, over a period that spanned half a century. The consequences of this incrementalism were the systematic and prolonged oppression of LGBTQ populations, by means of pathologisation, surveillance, regulation, discrimination and stigmatisation.

Can such a protracted form of marginalization be seen as progressive change, given that the APA was being confronted by first-wave gay liberation activists, as far back as the 1960s? Consider how different the outcome would have been had the APA dropped homosexuality outright from its DSM back then. Why did the APA consistently produce a series of new ambiguous classifications with which to continue to pathologise homosexuality over the next 40 years? What agenda was being followed and for the benefit of whom?

I contend that the changes on paraphilias featured in the DSM-5 can be considered another example of this incrementalist logic on the part of the APA. Although this edition no longer sweepingly deems the paraphilias to be mental disorders, structurally separating them as 'Paraphilias' and 'Paraphilic Disorders,' nevertheless this incremental shift is not altogether unproblematic. The mere presence of the category 'Paraphilias' in a diagnostic tool such as the DSM and their conflating descriptions as 'atypical sexual interests,'[29] serves to perpetuate their stigmatisation.

The 'Paraphilic Disorder' category is articulated along two fronts: personal distress on one hand, and sexual desires and behaviours that are harmful to others, and/or engaged in with unwilling partners on the other. In the absence

28 Andrea Daley and Nick J. Mulé, 'LGBTQs and the DSM-5: A Critical Queer Response.' *Journal of Homosexuality* 61, 9 (2014): 1291.

29 American Psychiatric Association (APA). 'Paraphilic Disorders.' *American Psychiatric Publishing*, last modified 2013c, Viewed September 14, 2014: <http://www.dsm5.org/Documents/Paraphilic%20Disorders%20Fact%20Sheet.pdf >, 1–2.

of scientific evidence to prove that such behaviours stem from or are engendered by a specific form of mental illness, the discoursive category in the DSM remains unsubstantiated and unmoored. Engaging in such sexual behaviours is already forbidden by Criminal Law, as sexual assault.

Yet, curiously, rape is not listed in the DSM, while other non-consensual sexual activities are.[30] The APA has to date not addressed these discrepancies or scientifically justified the inclusion of such categories in the realm of mental illnesses. The mere presence of these categories within the DSM, in essence, represents a misnomer from a BDSM perspective, as principles of safe, sane and consensual are not acknowledged.[31] Therefore, the consequence of this incrementalism can cause resentment for kinksters and confusion for the unfamiliar.

The specific response of 'feel[ing] personal distress about their interest, not merely distress resulting from society's disapproval,' under the Paraphilic Disorders category in the DSM-5 also requires some decontextualizing.[32] On its own, a response of this kind experienced by a hypothetical patient is devoid of the complexities of the patient's social location. Not taken into consideration are his/her capacity to reflexively negotiate her/his personal sexual interests with such matters as their gender, gender identity/expression, age, (dis)Ability, class, sexual orientation, race, ethnicity, religiosity, etc. In other words, framing the response in this way has the delimiting effect of hiding the reasons the patient may be presenting in this manner (not to mention its restrictiveness, as patients may present in ways that go far beyond this characterization).

Another example that shows how the APA reverts to a traditional, delimited, psychodynamic approach in the DSM-5 is its treatment of 'transvestic sexual arousal'. The manual states: 'clinical assessment of distress or impairment, like clinical assessment of transvestic sexual arousal, is usually dependent on the individual's self-report.[33] From a therapeutic perspective, this kind of psychodynamic approach neglects a critical therapeutic insight: an individual should

30 National Coalition for Sexual Freedom (NCSF), "DSM Revision White Paper: NCSF and the NCSF Foundation's Position on the Discriminatory Paraphilias Section in the DSM," N.D., Viewed April 19, 2015, <https://ncsfreedom.org/key-programs/dsm-v-revision-project/dsm-revision-white-paper.html >.

31 Jacques, Trevor. *On the Safe Edge: A Manual for SM Play*. (Toronto: WholeSM Publishing, 1993).

32 American Psychiatric Association (APA). *Diagnostic and Statistical Manual of Mental Disorders 5 (DSM – 5) – Paraphilic Disorders*. (Washington DC: APA, 2013a), accessed September 14, 2014.

33 Ibid, 703.

be assessed in the context of the society he or she lives and socializes in, and in the context of how she or he impacts her/his social environment, and vice versa.

The sole focus on a self-report undermines the patient's capacity to develop personal agency, through which one would be able to embrace one's sexual interests in healthy ways that include connecting with relevant supportive resources and others with similar interests. There is a difference between deeming a sexual interest that an individual has yet to come to terms with as pathological versus engaging in a supportive therapeutic process that explores the matter and assists the individual in understanding and accepting it.

7 Controversies within Psychiatry and Beyond

The critical queer analysis provided herein is certainly not limited to those on the outside of psychiatry. There is longstanding and growing unrest within psychiatry, pointing to significant divergences in politics on the DSM within the field. Debates have ensued, focusing on diverse issues. Some have revolved around empirical or evidence-based data to substantiate or challenge diagnoses;[34] others have gathered data on dimensional metrics devoid of moralizing judgement;[35] some have questioned the validity and utility of psychiatric diagnoses;[36] others have explored different behavioral and scientific sexological approaches to the DSM;[37] finally some have chosen to focus on the extent to which the implications of their work are helping patients, rather than harming individuals and their loved ones.[38]

During the preparation of the DSM-5 internal conflict within the field of psychiatry became apparent. Aldhous exposed the conflict in an article

34 Robert Carson, "Dilemmas in the Pathway of the DSM-IV." *Journal of Abnormal Psychology* 100 (1991): 302–307.

35 Robert Kendell, 'Five Criteria for an Improved Taxonomy of Mental Disorders.' in Defining *Psychopathology in the 21st Century DSM V and Beyond,* edited by John Helzer and James Hudziak, (Washington, DC: American Psychiatric Publishing, 2002), 3–18.

36 Robert Kendell and Assen Jablensky, 'Distinguishing Between the Validity and Utility of Psychiatric Diagnoses.' *American Journal of Psychiatry*, 74.1 (2003): 4–12.

37 Nathaniel McConaghy, 'Unresolved Issues in Scientific Sexology.' *Archives of Sexual Behavior*, 28.4 (1999): 285–318.

38 Peter Aldhous, 'Psychiatry's civil war.' *New Scientist*, 2738, Viewed December 11, 2009, <http://www.newscientist.com/article/mg20427381.300-psychiatrys-civil-war.html>; Editorial. 'Time's Up for Psychiatry's Bible.' *New Scientist*, 2738. Viewed December 17, 2009, <http://www.newscientist.com/article/mg20427382.400-times-up-for-psychiatrys-bible.html>.

revealingly entitled 'Psychiatry's Civil War,' and in related editorials, 'Time's Up for Psychiatry's Bible,' and 'Diagnosing the DSM'.[39] All raised serious questions as to the spuriousness of psychiatry's 'scientific methods' in determining mental disorders and its propensity towards over diagnosing, cautioning about the potential deleterious effects they may have on the public, and raising concerns furthered by recent observations and research.[40]

The APA's latest manual formulation was declared 'a sad day for psychiatry' by the Chair of the DSM-IV Task Force, Dr Allen Frances, who claimed processes used were flawed and may result in unsound scientific work and unsafe outcomes.[41] Another powerful critique had to do with changes in DSM-5 that emphasised a stronger pharmaceutical approach to treatment, reached without a cost-benefit analysis. This approach might have the effect of economically advantaging pharmaceutical corporations at the cost of increased human suffering for the diagnosed.[42] Upon its release, the DSM-5 was rejected by the National Institute of Mental Health (NIMH), who reached this decision because of the manual's poor diagnostic validity. The NIMH is currently creating

39 Peter Aldhous, 'Psychiatry's Civil War.' *New Scientist*, 2738, Viewed December 11, 2009,<http://www.newscientist.com/article/mg20427381.300-psychiatrys-civil-war.html>. Allen Frances, 'Diagnosing the DS,' *The New York Times* (New York, NY), May 11 2012a, Viewed September 18, 2014,<http://www.nytimes.com/2012/05/12/opinion/break-up-the-psychiatric-monopoly.html?_r=0>.

40 Megan Brooks, 'Published DSM-5 Field Trial Results Prompt Renewed Criticism.' *Medscape Today* (2012), Viewed January 2, 2013,<http://www.medscape.com/viewarticle/774475>; Brandon Gaudiano and Mark Zimmerman, 'Prevalence of Attenuated Psychotic Symptoms and Their Relationship With *DSM-IV* Diagnoses in a General Psychiatric Outpatient Clinic.' *Journal of Clinical Psychiatry*, 74.2 (2013): 149–155, Viewed January 2, 2013,<http://article.psychiatrist.com/dao_1login.asp?ID=10008052&RSID=90399506541510>.

41 Frances, Allen. 'DSM 5 Is Guide Not Bible—Ignore Its Ten Worst Changes: APA Approval of DSM-5 is a Sad Day for Psychiatry.' *Psychology Today*, 2 December 2012b, Viewed January 2, 2013,<http://www.psychologytoday.com/blog/dsm5-in-distress/201212/dsm-5-is-guide-not-bible-ignore-its-ten-worst-changes>.

42 Deborah Brauser, 'Experts React to DSM-5 Approval.' *Medscape Today*, (2012), Viewed December 2, 2012,<http://www.medscape.com/viewarticle/775526>; Allen Frances, 'How Many Billions a Year Will the DSM-5 Cost?' *Bloomberg*, 20 December 2012c, Viewed January 2, 2013,<http://www.bloomberg.com/news/2012-12-20/how-many-billions-a-year-will-the-dsm-5-cost-.html>; Rosie Mestel, 'Changes to the Psychiatrists' Bible, DSM: Some Reactions.' *LA Times*, (Los Angelas, CA) 9 December 2012, Viewed January 2, 2013, <http://www.latimes.com/health/boostershots/la-heb-dsm5-american-psychiatric-association-20121207,0,1392058.story>.

its own classification system,[43] and has embarked on the Research Domain Criteria (RDoC) project. The project investigates the importance of genetics, neuroscience, and behavioral science, to develop a new classification system within medicine that would address the problems in the DSM-5 in both reliability and validity.[44]

Internationally, the International Statistical Classification of Diseases (ICD) as administered through the World Health Organisation (WHO) conducts macro level research that tabulates disease and mortality rates in nation states.[45] Although not completely in parallel to the DSM, it too features pathological diagnoses based on gender identity and sexual orientation under the category of 'Disorders of Adult Personalities and Behaviours,' under the subsections of 'Gender Identity Disorders,' 'Disorders of Sexual Preference' (of which a series of paraphilias are featured), and 'Psychological and Behavioural Disorders Associated with Sexual Development and Orientation.'[46] Its latest diagnostic manual, the ICD-11, will be presented before the WHO in 2019 and scheduled for implentation in 2022.[47] It would be beyond the scope of this chapter to provide an analysis of the ICD texts, yet clearly careful study of these publications is necessary and worthwhile, to investigate new articulations that utilize an anti-oppressive approach to gender and sexual diversity in terms of identity, expression and behaviours.

Noteworthy, are the thematic concerns and points of interest related to the process and politics of what warrants inclusion as a diagnosis in the DSM-5 or forthcoming ICD-11, how these diagnoses are measured and, importantly, the implications of placing such a diagnosis on an individual. The process, particularly with regards to the APA and the DSM, is based on the tradition of its earlier iterations, which serves a conventional, restrictive, and conservative, normative agenda.

---

43 Thomas Insel, 'Director's Blog: Transforming Diagnosis.' *National Institute of Mental Health (NIMH)*. last modified 29 April 2013, Viewed September 18, 2014,<http://www.nimh.nih.gov/about/director/2013/transforming-diagnosis.shtml>.

44 National Institute for Mental Health (NIMH), "Research Domain Criteria (RDoC),"N.D., Viewed April 22, 2015,<http://www.nimh.nih.gov/research-priorities/rdoc/index.shtml>.

45 World Health Organisation (WHO), "International Classification of Diseases," N.D., Viewed April 22, 2015,<http://www.who.int/classifications/icd/en/>.

46 World Health Organisation (WHO), *ICD-10*, WHO, 1992.

47 World Health Organisation (WHO), "The International Classification of Diseases 11th Revision is due by 2017," 2012, Viewed April 22, 2015, <http://www.who.int/classifications/icd/revision/en/ >.

These are aimed at restricting and containing non-normative sexual interests, desires and behaviours that do not necessarily align with white, middle-class, heteronormative, and cisgenderist expectations of acceptability. Disturbingly, completely overlooked and not addressed is the potential damage inflicted on individuals whose sexual interests and desires may include BDSM, who through the process of diagnosis are being stigmatised by a system that chooses to label and pathologise rather than to be understanding and supportive. The continued classification of the paraphilias as clinical disorders constitutes the ongoing surveillance, pathologisation, and regulation of otherwise variant expressions of sexual behaviours. Such processes represent the antithesis to an anti-oppressive approach that recognises diversity, makes room for inclusion and works toward the strengthening of individuals.

What is apparent is that the discourse of 'unusual sexual interests or activities,' whether in the influential U.S. or internationally, requires critical interrogation to ensure that individuals who possess such interests and desires and who may enact them are sensitively addressed and not unnecessarily pathologised. The National Institute of Mental Health's critique and rejection of the DSM-5 is not unique: there is widespread questioning of the credibility of diagnostic classifications, and countries such as Denmark, Norway and Sweden have completely removed all consensual paraphilias from the list of mental health pathologies.[48]

Bodies that undertake such work must walk a fine line to ensure they are sensitively, properly and adequately addressing mental health concerns and not falling into oppressive exercises of pathologisation that create undue harm. Increasingly, within the APA and outside it, many are voicing dissent from scientific, ethical and social justice perspectives, undermining the legitimacy of the continued inclusion of the paraphilias in such diagnostic tools. I delve into such critiques in the next section.

8 Discussion

The Sexual and Gender Identity Disorders Work Group of the APA, that oversaw the revisions for the DSM-5, seemed to take seriously much paraphilia-related research that took place over the previous 14 years. A number of the

---

48 National Coalition for Sexual Freedom (NCSF), "Kinky is NOT a Diagnosis," N.D, Viewed April 22, 2015,<https://ncsfreedom.org/key-programs/dsm-v-revision-project/kinky-is-not-a-diagnosis.html >.

changes in the manual indeed reflected the many concerns raised by these studies.[49] Yet, from a critical queer analytical perspective, although progress can be discerned (particularly in the distinction between paraphilias and paraphilic disorders), a major shortcoming remains at the very foundation of its diagnostic tool. Its premise is steeped in traditional, conservative, white, middle class, heterosexist and cisgendered notions of a sexual 'normality' of desires and behaviours. Examples of such bias can be found in the language used in describing and addressing the paraphilias.

In the following sentence, the language used to describe the paraphilia are steeped in a judgmental and condescending tone, which inevitably entails a negative judgment for failing to ascribe to normative, typical standards:

> The term *paraphilia* denotes any intense and persistent sexual interest other than sexual interest in genital stimulation or preparatory fondling with phenotypically normal, physically mature, consenting human partners.[50]

Why would any sexual interests outside of the stimulation of genitals or pre-sex fondling be made suspect and why does 'phenotypically normal sex' have to be made the standard for 'normal' behaviour, given the vast array of sexual desires and practices that people engage in?

Similarly, the DSM-5 states: '... the term *paraphilia* may be defined as any sexual interest greater than or equal to normophilic sexual interests,' which is a clear attempt to create a hierarchical distinction between the 'good' and 'healthy' 'normal' sexual interest versus the 'abject,' 'unhealthy' and 'abnormal' sexual interests.[51] Transvestic disorders illustrate such polarities. The twice

---

49 American Psychiatric Association (APA). *Diagnostic and Statistical Manual of Mental Disorders 5 (DSM – 5) – Paraphilic Disorders.* (Washington DC: APA, 2013a), Viewed September 14, 2014,<http://dsm.psychiatryonline.org.ezproxy.library.yorku.ca/content.aspx?bookid=556&sectionid=41101785#103442326>; American Psychiatric Association (APA). "Highlights of Changes from DSM-IV-TR to DSM-5." American *Psychiatric Publishing,* 2013b, Viewed September 14, 2014,<http://www.dsm5.org/Documents/changes%20from%20dsm-iv-tr%20to%20dsm-5.pdf>; American Psychiatric Association (APA). 'Paraphilic Disorders.' *American Psychiatric Publishing,* 2013a, Viewed September 14, 2014, <http://www.dsm5.org/Documents/Paraphilic%20Disorders%20Fact%20Sheet.pdf>; Daley and Mulé, 'LGBTQs and the DSM-5,' 1306.

50 American Psychiatric Association (APA). *Diagnostic and Statistical Manual of Mental Disorders 5 (DSM – 5) – Paraphilic Disorders.* Washington DC: APA. 2013a, Viewed September 14, 2014, paragraph 3,<http://dsm.psychiatryonline.org.ezproxy.library.yorku.ca/content.aspx?bookid=556&sectionid=41101785#103442326>.

51 Ibid.,

emphasized abnormality of transvestitism is linked to the experiencing of 'significant distress and impairment,' 'because of their (patient's) behaviour,' (the emphasis in the parentheses is mine). This is a form of victim blaming in a society that has yet to loosen its grip on rigid binary gender expression.[52]

The language in the manual utilized to describe paraphilic disorders linked to breaking the Law is quite telling as well. The qualifying noun 'noxiousness' is used, as well as the descriptive statement of 'potential harm to others.'[53] 'Noxiousness' has moralistic connotations that allude to corruption, which is quite disturbing in a legal context. Foundational standards of normalcy are always conceived as white, middle class, heterosexual and cisgender, deeming all acts that fall outside of it as abnormal – and depending on their intensity – as potential paraphilic disorders. Although clinicians are provided with numerous extenuating circumstances regarding factors to consider in the diagnostic process (i.e. the usual life challenges most must deal with), the manual reverts to a traditional conventional framework for normative sexual desires and behaviour. An example of this is when the strength of a paraphilia is measured in relation to 'normophilic sexual interests or behaviours.'[54] What is of particular concern about such measures is the apparent lack of consideration given to potential gradients of sexual desires and behaviours and the possibility that for some, engaging in paraphilic sex may be their more heightened point of arousal.

Another problem has to do with the DSM-5's adoption of quantitative scales that can be arbitrarily and subjectively administered by clinicians as they attempt to understand the experiences of their clients, which may end up creating 'either or' scenarios between pathology and normality. The restrictive sets of questions that patients are asked to respond to (subject to how the patient is feeling that day) are also problematic.[55]

---

52 American Psychiatric Association (APA). 'Paraphilic Disorders.' *American Psychiatric Publishing*, Viewed September, 14 2014, paragraph 8,<http://www.dsm5.org/Documents/Paraphilic%20Disorders%20Fact%20Sheet.pdf>.

53 American Psychiatric Association (APA). *Diagnostic and Statistical Manual of Mental Disorders 5 (DSM – 5) – Paraphilic Disorders*. Washington DC: APA. 2013a, Viewed September 14, 2014, paragraph 1,<http://dsm.psychiatryonline.org.ezproxy.library.yorku.ca/content.aspx?bookid=556&sectionid=41101785#103442326>.

54 Ibid., paragraph 9.

55 Owen Whooley and Allan Horwitz, 'The Paradox of Professional Success: Grand Ambition, Furious Resistance, and the Derailment of the DSM-5 Revision Process.' *Making the DSM-5: Concepts and Controversies*, edited by Joel Paris and James Phillips, (New York: Springer, 2013): 75–92.

Further to this is the concern that APA references the controversial and disputed penile plethysmograph device, for measuring males' desires as well as viewing time in males and females.[56] This is a device that measures blood flow to the penis in relation to visual or audio stimuli and has been used in scientific and legal realms to assess sexual orientation and risk of sexual assaults on the part of sexual offenders. It is a controversial measuring tool due to its insufficient reliability.[57]

Others and I have argued that volumetric plethysmography testing, as a biomedical tool and interpretative model, is a radically reductionist means of 'diagnosing' erotic identities.[58] Time spent viewing images of paraphilic sex must also take into consideration its uniqueness, compared to mainstreamed sexual imagery. It is important that meaning-making activities tied to a complex phenomenology of desire not be overlooked. In other words, human development involves sexual development in terms of interests, desires, behaviours and activities. What arouses us can be fluid, and not always fully understood. Over time, and with encouragement and support, individuals develop meaning in relation to their sexual development, in a complex process that far exceeds the reductionist devices and interpretative modalities utilized in the questionable tests that use penile plethysmographs.

The responses from BDSM practitioners and LGBTQ communities are premised on understandings of how such diagnoses affect lives and recognizing the ideological debates that inform the highly politicized process of revising the DSM. The National Coalition for Sexual Freedom (NCSF) carried out a campaign that challenged including paraphilias in the DSM. When the changes were made and the DSM-5 was released, NCSF chose not to openly challenge the text, instead opting for a somewhat moderate approach. It recognized the incremental process the APA had engaged in and thanked the APA Paraphilias

56 W. Marshall, and Y. M. Fernandez, 'Phallometric Testing With Sex Offenders: Limits to its Value,' *Clinical Psychology Review,* 20 (2003): 807–822; William O'Donohue, Lisa Regev and Anne Hagstrom, 'Problems With the DSM-IV Diagnosis of Pedophilia,' *Sexual Abuse: A Journal of Research and Treatment* 12 (2000): 95–105; Walter Simon and Peter Shouten, 'Plethysography in the Assessment and Treatment of Sexual Deviance: An Overview.' *Archives of Sexual Behaviour,* 20, 1 (1991): 75–91.

57 Duhaime's Law Dictionary 'Penile Plethysmograph Definition,' Viewed June 26, 2015,<http://www.duhaime.org/LegalDictionary/P/PenilePlethysmograph.aspx>.

58 Daley and Mulé, 'LGBTQs and the DSM-5,' 1303.

Sub Work Group for differentiating between paraphilias and paraphilic disorders.[59]

In contrast, Keenan reached a more politicized, ironic and direct conclusion on the status of kinksters stating, 'Simply put, the *DSM V* will say that happy kinksters don't have a mental disorder. But unhappy kinksters do.'[60] She has argued that, 'The continued presence of the paraphilias (despite their superficial name change) in the ... *DSM V* is redundant, unscientific, unnecessary, and harmful to millions of kinksters.'[61]

The kink community has play standards and comportment guidelines premised on communication, safety, sanity and consensuality,[62] which are not necessarily present in 'normophilic' sexual engagements. It is important to tease out how political ideology informs sexual activism, and the influence of Neoliberalism within it. Thus it is helpful to place/locate these contrasting arguments along the political spectrum. The NCSF, for instance, falls on the right side of the spectrum: for this association the struggle is about the rights of good neoliberals to engage in kinky sex in private.[63]

Keenan, on the other hand, is interested in ousting the APA for its role in surveiling and regulating kink through the DSM, and ending such repressive practices, positioning her to the far left of the political spectrum. Variance in organised movements and the extent to which they take on publicly vocal political perspectives are dependent on a number of factors. Kinksters are not a homogeneous group, as they bring to the political arena the complexity of their own realities regarding being 'out.' Their goals for BDSM activism are influenced by whether they are interested in public advocacy. It is also important to point out that political organizing based on sexual behavior rather than on

59 National Coalition for Sexual Freedom (NCSF), 'DSM-V Revision Project,' N.D., Viewed April 20, 2015,<https://ncsfreedom.org/key-programs/dsm-v-revision-project/dsm-v-program-page.html >.

60 Jillian Keenan, 'We're Kinky, Not Crazy' *Slate.* last modified 7 March 2013, Viewed September 18, 2014,<http://www.slate.com/articles/health_and_science/medical_examiner/2013/03/sexual_kinks_in_the_dsm_v_paraphilic_disorders_describe_unhappy_kinksters.html>.

61 Ibid., 2.

62 Trevor Jacques, On the Safe Edge: A Manual for SM Play. (Toronto: WholeSM Publishing, 1993).

63 Margot D. Weiss, 'Gay shame and BDSM pride: neoliberalism, privacy and sexual politics,' *Radical History Review* 100, (2008): 86–101.

identity politics splinters the movement further and can create significant mobilization difficulties.[64]

Over the course of more than half a century, the DSM has grown into a powerful taxonomy. It has the power to define the 'normal' and the 'healthy,' effectively controlling modes of 'proper' sexual behavior, by labeling anything that falls outside of these restricted modalities as pathological and as mentally disordered. Although it is primarily influential in North America and parts of Europe, the DSM, having been translated into 22 languages, has a global impact that can extend to 'child custody decisions, self-esteem, whether individuals are hired or fired, receive security clearances, or have other rights or privileges curtailed.'[65]

Its inextricable link to the Law has been abused in numerous instances; its conservative political agendas have been furthered in the cultural realm and have impacted the governance of social institutions, such as families and the world of work; kinksters and LGBTQs alike have been oppressed, and such oppression has been justified by the equating of unusual sexual interests with psychiatric pathologies.[66]

Given this degree of influence, what is of great concern is the potential harm perpetrated on individuals whose sexual interests and desires are not considered 'normophilic,' resulting in stigmatisation by a system that labels and pathologises rather than accept a diversity of sexual practices. The behavioural norms in BDSM do not tolerate any acts that infringe on consent and cause distress: they cross the ethical line of acceptable paraphilic practices, and Laws to curtail and punish such behavior already exist. Therefore, why do paraphilic disorders need to be in the DSM?

I think that it is essential that the issue of power be addressed if this question is to be seriously considered. It can be surmised that removing the paraphilias outright from the DSM would in effect diminish the authoritative power

64 Deww Zhang, 'Dungeon Lives and Daily Lies: Navigating the Vanilla World,' *Erotic Subjects and Outlaws: Sketching the Borders of Sexual Citizenship*, in this volume.

65 Allen Frances, Saving Normal: An Insider's Revolt Against Out-of-Control Psychiatric Diagnosis, DSM-5, Big Pharma, and the Medicalization of Ordinary Life. (New York: Harper Collins Publishers, 2013); Charles Moser and Peggy Kleinplatz, 'DSM-IV-TR and the Paraphilias: An Argument for Removal,' *Sexual and Gender Diagnoses of the Diagnostic and Statistical Manual (DSM): A Reevaluation*, eds. Dan Karasic and Jack Drescher, (New York: Haworth Press, 2005), 91–109, 93.

66 Allen Frances, *Saving Normal: An Insider's Revolt Against Out-of-Control Psychiatric Diagnosis, DSM-5, Big Pharma, and the Medicalization of Ordinary Life*. (New York: Harper Collins Publishers, 2013).

the APA holds in sexual desires and practices, in society. Its self-ascribed role as ultimate authority on sexual pathologies allows it to define the paraphilias as it sees fit, – notwithstanding a lack of scientific evidence. The APA has the power to pathologise through surveillance, and in turn the ability to regulate and stigmatise through diagnosis.

It is a power of a highly impactful nature when one considers its influence on child custody cases, divorce disputes, arrests for obscenity, indecency, and the like.[67] Such influence affords the APA the ability to promulgate white, middle class, normophilic sexual activities that sit comfortably in Neoliberal agendas of sexual self-governance and privatized respectability. My analysis presumes that should the paraphilias ever be removed from the DSM, it would be an admission of error on the part of the APA for having had them there in the first place. Such an admission is not expected to take place. What we can expect and are already seeing is a gradual incrementalism, in which kink is slowly legitimised, an approach the APA has taken in the past, as in the case of homosexuality in the DSM.

The continued classification of paraphilias based on Criterion B as clinical paraphilic disorders contributes to and perpetuates negative, sinister and alarming characteristics that are the very antitheses of ethical definitions of BDSM.

- Why does the APA continue to define some sexual activities this way, given its history of not distinguishing between the paraphilias and paraphilic disorders in previous editions of the DSM?
- Why does the APA classify paraphilic disorders as pathological in the absence of scientific evidence?
- Is the APA's distinction into two paraphilic categories a means of justifying its own desire to continue to influence what it sees as 'normophilic' sexual behaviours?
- Is the APA reluctant to relinquish its power to pathologise, surveil, regulate and stigmatise 'unusual sexual behaviour' in order to uphold Neoliberal values?

I direct these questions not solely at the APA, although it has a responsibility to address them; I also pose them to society at large and question the need to continue to imbue the APA with diagnostic power over sexual matters.

67 National Coalition for Sexual Freedom (NCSF), "DSM Revision White Paper: NCSF and the NCSF Foundation's Position on the Discriminatory Paraphilias Section in the DSM," N.D. Viewed April 19, 2015,<https://ncsfreedom.org/key-programs/dsm-v-revision-project/dsm-revision-white-paper.html>.

9 Conclusion

By applying a critical queer analysis to the Paraphilias as a category in the DSM-5 I challenge hegemonic perspectives based on traditional, conventional thought on sexual interests and desires. In this chapter I provided a review of the prominence of the DSM and its influential impact on important sectors of society. I critiqued the highly questionable rationale for inclusion of the Paraphilias as a category in its taxonomy. I examined the changes in classification and the revisions that have occurred between the DSM-IV-TR to DSM-5.

Although separating out the Paraphilias from Paraphilic Disorders can be seen as a progressive move forward in depathologizing the category in general, it does not go far enough. I contend it continues to mis-label kinky acts as pathological, even though Laws currently exist to address any harm that might take place were such acts be of a non-consensual nature or if they harmed others. It fails to take seriously the stigmatizing effects it may have on those who question such desires in a society that can be rigid about such matters. Even when the APA takes society's disapproval into consideration, its traditional psychodynamic approach focuses solely on personal distress, and is unable to take into consideration the issue of sexual development and personal agency in acknowledging and accepting one's sexual interests.

From a critical queer analytical perspective, perhaps a sign of progress is the discontent that is surfacing from APA itself, as well as other mental health organisations. There is now widespread discussion of the validity of the APA's diagnostic manual, a challenge that stems from the lack of scientific evidence used to substantiate such diagnoses; challenged also are its questionable diagnostic model, and the deleterious effects such diagnosing may have on people's lives.

Underscoring such concerns is the increased regulatory role of psychiatric diagnosis that police individuals who express their sexual interests and desires in ways that fail to adhere to 'normophilic' beliefs, values and morals of dominant social groups. Challenged are traditional and contemporary biomedical and scientific efforts to classify, pathologise, and regulate 'unusual' sexual interests, desires and behaviours, as 'abnormal,' resulting in stigmatising implications that negatively intersect with law enforcement, the courts, family, careers and friends. I argue for affirming and sex positive – non-pathologising, deregulating, de-stigmatising and anti-oppressive – understandings of diverse sexual interests, desires and behaviours, in which kink is not unfairly targeted through conflation with sexual transgression.

Bibliography

American Psychiatric Association. *Diagnostic and Statistical Manual of Mental Disorders (DSM-IV)*. Washington DC: APA. 1994.

American Psychiatric Association. *Diagnostic and Statistical Manual of Mental Disorders (DSM-IV-TR)*. Washington DC: APA. 2000.

American Psychiatric Association. *Diagnostic and Statistical Manual of Mental Disorders 5 (DSM – 5) – Paraphilic Disorders*. Washington DC: APA. 2013a, accessed 14 September 2014,http://dsm.psychiatryonline.org.ezproxy.library.yorku.ca/content.aspx?bookid=556&sectionid=41101785#103442326.

American Psychiatric Association. "Highlights of Changes from DSM-IV-TR to DSM-5." *American Psychiatric Publishing*, accessed 2013b, http://www.dsm5.org/Documents/changes%20from%20dsm-iv-tr%20to%20dsm-5.pdf

American Psychiatric Association. "Paraphilic Disorders." *American Psychiatric Publishing*, last modified 2013c, accessed September 14 2014: http://www.dsm5.org/Documents/Paraphilic%20Disorders%20Fact%20Sheet.pdf

Blanchard, Ray. "The DSM Diagnostic Criteria for Pedophilia." *Archives of Sexual Behavior* 39, no. 4 (2009a): 304–316.

Blanchard, Ray. "The DSM Diagnostic Criteria for Transvestic Fetishism." *Archives of Sexual Behavior* 34, (2009b): 439–446.

Brauser, Deborah. "Experts React to DSM-5 Approval." *Medscape Today*, (2012), accessed 2 December, 2012, http://www.medscape.com/viewarticle/775526

Brooks, Megan. "Published DSM-5 Field Trial Results Prompt Renewed Criticism." *Medscape Today* (2012), last modified 14 November 2012, accessed 2 January 2013, http://www.medscape.com/viewarticle/774475

Bullough, Vern L. and Bullough, Bonnie. *Sin, Sickness, and Sanity*. New York: New American Library, 1977.

Butler, Judith. *Gender Trouble: Feminism and the Subversion of Identity*. New York: Routledge, 1999.

Carson, Robert. "Dilemmas in the Pathway of the DSM-IV." *Journal of Abnormal Psychology* 100 (1991): 302–307.

Daley, Andrea and Mulé, Nick J. "LGBTQs and the DSM-5: A Critical Queer Response." *Journal of Homosexuality* 61.9 (2014): 1288 – 1312.

Drescher, J*Theory, Culture & Society* "Queer Diagnoses: Parallels and Contrasts in the History of Homosexuality, Gender Variance, and the Diagnostic and Statistical Manual." *Archives of Sexual Behavior*, 39, 2 (2010): 427–60.

Editorial. "Time's Up for Psychiatry's Bible." *New Scientist*, 2738. accessed 17 December 2009, http://www.newscientist.com/article/mg20427382.400-times-up-for-psychiatrys-bible.html

Frances, Allen. "Diagnosing the DSM." *The New York Times* (New York, NY), May 11 2012a. Accessed 18 September 2014, http://www.nytimes.com/2012/05/12/opinion/break-up-the-psychiatric-monopoly.html?_r=0

Frances, Allen. "DSM 5 Is a Guide Not a Bible—Ignore Its Ten Worst Changes: APA Approval of DSM-5 is a Sad Day for Psychiatry." *Psychology Today*, 2 December 2012b. Accessed 2 January 2013,http://www.psychologytoday.com/blog/dsm5-in-distress/201212/dsm-5-is-guide-not-bible-ignore-its-ten-worst-changes

Frances, Allen. "How Many Billions a Year Will the DSM-5 Cost?" *Bloomberg*, 20 December 2012c. Accessed 2 January 2013,http://www.bloomberg.com/news/2012-12-20/how-many-billions-a-year-will-the-dsm-5-cost-.html

Frances, Allen. *Saving normal: An Insider's Revolt Against Out-of-Control Psychiatric Diagnosis, DSM-5, Big Pharma, and the Medicalization of Ordinary Life*. New York: Harper Collins Publishers., 2013.

Gabbard, Glen. *Gabbard's Treatments of Psychiatric Disorders*. American Psychiatric Press, 2007.

Gabbard, Glen, Moser, Charles, and Peggy Kleinplatz. "DSM-IV-TR and the Paraphilias: An Argument for Removal," *Sexual and Gender Diagnoses of the Diagnostic and Statistical Manual (DSM): A Reevaluation*, eds. Dan Karasic and Jack Drescher (New York: Haworth Press, 2005), 91–109.

Gaudiano, Brandon and Zimmerman, Mark. "Prevalence of Attenuated Psychotic Symptoms and Their Relationship With DSM-IV Diagnoses in a General Psychiatric Outpatient Clinic." *Journal of Clinical Psychatry*, 74.2 (2013): 149–155. Accessed 2 January 2013,http://article.psychiatrist.com/dao_1login.asp?ID=10008052&RSID=90399506541510

Insel, Thomas. "Director's Blog: Transforming Diagnosis." *National Institute of Mental Health (NIMH)*. last modified 29 April 2013. Accessed 18 September 2014, http://www.nimh.nih.gov/about/director/2013/transforming-diagnosis.shtml

Jacques, Trevor. *On the Safe Edge: A Manual for SM Play*. Toronto: WholeSM Publishing, 1993.

Karasic, Dan and Jack Drescher, eds. *Sexual and Gender Diagnoses of the Diagnostic and Statistical Manual (DSM): A Reevaluation*, (New York: Haworth Press, 2005)

Keenan, Jillian, "We're Kinky, Not Crazy" *Slate*. last modified 7 March 2013. Accessed 18 September 2014, http://www.slate.com/articles/health_and_science/medical_examiner/2013/03/sexual_kinks_in_the_dsm_v_paraphilic_disorders_describe_unhappy_kinksters.html

Kendell, Robert. and Jablensky, Assen. "Distinguishing Between the Validity and Utility of Psychiatric Diagnoses." *American Journal of Psychiatry*, 74.1 (2003): 4–12.

Kendell, Robert. "Five Criteria for an Improved Taxonomy of Mental Disorders." in Defining *Psychopathology in the 21st Century DSM V and Beyond*, edited by John Helzer and James Hudziak, 3–18. Washington, DC: American Psychiatric Publishing, 2002.

Marshall, W and Fernandez, Y M. "Phallometric Testing With Sex Offenders: Limits to its Value." *Clinical Psychology Review*, 20 (2003): 807–822.

McCammon, Susan., Knox, David, and Schacht, Caroline. *Choices in Sexuality*, Mason: Ohio, Atomic Dog Publishing, 2004.

McConaghy, Nathaniel. "Unresolved Issues in Scientific Sexology." *Archives of Sexual Behavior*, 28.4 (1999): 285–318.

Mestel, Rosie. "Changes to the Psychiatrists' Bible, DSM: Some Reactions." *LA Times*, (Los Angeles, CA) 9 December 2012. Accessed 2 January 2013, http://www.latimes.com/health/boostershots/la-heb-dsm5-american-psychiatric-association-20121207,0,1392058.story

Metzl, Johnathan. *The Protest Psychosis: How Schizophrenia Became a Black Disease.* Boston, MA: Beacon Press, 2009.

Money, John. *Gay, Straight, and In-Between: The Sexology of Erotic Orientation.* Oxford University Press. 1990.

Moser, Charles. and Kleinplatz, Peggy. "DSM-IV-TR and the Paraphilias: An Argument for Removal." In *Sexual and Gender Diagnoses of the Diagnostic and Statistical Manual (DSM): A Reevaluation*, edited by Dan Karasic and Jack Drescher, 91–109. New York: Haworth Press, 2005.

O'Donohue, William, Regev, Lisa and Hagstrom, Anne. (2000). "Problems With the DSM-IV Diagnosis of Pedophilia." *Sexual Abuse: A Journal of Research and Treatment* 12 (2000): 95–105.

Simon, Walter. And Shouten, Peter. "Plethysography in the Assessment and Treatment of Sexual Deviance: An Overview." *Archives of Sexual Behaviour*, 20.1 (1991): 75–91.

Spitzer, Robert. "Sexual and Gender Identity Disorders: Discussion of Questions for DSM-V". *Sexual and Gender Diagnoses of the Diagnostic and Statistical Manual (DSM): A Reevaluation*, edited by Dan Karasic and Jack Drescher, 111–116. New York: Haworth Press. 2005

Stekel, Wilhelm. *Sexual Aberrations: The Phenomenon of Fetishism in Relation to Sex*, translated from the 1922 original German edition by S. Parker. Liveright Publishing, 1930

Weiderman, Michael. "Paraphilia and Fetishism." *The Family Journal*, 11.3 (2003): 315–32.

Weiss, Margot D. "Gay Shame and BDSM Pride: Neoliberalism, Privacy and Sexual Politics," *Radical History Review* 100, (2008): 86–101.

Whooley, Owen, and Horwitz, Allan. "The Paradox of Professional Success: Grand Ambition, Furious Resistance, and the Derailment of the DSM-5 Revision Process." *Making the DSM-5: Concepts and Controversies*, edited by Joel Paris and James Phillips, 75–92. New York: Springer, 2013.

Zhang, Deww. “Dungeon Lives and Daily Lies: Navigating the Vanilla World.” *Erotic Subjects and Outlaws: Sketching the Borders of Sexual Citizenship*, edited by Serena Petrella, Brill.

Zucker, Ken. “Reports from the DSM-V Work Group on Sexual and Gender Identity Disorders.” *Archives of Sexual Behavior*, 39.2 (2010): 217–220.

CHAPTER 7

Bio-Politics in Sub-Saharan Africa: Re-Examining Prevention of Mother-to-Child Transmission Strategies for HIV

Abidemi Fasanmi

Abstract

Despite extensive investment of resources on HIV interventions in Sub-Saharan Africa, this area continues to be the greatest contributor of new infections that occur in adults and children across the world, with a disturbing trend of contagion for women that is three times higher than that of men. This chapter examines Prevention of Mother-to-Child Transmission (PMTCT) strategies for HIV adopted by the UN and WHO. These programs failure to attain the desired positive success rates in Sub-Saharan Africa, can be attributed to a lack of attention to the socio-cultural norms, values, and traditional practices that impact infection rates.

This chapter examines the ideological and epistemological framework of PMTCT strategies, offering an analysis of the bio-political dynamics that are at their core, ultimately creating barriers to treatment. I offer a close analysis of the social norms, the familial structures, relational gender dynamics, the traditional customs, the religious values and the patriarchal relations of power that constrain women's abilities to make decisions about their reproductive health to reduce infection.

In conclusion, I call for a critical dialogue for the development of appropriate and sustainable interventions that address the socio-economic, cultural and political peculiarities that these women face, so that PMTCT interventions and public health strategies can better serve one of the most vulnerable groups in this region.

Keywords

PMTCT strategies – women's health – sexuality – empowerment – bio- politics – bio-power – HIV – Sub-Saharan Africa – Nigeria

 | DOI:10.1163/9789004392298_009

1 Introduction

Since the discovery of HIV, a strenuous battle has been waged against transmission to roll back the tides of the infection that has reached pandemic proportions in Sub-Saharan Africa. This area of the globe is the greatest contributor of new infections, making up 95% of new infections in individuals in low and middle-income countries.[1] 71% of people living with HIV and 88% of children with HIV across the world can be found in this region.[2] The majority of HIV prevention strategies, including Prevention of Mother–to-Child Transmission (PMTCT) have mostly adopted a human rights and biomedical approach.

Approaching the problem of infection through a human rights lens has led authorities to target specific groups that had been deemed to be marginalized within a particular society (for instance, young wives and their children, but not their husbands), while a biomedical approach has privileged purely medical interventions, at the expense of more holistic strategies (that would take into consideration the cultural specificities and social dynamics of targeted groups).

An insufficient decrease in the rate of infection then led authorities to go through numerous revisions and re-developments of the guidelines for prevention and the treatment of HIV infection in many countries. What still appears to be missing from these new strategies is the resolve and willingness to engage in the cultural practices and traditional values that impact infection rates, and a serious examination of existing societal norms and behaviours that make it difficult for the most vulnerable groups, especially women, to make choices that would reduce their vulnerability to HIV infection.

This chapter offers a systematic analysis of PMTCT strategies' 'benign' bio-political agendas and their effects on the lives of marginalized women. I wish to make evident their ideological and epistemological shortcomings, which have dire harmful effects on the vulnerable populations that they seek to help. 'Bio-politics' is understood in Foucauldian terms here, as a control apparatus that is able to reach and govern an entire population,[3] and is tied to the notion of 'bio-power,' defined as 'an explosion of numerous and diverse techniques for achieving the subjugations of bodies and the control of

---

1 The Henry J. Kaiser Family Foundation 'Overview: The Global HIV/AIDS Epidemic', *Global Health Policy*, 30 November, 2015, viewed 21 April, 2014,http://kff.org/global-health-policy/fact-sheet/the-global-hivaids-epidemic/

2 Ibid.

3 Michel Foucault. *Security, Territory, Population: Lectures at the Collège de France 1977–1978*, trans. Graham Burchell (Basingstoke: Palgrave Macmillan, 2007), 243.

populations.'[4] Throughout the text, I offer an intersectional examination of the societal norms, the marital and familial structures, the traditional customs, and the moral and religious values of the region, to illustrate the ways in which biomedical interventions fail to address the socio-cultural contexts that shape the sexual and reproductive choices that place women and their children at greater risk of HIV infection, providing an exhaustive explanation of how and why PMTCT strategies, so far, have had such low success rates.

In the next section, I provide a brief description of the state of HIV infection in Sub-Saharan Africa, addressing the wide gender gap that can currently be found in the region. I argue that assessing risks uniquely within a biomedical framework poses significant problems: the impact of socio-cultural, economic and environmental factors as well as gendered dynamics, are largely ignored, placing the most vulnerable at risk. In section three, I discuss gendered dynamics in the region, and offer a critique of PMTCT strategies' assumptions that a woman is able to make specific decisions about her health and well-being, separately from her family and her community. I show the ways in which her existence is heavily constrained by patriarchal relations of power, and offer suggestions on how to re-organize medical care in a manner that would better serve those most at risk.

In section four, I discuss the concept of empowerment and illustrate how PMTCT strategies have adopted Feminist ideological frameworks that have been problematically 'exported' from the West, and have applied them in a context for which they are ill suited. The promise of economic empowerment has not necessarily brought freedom to women in these regions, and has not necessarily facilitated access to PMTCT care.

In section five, I argue that the biomedical framework that informs PMTCT strategies is part of a 'diffuse' governance tactic that specifically targets the health of marginalized groups, in this case women of reproductive age and their babies, at risk of HIV infection. Setting out to better the living conditions of these at-risk populations, these agencies make possible a shift in power management, away from the sovereign state in the region: power is ceded to non-governmental agencies that specialize in the management of health, and becomes bio-power. I discuss the role of the UN: in disseminating a specific type of 'privileged' scientific knowledge, it has helped shape *the norm* for HIV programming world-wide, inadvertently setting up epistemological hierarchies that worsen power imbalances between the West and the Global South.

4 Michel Foucault, *The History of Sexuality Vol. 1* (London: Penguin, [1978]1998), 140.

In section six, I discuss the issue of 'subjugated knowledge,' a process through which knowledge claims are organized into hierarchies that always privilege Western knowledge and deem local epistemologies as less important. Local indigenous researchers often find that making contributions is difficult, because they are routinely expected to align with the core assumptions that already inform medical strategies.

In section seven, I investigate the relationship between PMTCT strategies and the transnational pharmaceutical industry. I argue that Big Pharma has greatly benefited from this relationship, with the production of HIV related commodities (from condoms to high tech testing machinery), as well as HIV medical research trials. I discuss what I have termed *human drug trial labour*: pharmaceutical companies can easily compel local populations to participate in trials, especially HIV positive women, unethically exploiting them for profit.

In section eight, I discuss the effects of the bio-political interventions in the lives of women living with HIV in the administration of PMTCT care. On the one hand, PMTCT programs can provide opportunities for agency and survival for women living with HIV, through the creation of support groups that give them access to free health services, drugs, and financial empowerment, while also preventing HIV transmission to their babies. On the other hand, these programs subject the bodies of these women to a set of disciplinary interventions and actions, informed by the logic of its definitions of personhood, proper sexual behaviour, 'good' health and reproductive choices.

In conclusion, I call for a critical dialogue for the development of appropriate and sustainable interventions that address the socio-economic, cultural and political peculiarities that these women face, so that PMTCT interventions and public health strategies can better serve one of the most vulnerable groups in Sub-Saharan Africa.

2 Background

Klot and Nguyen have succinctly summed up how an individual's structural and intersectional location affects his or her fate in relation to HIV infection dynamics in Sub-Saharan Africa. They state:

> The HIV (immuno-deficiency virus) and AIDS (Acquired Immune Deficiency Syndrome) pandemic both fuels and is fuelled by inequalities across gender, race, ethnicity and class.[5]

5 Jennifer F. Klot and Vinh-Kim Nguyen, eds. *The Fourth Wave. Violence, Gender, Culture & HIV in the 21st Century* (UNESCO: Centre for Research in Ethnic Relations, 2009), 15.

The impact of HIV infection is increasingly disproportionate between genders, with young women between 15 and 24 years old being at least three times more likely to be HIV-positive than young men.[6] Nearly half the 30.8 million people living with HIV worldwide are women between the ages of 15 and 49. Between the ages of 15 and 24, gender disparities are even more extreme, with women 1.5 times more likely to be living with HIV than young men.[7]

To make matters worse, Sub-Saharan Africa has one of the highest rates of mother-to-child HIV transmission (MTCT).[8] UNESCO has investigated the failure to adequately protect women from infection in these areas, and shown that breakdowns in prevention stem from a lack of analysis of gender and ethno-cultural issues, and a dearth of critical, feminist and comparative approaches in the review of programming for HIV reduction.[9]

Risks relating to HIV were assessed in terms of 'vulnerable groups' based on 'high-risk of infectivity, by virtue of medically classified risky behaviours.'[10] These behaviours included having multiple sexual partners. Other risk factors are unsafe birthing and blood transfusion practices, where a HIV positive pregnant woman transmits HIV to her baby and medical practices, such as of unsafe blood transfusion practices of HIV infected blood to patients . These risks are pronounced for African women in places where certain cultural practices predispose them to obstretric or gynaecological problems that require surgical interventions. Examples of these practices are birthing practices that prevent women from seeking antenatal care from trained health professionals and pregnancy complications from extensive female genital cutting. Therefore,assessing risks uniquely within a biomedical framework poses significant problems, because it fails to recognize the influence of socio-cultural, structural, economic, political and environmental factors in shaping individual and group behaviour, which have the consequence of placing particular individuals and groups at disproportionate risk.[11] Institutions then develop a form of *biomedical tunnel vision*: even though they are aware, at least at the theoretical level, that HIV transmission patterns are multi-factorial, and have biomedical, structural and behavioural origins, in practice the

6 Ibid., 15.

7 Ibid.

8 AIDSTAR One, *Prevention of Mother-to-Child Transmission* (PMTCT) *of HIV*, Viewed 21 April 2014, http://www.aidstar-one.com/focus_areas/pmtct; World Health Organization (WHO), *Prevention of Mother-To-Child Transmission* (PMTCT) *Briefing Note*, (Geneva: WHO, Department of HIV/AIDS, 2007).

9 Klot and Nguyen, *The Fourth Wave*, 15.

10 Ibid., 16.

11 Ibid.

intervention strategies that they develop end up disproportionately emphasizing the biomedical component of HIV transmission. An emblematic example of biomedical tunnel vision in the implementation of HIV prevention strategies is the program for Prevention of Mother-to-Child Transmission.[12]

PMTCT is a strategy aimed at preventing the transmission of HIV from a pregnant or nursing woman to her child, during pregnancy, labour, delivery, and breastfeeding. This prevention strategy has several prongs for intervention that target women within specific phases of their life, but especially during their reproductive years. The four pronged approach program model is thought to be comprehensive and is being implemented worldwide, following the guidelines stipulated by the World Health Organization (WHO).[13]

Each of the four prongs targets a life stage for women at risk and offers a specific strategy for reducing HIV transmission: the first aims to prevent HIV infection in women of reproductive age, the second prevents unintended pregnancy in women with HIV, the third is aimed at preventing HIV transmission from mother to child, and the last offers ongoing care and support to mothers, their children, and families.[14] These interventions shared both a women-centred, human rights approach, and a biomedical focus.[15]

They unfortunately fail to grasp the complexities of the societal *fabric,* ignoring socio-economic and political dynamics, as well as the unique cultural environment of that society. Such interventions do not take place in a vacuum but instead are interwoven into cultural norms such as polygamy, religious beliefs, traditional practices and values. Emblematic examples are the patronage of Traditional Birth Attendants (TBAs) during childbirth, practices around breastfeeding, and other forms of family planning (i.e. an injunction on breastfeeding, deemed vital in traditional culture for the mother–child bond).[16] Breastfeeding is also strongly believed to prevent conception and forecloses the use of formula to reduce feeding costs. In the coming sections,

12 World Health Organization (WHO), *PMTCT Strategic Vision 2010–2015 Preventing Mother-To-Child Transmission of HIV To Reach The UNGASS And Millennium Development Goals Moving Towards The Elimination Of Paediatric HIV* (Geneva, WHO, 2010), 6.

13 Developed by the U.N. in 2001. United Nations Special Session on HIV/AIDS June 2002.

14 AIDSTAR One, *Prevention of Mother-to-Child Transmission* (PMTCT) *of HIV*.

15 Interventions targeted exclusively women for family planning services, ANC HIV clinics, micro finance (empowerment) programs, and emergency obstetrics plan designs (for pregnant women).

16 Emmanuel Monjok, Andrea Smesny, and E. James Essien. "HIV/AIDS–Related Stigma and Discrimination in Nigeria: Review of Research Studies and Future Directions for Prevention Strategies." *African journal of reproductive health* 13.3 (2009): 23.

I will present arguments that will make evident the fallacies of PMTCT strategies. I will assert that a strong focus on biomedical interventions, that targets solely women and adopts a human rights platform as well as economic empowerment frameworks, but continue to ignore the structural and cultural intricacies that impact HIV transmission, will achieve poor results in the African context, and especially in Sub-Saharan regions.

3 'Bargaining with Patriarchy,' Gender Performance and PMTCT

UNAIDS reports from 2015 indicate that:

> Without intervention, the risk of Mother-to-Child Transmission (MTCT) ranges from 20% to 45%. With specific interventions in non-breastfeeding populations, the risk of MTCT can be reduced to less than 2%, and to 5% or less in breastfeeding populations.[17]

And yet these interventions cannot be removed from the social, religious, economic, political and cultural realities that characterize women's status within African society.

To begin with, a woman's agency, in the African context, is intricately woven into the fabric of her social life, and heavily influenced by her structural locations,[18] which are strongly linked to her communal and familial connections, as well as her reproductive potentials.[19] Her existence is heavily constrained by patriarchal relations of power, which imbue the entire society. Unfortunately, the medical interventions promoted by internationally funded aid programs often favour individualistic decision making processes for women living with HIV. Such 'atomized' agency is simply not available to women in these contexts.

For example, PMTCT interventions focus on girls and women of reproductive age, pregnant women, mothers and their babies. These women are

17 World Health Organization (WHO), PMTCT *Strategic Vision 2010–2015*, 6.

18 Oyeronke Oyewumi, 'Conceptualizing Gender: The Eurocentric Foundations of Feminist Concepts and the Challenge of African Epistemologies', *Jenda: A Journal of Culture and African Woman Studies* 2 (2002), 1; see the chapters on gender and the economy, women, wealth, titles and power, gender and political organization in Ifi Amadiume. *Male Daughters, Female Husbands: Gender and Sex in an African Society* (New York: Zed, 1987).

19 Q. Ashton Action, ed. *Issues in Reproductive Medicine Research: 2011 Edition,* (Georgia Atlanta: Scholarly edition, 2011).

assumed to be able to make specific decisions about their health and well-being, as if they were the sole agents in charge, which simply is not the case. For instance, women are approached and encouraged to get tested after receiving counselling at family planning and ante-natal clinics, when they are alone, as they rarely would attend such clinics with their partners. But this individualistic approach is incongruous with African women's realities: they are unable to make such decisions alone, because in their culture, such decisions require the input and blessing of patriarchal agents of power. Thus, a woman's ability to employ agency requires, as Kandiyoti has powerfully argued, a constant 'bargaining with patriarchy.'[20]

The process of bargaining with patriarchy entails adopting various strategies to negotiate with structures of authority. Firstly, women need their husbands' permission to make financial, reproductive and health-related decisions. Attaining this financial or reproductive control entails a complex set of decisions and actions that these women must make in a manner that is consistent with the norms of their communities. A woman's social location in the contemporary family and society is thus a crucial component of this bargain.

Secondly, the social context is characterized by traditionally African and patriarchal norms. For instance, in Nigeria, sons are given great 'reproductive value,' while daughters end up having significantly less value. The high status afforded to sons encourages high fertility rates, polygamy, and wife rivalry: women who are married to the same husband end up competing with one another for resources, and their reproductive success in producing sons gives them power in accessing those resources.[21] Consequently, competition increases fertility rates and reduces interest in family planning. Family planning is, however, a key aspect of PMTCT intervention.

Thirdly, morality in the region strictly governs women's sexual expression and their modesty is highly esteemed in many religious and traditional

---

20 Deniz Kandiyoti, 'Bargaining with Patriarchy', *Gender and Society* 2.3 (1988), 279; through the adoption of this concept of 'bargaining patriarchy,' I wish to explore various ideological constructs of a woman's social location in relation to PMTCT strategies. These create structures of oppression that both afford her a subject position but at the same time objectify her.

21 Betsy Hartmann. 'Security and Survival: Why Do Poor People Have Many Children,' *The Post-Colonial Science and Technology Reader*, edited by Sandra Harding, 310–317 (Durham and London: Duke University Press, 2011); Ian M. Timæus and Angela Reynar, 'Polygynists and Their Wives in Sub-Saharan Africa: An Analysis of Five Demographic and Health Surveys', *Population Studies* 52.2 (1998), 3–5; William Jankowiak, Monika Sudakov and Benjamin C. Wilreker, 'Co-Wife Conflict and Co-operation', *Ethnology* 44.1(2005), 1,89.

customs in Africa.[22] The identity of a woman in Nigerian society is strongly tied to norms relating to morality, chastity and reproduction. The culture of morality and chastity in Nigeria is not only ingrained in traditional norms but also in religious norms.[23] Thus, sexuality is regarded as a *sacred and unspoken subject*, one that should never be openly discussed. It is women who are tasked and held strictly responsible for maintaining the order of morality and chastity before and after marriage, through their demeanour.

These issues are pertinent to an aspect of the strategy for PMTCT, which specifically targets girls and women of reproductive age and aims at preventing infection with HIV. Studies have shown that most HIV intervention programs emphasize abstinence as a technique for prevention, even though studies have shown a high percentage of early sexual debuts in girls.[24] Moreover, fewer girls than boys receive sex education. This is due in part to the secrecy in which sexuality is enshrouded, especially with regards to females, as well as the moral and religious values tied to sex within the culture of the region.[25]

Given that HIV infection occurs in the majority of cases through sexual transmission, women living with HIV are inevitably morally judged and stigmatized once their HIV status becomes disclosed.[26] The predictable result is that people tend to hide their status and rarely disclose whether they are HIV positive to their partners. An additional issue has to do with familial dissolution: divorce or separation are often frowned upon in African society,[27] and this makes it difficult for women to freely exercise their rights within marital relationships, or in the event of intimate partner violence that can result with a disclosure of HIV positive status. Thus, women's ability to negotiate their rights and power are severely diminished, because of their unwillingness to divorce.[28]

---

22 Shanti A. Parikh, 'The Political Economy of Marriage and HIV: The ABC Approach, 'Safe' Infidelity, and Managing Moral Risk in Uganda', *American Journal of Public Health* 97.7 (2007), 1198.

23 K. Winskell, P. J. Brown, A. E. Patterson, C. Burkot and B. C. Mbakwem, 'Making Sense of HIV in South eastern Nigeria', *Medical Anthropology Quarterly*, 27(2013), 208.

24 UNAIDS. *Impact of HIV and Sexual Health Education on the Sexual Behaviour of Young People: A Review Update* (Geneva, 1997), 8.

25 UNAIDS. *Impact of HIV and Sexual Health Education*,8; Winskell et al., 'Making Sense of HIV', 207.

26 Ibid.

27 Love Obiani Arugu, 'Social Indicators and Effects of Marriage Divorce in African Societies', *The Business & Management Review* 4.4 (2014), 382.

28 Ibid.

Lastly, varying forms of hierarchical relationships exist in African society.[29] These hierarchies introduce unique intersectionalities that complicate the ways in which women are empowered or disempowered. For example, in South Western Nigeria, a young wife in an extended family system is subordinate to older wives and other members of the family she marries, regardless of age differences. For example, a *Gogo* (grandmother) in Hausa-Fulani communities has as much authority as some men. Therefore, these unique hierarchical relationships create power relations among women in these settings that place some of them into further subjection within the context of the household.

Schippers' conceptualization of 'multiple hierarchical femininities' provides a compelling and empirically useful framework to analyse the centrality of hegemonic femininity and multiple hierarchical femininities in patriarchal gender relations.[30] This framework, though not yet utilized for research in Africa, is rife for exploration because it can prove useful in examining and analysing gendered social relations with respect to PMTCT intervention design, across settings and locations in different African countries. It could potentially broaden our understanding of how gender is complicated by the intersections of age and social position within the family, as well as class and ethnicity.

To understand further the contextual gender dynamics that impact specific behaviours that affect health and HIV transmission, it is important to explore intersectional power dynamics at the heart of norms in the African context, and Connell and Messerschmidt's concept of 'multiple masculinities'[31] can be a pertinent framework for analysis. The theorists' framework can offer illuminating insights to understand the patterns of higher rates of HIV infection among women in Sub-Saharan Africa, and might offer alternative solutions in addressing the PMTCT gap, which can be defined as the gap between the number of HIV positive pregnant women who need prophylaxis in developing countries, and those who actually receive it.[32]

---

29 Patricia Hill Collins, 'It's All in the Family: Intersections of Gender, Race, and Nation', *Hypatia* 13 (1998), 64; Kandiyoti, 'Bargaining with Patriarchy,' 278- 279.

30 Mimi Schippers, 'Recovering The Feminine Other: Masculinity, Femininity, And Gender Hegemony', *Theory and Society* 36.1 (2007), 85.

31 R.W. Connell and James W. Messerschmidt. 'Hegemonic Masculinity: Rethinking the Concept.' *Gender & Society* 19 .6 (2005), 829–859.

32 Oladokun R. E., Ige O. and Osinusi Kikelomo. 'Gaps in Preventing Mother to Child Transmission (PMTCT) and Human Immune Deficiency Virus (HIV) Exposure Among Infants in a Nigerian City: Implications for Health Systems Strengthening,' *Journal of AIDS and HIV Research*, 5.7 (2013), 254.

Norms about the performance of masculinity greatly impact HIV infection.[33] For example, couple counselling is a challenging endeavour due to men's poor health seeking behaviours in Nigeria. Masculine attributes of toughness are often associated with the ability to endure physically, and therefore men tend to tolerate illnesses because a demonstration of being physically incapacitated would be an admission of weakness.[34]

In addition, men who have sex with men (MSMs) in Nigeria often identify as heterosexual, although their sexual attraction is clearly not confined to members of the opposite gender. This is partly due to societal pressures to conform to normative heterosexuality. MSMs' identity in Nigeria is therefore wrought with ambiguities that make precision in intervention design difficult. Firstly, MSMs have to live covertly, for fear of being stigmatized, and secondly, they are not likely to disclose their homosexual or bisexual orientations to people outside their network or their female spouses. Thus, it becomes difficult for them to consider partner counselling, for fear they would have to disclose their true sexual orientation. This becomes a barrier to testing and counselling opportunities.[35] Avoidance of counselling in turn becomes a barrier for MSMs seeking general health services for or with their sex partner, and this ends up exposing them to higher risks of infection with HIV.

Hence, an understanding of the intersectionality of gender, age, class, HIV status, religion, and cultural norms can provide insights on how the normalization of gender[36] and sexual identities influences women's ability to accept, obtain and access PMTCT services across different communities. It could also provide an explanation for the high rates of HIV infection and their gendered trends across the region, and offer insights on how to reduce the PMTCT gap.

---

33 G., Barker, C. Ricardo, M. Nascimento, A. Olukoya, and C. Santos, 'Questioning Gender Norms with Men to Improve Health Outcomes: Evidence of Impact', *Global Public Health* 5.5 (2010), 539, 541; Will H., Courtenay, 'Constructions of Masculinity and Their Influence on Men's Well-Being: A Theory of Gender and Health', Social Science and Medicine 50.10 (2000), 1385; Morten, Skovdal et al., 'Masculinity as a Barrier to Men's Use of HIV Services in Zimbabwe', *Globalization and Health* 7.13 (2011), Viewed 21 April, 2014,http://www.globalizationandhealth.com/content/7/1/13.

34 Skovdal et al., 'Masculinity as a Barrier', 13.

35 The observations I provide here on the dilemma of multiple masculinities using the case of men having sex with men is based on my work with this vulnerable group on a program I participated in for sexual prevention of HIV infection Global HIV/AIDS Initiative in Nigeria (GHAIN)), in Nigeria from 2009 to 2011.

36 Will H., Courtenay, 'Constructions of Masculinity', 1385; Schippers, 'Recovering the Feminist Other,'85.

Thus, approaches that are only targeting women, are rights-based, or follow a program of economic empowerment that exclude men, end up failing to address problems. They are unable to comprehend the power dynamics in women's lives and are insensitive to the complexities of the power struggles they have to contend with. They endanger women's health outcomes, threatening their survival in that environment.

4 Western Liberal Feminism, PMTCT and the Issue of 'Empowerment'

The ideology of Feminism, since the liberal Feminist movements of the 1960s, has undergone significant transformations. Feminist epistemologies have splintered and come to inform and problematize the issue of emancipation in disparate ways. The meaning of 'liberation' and the different articulations of what constitutes 'women's rights' have greatly affected the concept of female empowerment, and the praxes that should be invoked and followed to achieve it.

The introduction of the concept of 'intersectionality' has been extremely useful to contextualize and better understand not only the spread of HIV in Sub-Saharan Africa but also the political and ideological dynamics that inform interventions in this area. Intersectionality allows one to problematize the ideological frameworks that have been problematically 'exported' from the West, and applied in a context for which they are ill suited, having the inevitable consequences of failing to reduce HIV infection.

Intersectionality allows a systematic analysis of the dynamics of infection, and explicates how rates of contagion in the area are greatly affected by the structures of race and ethnicity, class, gender, age and sexual orientation. But just as importantly, it offers an interpretive framework for the concepts of 'empowerment' and 'liberation' through a critical race lens. I can analyze the ideological blind spots that mire Western based strategies for medical intervention in HIV prevention strategies. Thus it makes possible a two-pronged analysis of the social context as well as the ideological framework that informs intervention, simultaneously, and how each realm is affected by socially, historically, politically and contextually contingent factors.

According to Goderema,[37] an African feminist, the appearance of racial and cultural tensions among feminists has led to a critique by African researchers and

37 Ruvimbo Goredema, 'African Feminism: The African Woman's Struggle for Identity', *African Yearbook of Rhetoric: Gender Rhetoric, North-South* 1 (2010), 34.

theorists of Western Feminist's principles of liberation and rights-based politics. Oyewumi cynically describes Western Feminist efforts in these terms:

> Historically recent Europe[an] and America[n] social movements were founded to struggle for female equality and subsequently carried forward in an imperial march across the globe.[38]

Not always have these well-meaning but naïve efforts been taken as useful praxes to approach an analysis of gender dynamics in non-Western contexts.

In this section, I argue that this 'imperialist march' has unintentionally embedded PMTCT strategies, especially with regards to Sub-Saharan Africa, in a bio-political sphere, which has had both positive and negative consequences. I am here making reference to the concept of female empowerment that permeates development efforts in Africa. It is primarily premised on a Western Liberal Feminist trope related to rights-based politics and economic empowerment. This trope posits women as the *necessary gateway* to liberation, citizens to be *equipped* with rights, and given access to funds, processes that in turn will transform them into agentic decision-making subjects with choices.[39]

Studies have shown that the assumption that 'economic empowerment is the gateway to liberation'–that women with rights and financial support are transformed into agents–has been possible in some instances but has not been successful in others.[40] On the one hand, women's economic empowerment has been shown to improve women's bargaining power in the household,[41]

38 Oyeronke Oyewumi, *African Woman and Feminism: Reflecting on the Politics of Sisterhood* (Trenton New Jersey: Africa World Press Inc., 2003), 1; Goredema, 'African Feminism', 344.

39 Maitrayee Mukhopadhyay and Shamim Meer (eds), 'Gender, Society & Development: Gender, Rights and Development a Global sourcebook', (Amsterdam: KIT, 2008). The authors explore various uses and interpretations of rights and empowerment platforms from various regional programs and perspectives and, in so doing, they demonstrate the problems of adopting a universal rights based approach, as it intertwines with female empowerment. They also illustrate the challenges that women face and their ingenuity in overcoming them.

40 Sara Hlupekile, Longwe, 'Towards Realistic Strategies for Women's Political Empowerment in Africa', *Gender and Development* 8.3 (2000), 24; Linda Mayoux, 'Women's Empowerment through Sustainable Microfinance: Rethinking "Best Practice"', *Discussion Draft, February 2006*, Viewed 19 November 2014, http://www.genfinance.info/Documents/Mayoux_Backgroundpaper.pdf

41 Naila Kabeer, 'Resources, Agency, Achievements: Reflections on the Measurement of Women's Empowerment', *Development and Change* 30 (1999), 451; Sarah Mosedale, 'Assessing Women's Empowerment: Towards a Conceptual Framework', *Journal of International*

and provided access to external social support,[42] thanks to their participation in micro-financing programs. On the other hand, economic empowerment of women alone has been shown not to address the structural or cultural challenges that women living with HIV face daily, nor provide the proper environment to enable them to make the right choices.[43]

Numerous studies have proven that economic empowerment may have significant detrimental effect on the lives of women, by exposing them to greater risks for violence,[44] because of shifts in household economic power dynamics. These shifts may bring men to perceive a loss of status and to consequently overreact, in an attempt to regain a sense of control.[45] Women's economic empowerment, according to research, may also increase expectations and demands for their labour, thus burdening them further, and effect has been termed a 'triple burden.' Kabeer has demonstrated that this triple burden has economic, productive and reproductive consequences. Women are made responsible for income generation well beyond their original production responsibilities, while their reproductive labour remains unchanged. They are still expected to have a high number of children and raise them.[46]

Institutional mechanisms to introduce policies that would secure women's rights and legally protect them still remain underdeveloped in Sub-Saharan Africa, and governmental obligations remain weak. Also, research efforts to truly measure to what extent women's empowerment has taken place remain inadequate. Researches are cognizant on this issue, and are currently re-examining their analytical frameworks, to better capture the aspects of women's lives that actually reflect positive improvement.[47] It remains to be seen whether other

---

Development 17. 2 (2005), 245. Karim, Lamia. 'Micro Finance and Its Discontent: Women in Debts in Bangladesh.' Minneapolis: University of Minnesota Press, 2011.

42 Kabeer, 'Resources, Agency, Achievements', 454, 455.

43 Ibid.

44 Karim, Lamia *Micro Finance and Its Discontent: Women in Debts in Bangladesh* (Minneapolis: University of Minnesota Press, 2011) 444; England, 'Conceptualizing Women's Empowerment,' 61.

45 S.R. Schuler, S.M. Hashemi and S.H. Badal, 'Men's Violence Against Women in Rural Bangladesh: Undermined or Exacerbated By Microcredit Programmes?', *Development in Practice* 8.2 (1998), 148.

46 Naila Kabeer, 'Triple Roles, Gender Roles, Social Relations: The Political Sub-Text of Gender Training,' in Kabeer. *Reversed Realities Gender Hierarchies in Development Thought* (London: Verso, 1994), 264–306.

47 Valentine Moghadam and Lucie Senftova, 'Measuring Women's Empowerment: Participation and Rights in Civil, Political, Social, Economic, and Cultural Domains', *International Social Science Journal* 184 (2005), 390.

forms of empowerment, through action by religious institutions[48] or other legal instruments, such as customary laws,[49] in given societies could be more effective.

England has argued that the availability of economic supports, the introduction of laws that extend rights, and the existence of institutional norms do not necessarily equate to straightforward empowerment in women's lives. She has stated:

> Economic resources, laws, institutional rules and norms held by others in one's environment as an objective basis of power, but the subjective states of self-efficacy and entitlement to effect the way in which power is exercised, i.e. one may have an objective bases of power but not exercise it.[50]

This argument is true for women in many countries and cultures around the world who are constantly 'bargaining with patriarchy,' as illustrated in detail in the discussion in the previous section.

Feminist social scientists have argued that a woman's ability to make choices is the best measure to discern if she has access to human rights and to gage the degree of empowerment she has achieved. Even though a woman's ability to make choices has been proven to have important life-long impacts, it remains difficult to measure.[51] Yet such choices may greatly increase risks of mother-to-child transmission of HIV.

Kabeer's focus on 'choice' as a significant measure for empowerment opens up for debate the types of choices women make, the interpretation of the processes that are undertaken to reach those choices, and whether or not they are empowering. And yet Kandiyoti's concept of 'bargaining with patriarchy' highlights how problematic it is to equate 'choice' with 'empowerment.' She argues:

---

48 Saba Mahmood. *Politics of Piety: The Islamic Revival and the Feminist Subject* (Princeton: Princeton UP, 2005) xi; Charlotte Spinks, 2003 'Panacea or Painkiller? The Impact of Pentecostal Christianity on Women in Africa', in *The Impact of Religion on Women in the Development Process, Critical Half: Annual Journal of Women for Women International* 1(1): 22–23.

49 A report by the International Development Labour Organization includes case studies on legal empowerment in nine countries; International Development Labour Organization (IDLO), 'Accessing Justice: Models, Strategies and Best Practices on Women's Empowerment' (Rome and New York, 2013), 1–74.

50 England, 'Conceptualizing Women's Empowerment', 61.

51 Moghadam & Senftova, 'Measuring Women's Empowerment', 390; Kabeer, 'Resources, Agency, Achievements', 436; Kabeer, 'Conflicts Over Credit', 79.

> Women strategize within a set of concrete constraints through patriarchal bargains to maximize security and optimize life options with varying potential for active or passive resistance in the face of oppression.[52]

It is possible to conclude that empowerment through economic means alone will not ensure adequate protection for women in the implementation of current PMTCT strategies in the Sub-Saharan context. Therefore, it becomes necessary to explore and develop appropriate PMTCT strategy interventions that truly empower women, by addressing those contextual factors that influence how women consider and make reproductive choices. These contextual factors and their solutions can be elicited through community based participatory approaches, which may also enable sustainability and reduce dependency on transnational funding.

5 Transnational Bio-politics and PMTCT Strategies

This section explores the links between feminist epistemologies and the economics of HIV prevention programming through transnational funding. I argue that these discoursive positions inadvertently become entangled in a political logic that attempts to control the health of populations, through a process that Foucault has termed bio-politics.[53]

A Nigerian proverb astutely states: *'he who pays the piper dictates the tune of his music;'* it succinctly sums up the operational methods of transnational development programs, including PMTCT strategies. Epistemologically, PMTCT strategies' framework is informed by a Western Liberal Feminist lens that envisions a future in which women will gain reproductive control of their bodies and their lives through a process of female empowerment that is ensured by the introduction of human rights codification in the legal system. This stance was emblematic of the 'second wave' Feminism of the 80s, which coincided with the early period of research into AIDS and the discovery of HIV in 1983.

This political stance has an 'individualistic' slant, making *the individual* the recipient of such rights. Such a slant came to permeate most discourses geared towards the betterment of human life, including the medical sphere and HIV prevention. Thus it became the key approach for interventions on women, even in African contexts, although it was in stark contrast to the traditional values

52 Kandiyoti, 'Bargaining With Patriarchy', 275.

53 Foucault, 'Security, Territory, Population', 243.

and cultures of the Sub-Saharan region, which do not privilege the individual, but rather conceive of society in more communitarian terms. Therefore, emphasis for interventions was placed on individuals (women of reproductive age), not groups (families and communities): this bias greatly compromised efficacy.

Moreover, a biomedical approach to prevention was utilized, which organized interventions in the context of medical facilities (existing hospitals), and programs within the existing health system, regardless of whether these spaces and programs were likely to be used by or were actually accessible to target populations.

Through these manoeuvres, PMTCT strategies were colonized by a form of 'bio-politics,' that was strongly imbued by Western economic ideologies and Feminist emancipation-driven values. Women became the objects of a medicalized epistemology, due to their reproductive role and their social reproductive functions. This inadvertently led to the exercise of bio-power on their bodies, which came to be understood, disciplined and intervened upon through a global strategy for PMTCT strategies to control HIV infection.[54] A *biomedicalized* PMTCT strategy forced the bodies of women in general, and women infected with HIV in particular, to enter into the political. As HIV infection and AIDS became a pandemic in Sub-Saharan Africa, local, national and international attention became drawn to safeguarding the survival of the next generation.

Historically, transnational discourses on women in Africa have affected the way they are perceived and have also determined frameworks for types of interventions that they require, in transnational aid, HIV prevention, as well as economic empowerment programs. However, as Foucault has conclusively argued, these forms of trans-territorial actions often lead to the co-production of bio-power and bio-politics that ultimately came to perpetrate social injustices.[55] These *unintended consequences* found their origins in altruistically conceived actions, but had dire negative effects, regardless of their benevolent origins. Furthermore, because PMTCT strategies had their epistemological origins in the office of the United Nations (UN), an institutional giant, a global authority was constituted, which had immense power and the ability to enforce its implementation world-wide, in the name of *fostering life*.

Foster has argued that bio-power operates by shifting the mechanisms of power from a nation with sovereign authority to take life, to a more dispersed

54 Ibid., 401.

55 Ibid.

institutional setting that can reach beyond borders, with the power to foster life. This bio-power can then be used to administer and regulate the biological existence of populations. In this manner, bodies are subjected to techniques of power through diverse institutions.[56]

I argue that the UN, as an institution of world-wide import, has acquired such bio-power: its role as one of the most important administering and regulatory bodies on development issues in the world should not be ignored. Its prominent role in formulating strategies and directing frameworks for intervention on issues of global importance, such as HIV prevention and treatment, make evident its institutional power over entire populations. Arguably, it can also be indicted for exacerbating the bio-power imbalance between the West and the Global South.

I contend that the UN's role in disseminating a specific type of scientific knowledge helped shape *the norm* for HIV programming. This norm forms the basis for HIV prevention guidelines, including PMTCT strategies, which inadvertently set up epistemological hierarchies that worsen power imbalances and imbue policies and guidelines, as well as strategies, with a strong Western bio-political bias. I am also of the opinion that the bio-power and bio-politics that set up this *ethico-legal norm,*[57] in the form of international and national policies, guidelines and strategies for HIV prevention, also play a role in undermining local forms of knowledge production,[58] which have the inadvisable effect of oppressing the marginalized and vulnerable populations that the strategies are attempting to help in the first place in the fight against the spread of HIV. These issues will be discussed in the next section.

6 Hierarchies of Knowledge Production and PMTCT

In the coming paragraphs, I will offer an analysis of the deleterious effects of Western bias, and illustrate how the extensive capital investment in PMTCT programs in some communities has been unable to reach a commensurate level of success in reducing the incidence of HIV in babies born to infected mothers. This lack of success calls into question the sustainability of such programs

56 Laura A. Foster, 'Patents, Bio-politics, and Feminisms: Locating Patent Law Struggles Over Breast Cancer Genes and the Hoodia Plant', *International Journal of Cultural Property* 19 (2012), 374.

57 Emphasis mine.

58 Foster, 'Patents, Bio-Politics, and Feminisms', 374.

in countries in the Global South once these projects come to an end, especially when funded by international or bi-lateral donors.[59]

Although some would argue that the UN has attempted to include local cultural content to the strategies it has promoted, questions remain about the production of such knowledge and the motivation for its production, given that it cannot be extricated from its funding source. Are the indigenous researchers involved, I ask, truly able to make useful contributions to the knowledge produced? Or are they forced to comply to a bio-political optic selected in advance, and required to align themselves with the core assumptions that already tinge the strategies in place? Dorothy Roberts has powerfully made this point in her study of 'medical stereotyping,' where a certain kind of knowledge is rejected because it is not 'politically correct,'[60] and so has Jenny Readon in her work on the politics of epistemological inclusivity in the science of genomics.[61]

An important issue that needs to be addressed is the hierarchical organization of knowledge claims in a manner that always privileges Western knowledge and deems local epistemologies as less important, a labelling process that Gayatri Chakravorty Spivak calls the 'epistemology of the subaltern.' In a related manner, the indigenous researcher is also considered a 'subaltern' in this space.[62] The adoption of community based participatory research and multi-sited ethnographic approaches is essential in order to acknowledge previously 'subjugated knowledge,' for achieving meaningful successes in PMTCT interventions in Sub-Saharan African countries.[63]

In the coming paragraphs, I explore the dynamics of knowledge production and investigate which types of knowledge are promoted and which become subjugated in the arena of international development discourse. I will argue that such warped dynamics of knowledge production end up informing PMTCT strategies in a manner that affects their outcomes in developing countries.

As the numbers of newly infected HIV people and HIV rates increased in Sub-Saharan Africa, the management of its spread took on a marked

59 The term 'bi-lateral donor' usually refers to assistance given directly from a single donor organization or government, directly to a recipient country.

60 Dorothy Roberts, *Fatal Intervention: How Science, Politics and Big Business Re-Create Race In The Twenty-First Century* (New York, London: The New Press, 2011), 97.

61 Jenny Reardon. *Race to Finish: Identity and Governance in an Age of Genomics* (Princeton: University Press, 2005), 36.

62 Gayatri Chakravorty Spivak, 'Can the Subaltern Speak?' in *The Postcolonial Studies Reader* eds. Bill Ashcroft, Gareth Griffiths and Helen Tiffined (London and New York: Routledge, 1995), 25.

63 Spivak, 'Can the Subaltern Speak?', 25.

urgency, given the poor access to treatment that was available to local populations. The task of treating and preventing AIDS in Sub-Saharan Africa became a problematic, *prescribed intervention* which unfortunately overlooked or underestimated the structural, cultural and religious differences in sexual behaviour, gender dynamics and social norms between the West and Sub-Saharan nations.

The emphasis on Western driven approaches to HIV prevention and treatment programs, and the lack of consideration for the peculiar 'socio-sexual geography'[64] of African societies has also not helped. This is because the 'subjugated knowledge' of local and indigenous people were often considered not objective, empirical and not replicable, at times even 'mystical' or 'illogical.'[65] Therefore, attempts were made, as in the case of HIV prevention, to 'civilize' the subjects or the populations with [high HIV prevalence through 'proper'] education on sexual behaviours.[66]

These approaches, usually based on scientifically proven intervention studies, were divorced from the contextual realities in which these populations exist, often dissociating culture from science. Ashley Montagu has discussed the dangers of this attitude, and insisted humans should be 're-conceived as an amalgam of biology and culture;'[67] an inability to do so may have drastic deleterious effects on the success rates of HIV prevention in these contexts.

In a similar vein, Mohanty has pointed out that it is essential to embrace the 'intellectual and political constructions of third world feminisms' in constructing a more strategic approach for preventing mother to child transmission of HIV in Africa.[68] Current definitions of womanhood in HIV prevention strategies, as I argued earlier, are erroneously based on an individualised rights based approach that has a strong Western bias.

I therefore align with the position taken by Kavita Philip on 'mixed modernity:' it is important not to encourage the annulment of scientific reasoning in terms of treatment, but to build a local context approach in applying

64 I adopt the term 'socio-sexual geographies' from J. Hirsch et al., 'The Inevitability of Infidelity: Sexual Reputation, Social Geographies, and Marital HIV Risk in Rural Mexico', *Am J Public Health* 97.6 (2007), 986.

65 Colin Scott, 'Science for the West' in *The Post-Colonial Science and Technology Reader*, ed. Sandra Harding (Durham and London: Duke University Press, 2011), 176.

66 Kavita Philip, *Civilizing Natures: Race, Resources and Modernity in Colonial South India* (New Brunswick, New Jersey: Rutgers University Press, 2004), 64.

67 Reardon, 'Race to Finish,' 36.

68 Chandra Mohanty, Ann Russo, and Lourdes Torres, eds., *Third World Women and The Politics of Feminism* (Bloomington and Indianapolis: Indiana University Press, 1991), 51.

internationally prescribed recommendations, while at the same time, adopting culturally minded approaches that are based on local knowledge.[69]

7 Big Pharma in the Transnational Context: Commoditization and Human Drug-Trial Labour in HIV Prevention Strategies

In this section, I analyse the relationship between PMTCT strategies and the transnational pharmaceutical industry. I argue that the forms of bio-politics at the heart of HIV prevention strategies have greatly advantaged this industry, and led to a veritable explosion in the production of HIV related commodities (from condoms to high tech testing machinery), as well as HIV medical research trials, and the unethical treatment of research subjects for these trials.

In his analysis of Jamaican society, Burnard has argued that the economics of labour, reproduction and the politics of production both in the public and private spheres created a gender divide, but were also instrumental for the fostering of agency for women in Jamaica.[70] These insights are applicable in my analysis of PMTCT strategies in Sub-Sharan Africa: the economics of labour, reproduction and politics of production in this context not only create racial and class divides, but also a gender divide in the regulation of the bodies of women living with HIV and women in general.

Transnational institutions came to be produced together with the tools and the programming for sustaining them and for justifying their existence, as well as the machinery for the distribution of their goods and services, which in turn impacted labour strategies[71] around HIV prevention and treatment. For example, the proliferation of Non-Governmental Organizations (NGOs) that focused exclusively on HIV programs locally and internationally was problematic because of its 'single-disease' focus. This singular treatment optic compromised the effectiveness of the delivery of their programming. As discussed earlier, the programming strategies and interventions of these NGOs were ignorant of the structural (social, cultural, economic and political) positioning of their

69 Philip, *Civilizing Natures*, 162.

70 Burnard, 'Evaluating Gender', 82–83.

71 Melinda Cooper, 'Double Exposure–Sex Workers, Biomedical Prevention Trials and the Dual Logic of Global Public Health', *Science and Feminist Online* 11.3 (2013), 3, Viewed 19 November, 2014,http://sfonline.barnard.edu/life-un-ltd-feminism-bioscience-race/double-exposure-sex-workers-biomedical-prevention-trials-and-the-dual-logic-of-global-public-health/#sthash.y2JR9PrM;Foster 'Patents, Bio-politics, and Feminisms,' 381–382.

clients. They introduced economically exploitative practices: they fostered the creation of a market for commodities specifically geared towards HIV prevention that were ill suited in the fight to maximise HIV prevention.

For instance, HIV prevention programs created markets for commodities, like male and female condoms, lubricants, antiretroviral drugs and an array of HIV related equipment. Unfortunately, they lacked effective programming for the timely delivery of such products: for example, condoms procured from foreign companies would take too long be delivered or cleared for importation, and ended up being expired upon arrival. Another problematic issue had to do with high tech equipment. Often such delicate and difficult to use equipment, which are technologically complex and require specific conditions for their proper use, were completely unsuitable for use in remote communities and the medical facilities available. For example, some equipment was procured without ensuring that it could actually be used in that particular setting: at times there were no skilled workers to operate them; at times they could not function because the community did not have electricity or, if it did, it was not reliable enough for use.

Another problematic economic practice ushered in by HIV prevention interventions in Sub-Saharan Africa, according to Cooper, were the numerous research trials that targeted specific bodies, on the basis that these populations had high HIV prevalence rates.[72] This has led to the exploitation of vulnerable populations, in what I refer as *human drug trial labour*: at-risk individuals were co-opted into drug trials testing, creating what I call the *human-pharmaceutical industrial complex*. Local populations were exploited, ending up selling their labour force to Big Pharma at very low cost, in a manner that was greatly advantageous for pharmaceuticals companies, who would not be able to carry out similar trials in Western contexts, for such low costs.

Pharmaceutical companies could easily compel local populations to participate in these trials, by offering payments. The individuals targeted, people living with HIV, were usually in difficult financial circumstances and could be very easily compelled: they used trial studies as an alternative source of income. In these cases, women were particularly vulnerable, because of their inferior social location in society, and also because they had much higher rates of HIV infection. They also experienced high cultural pressures to take on a reproductive role, because society burdened them with the responsibility of producing the next generation through their reproductive labour, thus heightening their HIV infection risks and those of their children.

72 Cooper, 'Double Exposure', 1.

8 The Effects of Bio-Politics on the Lives of Women

In the context of Sub-Saharan Africa and the cultural practice of 'bargaining with patriarchy,' the reproductive labour of a woman is *key* to her survival and her status in society. As such, her reproductive labour can both be the platform of her subjection as well as her empowerment and agency. Often times, a woman's reproductive capability determines her access to resources, such as land or financial rewards. For example, a woman who has conceived one or more sons has greater access to economic resources, especially in communities that are organized around patriarchal familial hierarchies, like many communities in Nigeria.

Certain cultural practices place a high value on attributes that are considered to be 'good mothering,' such as breastfeeding. A woman who fails to breastfeed is perceived as incompetent in the caring for her baby, and can be easily stigmatized as 'negligent.' This influences negative perceptions of her personhood and thus can affect her social relations and standing with members of her family, and especially her in-laws. She is usually assumed to have contracted HIV, and immediately stigmatized.

The repeated and sometimes contradictory changes in PMTCT strategies and paediatric guidelines on breastfeeding and weaning practices have often been extremely confusing, and have ended up having dire deleterious effects on at-risk populations. They not only sent conflicting messages to the public but also further worsened the stereotypes that link HIV infection and breastfeeding.[73]

PMTCT strategies have not been consistent on this matter: in the early stages of their implementation HIV positive mothers were advised not to breast feed their babies, but later on these approaches were modified, due to increasing mortality rates in babies of mothers living with HIV as a result of either malnutrition or diarrhoea. Asking women not to breastfeed resulted in a spike in malnutrition and intestinal tract infections: mothers were not able to provide proper nutrition to their babies, as they lived in areas without portable water, were poor and thus unable to afford supplementary milk. These conditions were prevalent in many under-developed and resource poor environments; an injunction not to breastfeed resulted in higher mortality rates in infants.

A sole focus on a biomedical approach and a strategy that deals with individuals rather than communities, by the uncritical adoption of Feminist

73 My work of over ten years in the area of epidemiological prevention has made me a witness to some of these challenges in HIV intervention programs.

ideologies that insists on a woman's right to access PMTCT, are problematic. A close analysis of the structural constraints that women in these communities face on a daily basis is essential, so that the consequences of any form of constraint placed on her choice to bear children and mother are fully understood in their social and cultural contexts.

Thus, Beauvoir's book *The Second Sex* offers profound insight on the intricate ways in which reproduction constantly undermine women's ultimate desire and or capacity for liberty, giving credence that for women living with HIV in these African contexts, true liberation in the areas of sexuality and reproduction may not be possible, especially when child bearing and mothering are involved.[74] It is also possibly to question, as Rich has done, whether women's taking control of their sexual and reproductive rights actually means access to true liberty.[75]

When addressing women's reproduction, HIV infection and related PMTCT strategies, I have shown that bio-political interventions went hand in hand with the creation of scientific knowledge, technology and pharmaceutical products, machinery and testing production, that sadly did not take into account the societal norms, cultural values and traditional morality. And now I conclude with a reckoning and offer a recapitulation of the gains and losses for women in PMTCT programs in the context of Sub-Saharan Africa.

On the one hand PMTCT programs provided opportunities for agency and survival for women living with HIV, through the creation of support groups that gave them access to free health services, drugs, and financial empowerment, while also preventing HIV transmission to their babies. On the other hand, these programs subjected the bodies of these women to a set of disciplinary interventions and actions, informed by the logic of its definitions of personhood, proper sexual behaviour, 'good' health and reproductive choices.

A focus on women in PMTCT strategies and programs made women responsible for their HIV status, and the epidemiological status of their babies. Thus, while they attempted to overcome the challenges to accessing health services, women were caught in a web of personal and socially imposed bodily surveillance practices. They were still not free from the constraining rules enforced on them by their culture and social contexts that affected the manner in which they could participate in PMTCT programs. These normative interventions inadvertently made them vulnerable to societal stigma, thus compromising their

74 de Beauvoir, Simone. *The Second Sex* (New York: Vintage Books, 1989), 696–697.

75 Adrienne Rich. *Of Woman Born, Motherhood as Experience and Institution* (New York: W.W. Norton and Company Inc., 1986), 13.

ability to remain engaged with the programs and continue to receive medical supports. And thus:

> The best-intentioned projects, including feminist ones, can betray their emancipatory goals by creating "*dependent subjects*" and by reproducing the depoliticizing and regulating social norms of liberalism.[76]

Mardossian's quote above justifies how normative formulations in PMTCT policy have divorced bodies from the materiality of their existence: the way in which the programs were conceptualized have objectified women within a biomedical framework, removing them from their social realities. This in turn has impacted the effectiveness and efficiency of the prescribed programs, while it also endangered women's agency.

9 Conclusion

In this essay, I have conclusively argued that current PMTCT strategies, as they are presently formulated, will not be able to make much of a difference in the spread of HIV in Sub-Saharan Africa, as they are steeped in ideological frameworks that are ill suited to address the cultural and social dynamics in the region. Their rights-based, individual-based assumptions for empowerment, strongly steeped in Liberal Feminism and an assumption on the primacy of economic resilience, ignore the communal and familial structures that organize life, sexuality and reproduction in the region.

The insistence to deal with infection through a uniquely biomedical approach, which privileges purely medical interventions, at the expense of more holistic strategies, that would take into consideration the cultural specificities and social dynamics of targeted groups, has impacted access to care negatively. I have provided a close analysis of the social norms, the familial structures, relational gender dynamics, the traditional customs, and the religious values, examining how they intersect with one another, showing how women's existence is heavily constrained by patriarchal relations of power. I have argued that it is through these constraints that they have to make specific decisions about their health and well-being, always in conjunction with their families and communities.

76 Carine M. Mardorossian, 'Toward a New Feminist Theory of Rape', *Signs* 27.3 (2002), 759.

In conclusion I call for a critical dialogue for the development of appropriate and sustainable interventions that address the socio-economic, cultural and political peculiarities that these women face, so that PMTCT interventions and public health strategies can better serve one of the most vulnerable groups in this region. I believe that beyond an overhaul of PMTCT strategies, the ethics of public health practices, transnational aid and the activities of pharmaceutical industries should be questioned with a close awareness of the pressures exerted by global Neo-liberalism. The examination of Western bias, a Liberal Feminist rights-based slant and the insistence on an overly medicalized approach in PMTCT strategies that I have provided in this chapter has made evident how *the personal has been made political through transnational bio-politics*.

I conclude this chapter with the insightful words of Van Oudenhoven and Wazir on transnational collaborative partnerships for research and intervention: it is necessary to break through the divisive boundaries between 'technical experts' and the 'recipient subjects,' so that a process of reciprocal and mutual learning can be achieved, one that encourages 'respectful listening,' and is thus able to balance relations of power and foster sharing.[77] This *true* partnership will assist in developing appropriate interventions that would have much better success in curbing mother-to-child transmission of HIV in Sub-Saharan Africa.

Acknowledgements

I wish to thank Professor Kathryn Yount for her review of an earlier version of the manuscript and for her constructive comments and continued encouragement.

Bibliography

Action, Q. Ashton. ed. *Issues in Reproductive Medicine Research*. Atlanta, Georgia: Scholarly Edition, 2011.

AIDSTAR One. 'Prevention of Mother-to-Child Transmission (PMTCT) of HIV'. Viewed 5 November 2014. http://www.aidstar-one.com/focus_areas/pmtct

77 Nico van Oudenhoven and Rekha Wazir, 'Replicating Social Programmes: Approaches, Strategies and Conceptual Issues', *Management of Social Transformation, Discussion Paper Series*, 18.3 (Paris: UNESCO), Viewed 21 April, 2014.

Amadiume, Ifi. *Male Daughters, Female Husbands: Gender and Sex in an African Society*. New York: Zed, 1987.

Arugu, Love Obiani. 'Social Indicators and Effects of Marriage Divorce in African Societies.' *The Business & Management Review* 4 .4 (2014): 374–383.

Ashcroft, Bill, Gareth Griffiths, and Helen Tiffined, eds. *The Postcolonial Studies Reader.* London and New York: Routledge, 1995.

Barker, G., Ricardo, C., Nascimento, M., Olukoya, A., and C. Santos. 'Questioning Gender Norms with Men to Improve Health Outcomes: Evidence of Impact.' *Global Public Health* 5.5 (2010): 539–553.

Burnard, Trevor. 'Evaluating Gender in Early Jamaica, 1674–1784.' *History of the Family* 12 (2007): 81–91.

Collins, Patricia Hill. *Black Feminist Thought: Knowledge, Consciousness and the Politics of Empowerment.* New York and London: Routledge, 1990.

Collins, Patricia Hill. 'It's All in the Family: Intersections of Gender, Race, and Nation.' *Hypatia* 13 (1998): 62–82.

Collins, Patricia Hill. *Black Sexual Politics: African Americans, Gender, and the New Racism*. New York and London: Routledge, 2005.

Connell, R. W. and James W. Messerschmidt. 'Hegemonic Masculinity: Rethinking the Concept.' *Gender & Society* 19 .6 (2005): 829–859.

Cooper, Melinda. 'Double Exposure–Sex Workers, Biomedical Prevention Trials and the Dual Logic of Global Public Health.' *Science and Feminist Online*, 11.3 (2013). Viewed 4 April 2014. http://sfonline.barnard.edu/life-un-ltd-feminism-bioscience-race/double-exposure-sex-workers-biomedical-prevention-trials-and-the-dual-logic-of-global-public-health/#sthash.y2JR9PrM

Courtenay, Will H. 'Constructions of Masculinity and Their Influence on Men's Well-Being: A Theory of Gender and Health.' *Social Science and Medicine* 50.10 (2000): 1385–1401.

de Beauvoir, Simone. *The Second Sex*. New York: Vintage Books, 1989.

England, Paula. 'Conceptualizing Women's Empowerment in Countries of the North.' In *Women's Empowerment and Demographic Processes: Moving Beyond Cairo*, edited by H.B Presser and G. Sen, 37–65. Oxford: Oxford University Press, 2000.

Foster, Laura A. 'Patents, Bio politics, and Feminisms: Locating Patent Law Struggles over Breast Cancer Genes and the Hoodia Plant.' *International Journal of Cultural Property* 19(2012): 371–400.

Foucault, Michel. *The History of Sexuality Vol. 1*. London: Penguin, [1978]1998.

Foucault, Michel. *Security, Territory, Population: Lectures at the Collège de France 1977–1978*, trans. Graham Burchell. Basingstoke: Palgrave Macmillan, 2007.

Goredema, Ruvimbo. 'African Feminism: The African Woman's Struggle for Identity'. *African Yearbook of Rhetoric: Gender Rhetoric, North-South* 1 (2010): 33–41.

Harding, Sandra, ed. *The Post-Colonial Science and Technology Reader.* Durham and London: Duke University Press, 2011.

Hartmann, Betsy. 'Security and Survival: Why Does Poor People Have Many Children,' *The Post-Colonial Science and Technology Reader*, edited by Sandra Harding, 310–317. Durham and London: Duke University Press, 2011.

Hirsch, Jennifer S., Sergio Meneses, Brenda Thompson, Mirka Negroni, Blanca Pelcastre, and Carlos del Rio. 'The Inevitability of Infidelity: Sexual Reputation, Social Geographies, and Marital HIV Risk in Rural Mexico.' *Am J Public Health* 97.6 (2007): 986–996.

Jankowiak, William, Monika Sudakov and Benjamin C. Wilreker. 'Co-Wife Conflict and Co-operation.' *Ethnology* 44.1 (2005): 81–98.

Kandiyoti, Deniz. 'Bargaining with Patriarchy.' *Gender and Society* 2.3 (1988): 274–290.

Kabeer, Naila. 'Triple Roles, Gender Roles, Social Relations: The Political Sub-Text of Gender Training,' in Kabeer, N. Reversed Realities Gender Hierarchies in Development Thought, (London: Verso, 1994), 264–306.

Kabeer, Naila. 'Resources, Agency, Achievements: Reflections on the Measurement of Women's Empowerment.' *Development and Change* 30 (1999): 435–462.

Kabeer, Naila. 'Conflicts Over Credit: Re-Evaluating the Empowerment Potential of Loans to Women in Rural Bangladesh.' *World Development* 29.1 (2001): 63–84.

Karim, Lamia. *Micro Finance and Its Discontent: Women in Debts in Bangladesh.* Minneapolis: University of Minnesota Press, 2011.

Klot, Jennifer F. and Vinh-Kim Nguyen, eds., *The Fourth Wave Violence, Gender, Culture & HIV in the 21st Century.* UNESCO: Centre for Research in Ethnic Relations, 2009.

Longwe, Sara Hlupekile. 'Towards Realistic Strategies for Women's Political Empowerment in Africa.' *Gender and Development* 8.3 (2000): 24–30.

Mahmood, Saba. *Politics of Piety: The Islamic Revival and the Feminist Subject.* Princeton: Princeton UP, 2005.

Mardorossian, Carine M. 'Toward a New Feminist Theory of Rape', *Signs*, 27.3 (2002): 743–775.

Mayoux, Linda. 'Women's Empowerment through Sustainable Microfinance: Rethinking "Best Practice".' *Discussion Draft February 2006.* Viewed 4 April 2014. http://www.genfinance.info/Documents/Mayoux_Backgroundpaper.pdf.

Moghadam, Valentine M. and Lucie Senftova. 'Measuring Women's Empowerment: Participation and Rights in Civil, Political, Social, Economic, and Cultural Domains.' *International Social Science Journal* 184(2005): 389–412.

Mohanty, Chandra Talpade. 'Under The Western Eye' Revisited: Feminist Solidarity Through Anti-Capitalist Struggles.' *Signs* 28.2 (2003): 499–535.

Mohanty, Chandra, Russo, Ann and Lourdes, Torres, eds. *Third World Women and the Politics of Feminism.* Bloomington and Indianapolis: Indiana University Press, 1991.

Monjok, Emmanuel, Andrea Smesny and E. James Essien. 'HIV/AIDS-Related Stigma and Discrimination in Nigeria: Review of Research Studies and Future Directions for Prevention Strategies.' *African Journal of Reproductive Health* 13.3 (2009): 21–35.

Mosedale, Sarah. 'Assessing Women's Empowerment: Towards A Conceptual Framework.' *Journal of International Development* 17.2 (2005): 243–257.

Oladokun R. E., Ige O. and Osinusi Kikelomo. 'Gaps in Preventing Mother to Child Transmission (PMTCT) and Human Immune Deficiency Virus (HIV) Exposure Among Infants in a Nigerian City: Implications for Health Systems Strengthening,' *Journal of AIDS and HIV Research*, 5.7 (2013), 254–259.

Oyeronke, Oyewumi. 'Conceptualizing Gender: The Eurocentric Foundations of Feminist Concepts and the Challenge of African Epistemologies.' *Jenda: A Journal of Culture and African Woman Studies*, 2 (2002), 1–5.

Oyeronke, Oyewumi. *African Woman and Feminism: Reflecting on the Politics of Sisterhood.* Trenton New Jersey: Africa World Press Inc., 2003.

Parikh, Shanti A. 'The Political Economy of Marriage and HIV: The ABC Approach, "Safe" Infidelity, and Managing Moral Risk in Uganda'. *American Journal of Public Health* 97.7 (2007): 1198–1208.

Philip, Kavita. *Civilizing Natures: Race, Resources and Modernity in Colonial South India.* New Brunswick, New Jersey: Rutgers University Press, 2004.

Presser, H. B. and G. Sen, eds. *Women's Empowerment and Demographic Processes: Moving Beyond Cairo.* Oxford: Oxford University Press, 2000.

Reardon, Jenny. *Race to Finish: Identity and Governance in an Age of Genomics.* Princeton University Press, 2005.

Rich, Adrienne. *Of Woman Born, Motherhood as Experience and Institution.* New York: W.W. Norton and Company Inc., 1986.

Roberts, Dorothy. *Fatal Intervention: How Science, Politics and Big Business Re-Create Race in The Twenty-First Century.* New York, London: The New Press, 2011.

Schippers, Mimi. 'Recovering the Feminine Other: Masculinity, Femininity, and Gender Hegemony.' *Theory and Society* 36.1 (2007): 85–102.

Schuler, S.R., Hashemi, S.M., S.H., Badal. 'Men's Violence against Women in Rural Bangladesh: Undermined or Exacerbated By Microcredit Programmes?' *Development in Practice* 8.2 (1998): 148–57.

Scott, Colin. 'Science for the West' in *The Post-Colonial Science and Technology Reader*, edited by Sandra Harding, 175–197. Durham and London: Duke University Press, 2011.

Skovdal, Morten, Campbell Catherine, Claudius Madanhire, Zivai Mupambireyi, Constance Nyamukapa, Simon Gregson. 'Masculinity as a Barrier to Men's Use of HIV Services in Zimbabwe.' *Globalization and Health*, 7:13 (2011): doi: 10.1186/1744-8603-7-13.Viewed 6 April 2016.http://www.globalizationandhealth.com/content/7/1/13

Spivak, Gayatri Chakravorty. 'Can the Subaltern Speak?' In *The Postcolonial Studies Reader*, edited by Bill Ashcroft, Gareth Griffiths and Helen Tiffined, 24- 28. London and New York: Routledge, 1995.

The Henry J. Kaiser Family Foundation 'Overview: The Global HIV/AIDS Epidemic', *Global Health Policy*, 30 November, 2015. Viewed 21 April, 2014.http://kff.org/global-health-policy/fact-sheet/the-global-hivaids-epidemic/

Timæus, Ian M. and Angela Reynar. 'Polygynists and Their Wives in Sub-Saharan Africa: An Analysis of Five Demographic and Health Surveys.' *Population Studies* 52.2 (1998): 145–162.

UNAIDS. *Impact of HIV and Sexual Health Education on the Sexual Behaviour of Young People: A Review Update*. Geneva, 1997.

United Nations Special Session on HIV/AIDS June 2002.

Van Oudenhoven, Nico and Rekha Wazir. 'Replicating Social Programmes: Approaches, Strategies and Conceptual Issues.' *Management of Social Transformation Discussion Paper Series* 18. 3 (Paris: UNESCO). Viewed 06 April 2016. http://www.unesco.org/most/dsp18.htm.

Winskell, K., P. J. Brown, A. E. Patterson, C. Burkot and B. C. Mbakwem, 'Making Sense of HIV in South eastern Nigeria'. *Medical Anthropology Quarterly*, 27(2013): 193–214.

World Health Organization. 'Taking Stock: Health Worker Shortages and the Response to AIDS.' Geneva: WHO, 2006.

World Health Organization. 'Prevention of Mother-To-Child Transmission (PMTCT) Briefing Note.' Geneva: WHO, Department of HIV/AIDS, 2007.

World Health Organization. *PMTCT Strategic Vision 2010–2015 Preventing Mother-To-Child Transmission of HIV To Reach The UNGASS And Millennium Development Goals Moving Towards The Elimination Of Paediatric HIV* Geneva, WHO, 2010.

CHAPTER 8

Dungeon Lives and Daily Lies: Navigating The Vanilla World

Deww Zhang

Abstract

21 self-identifying kinksters who regularly attend public BDSM events in New Zealand were interviewed as part of an ethnographic inquiry into the Auckland kink scene. They shared various aspects of their kink journeys, including their experiences and reflections about kink becoming increasingly mainstream. While they continue to contend with negative messages perpetuated by the media and contest inaccurate assumptions about kinksters that are circulating in the public consciousness, they are aware of the changing image of BDSM in the public sphere and the potential impact that a paradigm shift towards tolerance and acceptance could have on their lives. This section explores how kinky 'outlaws' perceive and navigate the vanilla or 'real' world. It seeks to address questions such as: what are the popular (mis)representations of kink that have facilitated (or derailed) open dialogue about BDSM? How mainstream, sanitised and 'vanillarised' has kink become, while also simultaneously hypersexualised? Has anything been lost in the process? This chapter also seeks to establish whether kinksters have been receptive to those depictions of BDSM in the media that, on the surface, seem to give a positive spin to the practice. Ultimately this chapter wishes to address how Kiwi kinksters negotiate the beliefs, opinions and attitudes that vanilla people have about BDSM and BDSM practitioners.

Keywords

BDSM – ethnography – kink – sadomasochism – sexual citizenship

 | DOI:10.1163/9789004392298_010

1 Introduction

To query the state of BDSM in Auckland, New Zealand, an ethnographic study, involving researcher immersion among BDSM practitioners in BDSM spaces, was conducted and 21 self-identified kinksters were interviewed. Interviewees shared various aspects of their kink journeys, including their experiences and reflections about kink becoming increasingly mainstream. While they continue to contend with negative messages perpetuated by the media and contest inaccurate assumptions about kinksters that are circulating in the public consciousness, they are aware of the changing image of BDSM in the public sphere and the potential impact that a paradigm shift towards tolerance and acceptance could have on their lives. This chapter explores how kinky 'outlaws' perceive and navigate the vanilla or 'real' world. This section seeks to assess how receptive Kiwi kinksters have been to those depictions of BDSM in the media that, on the surface, seem to give a positive spin to the practice. Also important is how Kiwi kinksters negotiate the beliefs, opinions and attitudes that the general public has about BDSM and BDSM practitioners. This essay is subdivided into nine sections. Section two introduces the concept of sexual politics and sexual citizenship, and section three describes the difficulties involved in contesting citizenship for BDSM practitioners. The following four sections discuss in detail the findings of the ethnographic study, departing from the methodology and continuing into the analysis, and offering concluding thoughts in section nine. I begin my discussion outlining the concept of sexual citizenship and how it pertains to BDSM.

2 *In* or *out*? Erotic Citizenship and the Politics of Inclusion for BDSM

At its core, sexual citizenship politics problematises the privileged position of heteronormative identities, lifestyles and practices, and fights for the inclusion of alternative sexualities. It is a rights-based demand of recognition and respect, empowering an individual to be able to make an identity claim, such as 'I am queer,' and campaigning to be accorded the same rights (to marriage, adoption, child custody, bequeathing in cases without a will, and so on) as the heteronormative-conforming population.[1] Such rights-based positioning

1 Jeffrey Weeks, "The Sexual Citizen," *Theory, Culture & Society* 15.3 (1998) 36; Leticia Sabsay, "Sexual Citizenship and Cultural Imperialism," in *Routledge Handbook of Global Citizenship Studies* eds. Engin F. Isin and Peter Nyers (Oxford: Routledge, 2014), 98.

is founded on the central tenet of equality, where a range of ways of doing, being, and embodying sexualities ought to be considered as differences along a horizontal spectrum, rather than a temporally or societally-imposed hierarchy, from superior (normal, natural, acceptable, morally sound) to inferior (abnormal, unnatural, unacceptable, morally objectionable) practices: in other words, different rather than 'better' or 'worse' cultures.[2]

The ultimate goal of attaining sexual citizenship extends beyond formal recognition, which could for example be demonstrated through passing a marriage equality bill through parliament. Ideally, fully inclusive sexual citizenship would allow anyone to adopt any sexual identity and/or engage in a range of sexual practices without fear of legal, medical, and/or moral censure, and without fear of being negatively judged, discriminated against, ostracised, and/or persecuted by others. To use the above example, a world which recognises marriage equality is qualitatively different from a world where a less conventional couple or polyamorous group cannot display affection in a public space without garnering unwanted attention from any passers-by.

However, experts on sexuality and mental illness, since the birth of the disciplines of Psychiatry and Sexology, *circa* 1800s, have pathologised BDSM practices. This trend began with the publication of Richard von Krafft-Ebing's seminal diagnostic tome in 1886, *Psychopathia Sexualis*, and has fundamentally remained unchanged. This vilification has had significant negative impact on BDSM practitioners. The consequences have been dire for those whose proclivities are made publicly known. Social, legal, and medical persecution and prosecution have followed, the ramifications of which have included: loss of jobs, child custody battles, long term relationships as well as friendships, and a reluctance to seek professional medical advice and services if sporting scars, bruises and welts from BDSM-related activities.[3] The persistent label of BDSM inclinations as indicative of some form of underlying individual psychopathology, despite the prevalence of kinky fantasies and BDSM imagery in popular media, has hampered efforts to incorporate BDSM practitioners as legitimate sexual citizens within society.[4] This is despite claims from those within and

2 Gayle Rubin, "Thinking Sex: Notes for a Radical Theory of the Politics of Sexuality," in *Social Perspectives in Lesbian and Gay Studies: A Reader*, eds. Peter M. Nardi and Beth E. Schneider (USA: Routledge, 1998), 108–109.

3 Susan Wright, "Survey of Violence & Discrimination Against Sexual Minorities: Fast Facts," *Ncsfreedom.org*, 2008, accessed March 29, 2015, https://ncsfreedom.org/resources/bdsm-survey/2008-bdsm-survey-fast-facts.html.

4 Darren Langdridge, "Voices from the Margin: Sadomasochism and Sexual Citizenship," *Citizenship Studies* 10.4 (2006): 374.

outside of medicine who oppose the inclusion of sexual/paraphilic categories (the official classification for BDSM practices), as mental illnesses.

The permutations of diagnoses of alternative expressions of sexualities over the years and editions of diagnostic manuals, such as the American Psychiatric Association's Diagnostic and Statistical Manual of Mental Disorders (DSM) and the World Health Organisation's International Classification of Diseases (ICD), have been used as a means of empowering medicine as an entity capable of delineating what is 'morally acceptable' and thus 'normal' for a given societal context.[5]

In contemporary society, the campaign for sexual citizenship involves demanding the right to adopt sexual identities and perform sexual activities outside the heteronormative paradigm. Hegemonic heteronormativity endorses current institutionalised sexual norms and practices, such as a monogamous long-term relationship between a cisgendered, heterosexual-identifying man and woman, or having sex for procreation rather than recreational purposes. These are discursively elevated to the status of ideal practices, and organized around a 'natural,' 'normal' and 'moral' nexus, excluding all other forms of sexual possibilities (now considered 'deviancies'), thereby systematically invalidating non-normative sexual practices.[6]

The concept of pleasure exists in a false dichotomy with productivity: in a society that is driven by capitalistic notions of production and consumption, pleasure is viewed as antithetical to productivity and efficiency, and must necessarily be productive lest it be considered disruptive to that society.[7] The focus of BDSM on erotic/sensual pleasure thus falls into that disruptive category, a marginalised 'other' that values consensual exploration and experimentation in the pursuit of mutual pleasure. The kinkster challenges, subverts, and transgresses *status quo* erotic norms, further impeding practitioners' claim for sexual citizenship.[8]

5 For a detailed discussion on these topics, and a critique of the inclusion of the paraphilias in Psychiatric diagnostic manuals, Nick Mulé's "Kink and the DSM-5: Pathologisation, Regulation, Stigmatisation," chapter six in this volume.

6 Diane Richardson, "Constructing Sexual Citizenship: Theorising Sexual Rights," *Critical Social Policy* 20.1 (2000): 109.

7 Karmen MacKendrick, *Counterpleasures* (New York: State University of New York Press, 1999), 3.

8 Darren Langdridge and Trevor Butt, "The Erotic Construction of Power Exchange," *Journal of Constructivist Psychology* 18.1 (2005): 68.

3 Disruptive Pleasures, Erotic Outlaws

In light of this, it would appear to be more prudent to strive to legitimise BDSM identities rather than BDSM activities, similar to the political action undertaken by the LGBTQ movement, which has campaigned largely on the (not unproblematic) basis of essentialist paradigms of being born/innately different from the heteronormative population, for a range of queer identities to be accorded due recognition. However, the notion of 'sexual identity' is fraught with difficulties particularly for BDSM practitioners. Unlike other sexual minorities, who are more publicly visible, BDSM practitioners can inhabit an 'invisible closet.' Even the act of 'coming out' may be difficult, because it might involve hinting at or outright disclosing details of private and intimate activities. Kinksters have the option of blending in with the mainstream crowd, and need not worry about the same discrimination that, for example, a same-sex couple wanting to have children might face.[9]

One illustrative survey has revealed that at least 70% of the participants polled in the sample chose to remain selectively closeted,[10] in part due to the perceived social stigma and the fear of being subjected to discriminatory practices. The lack of knowledge about peoples' phenomenological experiences of BDSM and relative invisibility of their narratives has also influenced considerations for whether there is a pressing need for anti-discrimination laws to be enacted, despite the hostility inherent in the mainstream environment.[11] The absence of an international social movement and a global, united, vocal activist front for BDSM practitioners could stem from multiple factors, including:

- Fragmented communities with different goals – not everyone is interested in political organising or campaigning for emancipation for sexual citizenship and recognition.
- Different countries and cultures are at different stages of social acceptance and legal recognition for dealing with BDSM;[12] even if individual local communities were to agree on what they wanted to campaign for, their goals would differ across social contexts and geographical locations.

---

9 Joe Weinberg, "The Invisible Closet: Pressure and Difficulties of the 'Fringe-Queer' Community," *Rupkatha Journal: On Interdisciplinary Studies in Humanities* VI.1 (2014): 20.

10 Susan Wright, "Discrimination of SM-Identified Individuals," *Journal of Homosexuality* 50.2–3 (2006): 219.

11 Eleanor Wilkinson, "'Extreme Pornography' and the Contested Spaces of Virtual Citizenship," *Social & Cultural Geography* 12.5 (2011): 494.

12 SM International, "SM International," *Journal of Homosexuality* 50.2–3 (2006): 263–280.

- Some practitioners prefer to indulge in BDSM privately and/or within their own communities – for every visible BDSM practitioner there are untold numbers of others who are closeted or do not wish to engage in public dialogue about legitimising BDSM practitioners as sexual citizens.
- Given the history of the state's reaction to other sexual minorities (e.g. the official draconian response and the unofficial bullying, harassment and discrimination of homosexuals following the acknowledgement of HIV/AIDS in the 1980s), practitioners may be reluctant to raise awareness of their practices, fearing that authorities might clamp down on BDSM-facilitating establishments and practices.
- Pervasive BDSM imagery in various media avenues, compounded with the popularity of kinky fictional narratives, could lead to some practitioners overestimating how widely and readily their practices are accepted, leading to a general sense of apathy on the political front.

The absence of a strong political voice, in terms of visibility (certainly nothing comes close to the scale of, for example, the marriage equality movement) is one of several factors contributing to apparent complacency and apathy, fuelling the permissive attitude in allowing discriminatory practices to continue in the workplace, on the legal front, and within medicine, as well as its continued pathologisation in the DSM-V. This is compounded by the fact that addressing sexual citizenship is not a straightforward matter when people are selectively self-identifying as BDSM practitioners.[13] There are those who think of themselves as 'kinky people' inhabiting a 'kinkster' identity, and there are those who simply 'do kinky things.' Then, among those who 'do kinky things,' there are people who adopt various strategies to be able to claim that they are 'normal' and not interested in '*real* kinky things,' because of its associated negative implications.[14]

Different BDSM communities and practitioners have different aims – some want to be able to engage in BDSM activities in private without fear of persecution, others want complete societal acceptance, and still others lament how S&M has evolved since the 1950s, resent the recent trends of mainstreaming kink, and enjoy the secretive, transgressive nature of BDSM. It should be noted that sometimes the same individual might want different things depending on their circumstances.[15] Increasing awareness of BDSM in the courtroom may

---

13 Bela B. Chatterjee, 'Pay v UK, the Probation Service and Consensual BDSM Sexual Citizenship,' *Sexualities* 15.5/6 (2012): 741.

14 Rebecca F. Plante, 'Sexual Spanking, the Self, and the Construction of Deviance,' *Journal of Homosexuality* 50.2–3 (2006): 72–73.

15 Langdridge, 'Voices from the Margin,' 379–381.

be of little interest to a BDSM practitioner until he/she is prosecuted for assault, or are disadvantaged in a child custody battle. Despite the well-intended campaign for sexual citizenship to reduce discrimination, decrease social stigma and increase social acceptance, given the fragmented, disparate nature of BDSM membership and the varied type of community kinksters inhabit, it may be difficult to find a solution that caters to everyone's needs and desires.

The coming sections seek to provide a context to the question 'where to from here?' by exploring the current state of BDSM in the public sphere or the 'vanilla world,' in contemporary New Zealand society. It is important to compare previous prominent ethnographic studies conducted in other developed countries, which have canvassed samples that have been predominantly white, educated, and middle-/upper-class, to New Zealand. The point of this investigation would be to ascertain whether the status of BDSM might be different, and yet not necessarily unique, while acknowledging there also might be differences within New Zealand itself.

It is hoped that the ways in which Auckland kinksters are grappling with the status of 'sexual outlaw' to that of 'sexual borderline acceptable minority' will provide additional insights into the global response to the legitimising trajectory that BDSM has been enjoying in the mainstream. It may well be the case that the differences between practitioners and non-practitioners are exaggerated through the demarcation process of distinguishing between the in-group and out-group, or that non-practitioners are far more critical about BDSM than practitioners have been led to believe. Regardless, what is important to practitioners, as we are about to find out, is their own perceptions of the vanilla world as opposed to how vanilla people *actually* perceive and treat them. This will be the focus of the coming sections.

4 Methodology

Ethnography is a research method where the researchers immerse themselves fully into the culture and community being studied, collecting data through field-notes about observations and first-hand experiences, and by interviewing the locals.[16] Traditionally thought of as lone anthropologists spending extended periods of time in remote tribes, in the past century the ethnographic

16 John W. Creswell, *Research Design: Qualitative, Quantitative, and Mixed Methods Approaches (4th Edition)* (London: SAGE, 2014), 13–14.

method has been successfully appropriated for researching contemporary urban cultures and subcultures.[17]

Ethnography is a relevant approach for marginalised, vulnerable populations. BDSM practitioners wary of being judged or discriminated against may be reluctant to speak to an 'outsider' researcher, and those who are willing may not respond in the same way as they would to an 'insider' (though these 'outsider' and 'insider' terms are debatable). Becoming an 'insider' also gives the researcher access to a shared language, shared experiences and shared knowledge about the inner workings of the culture and community, which can then be drawn upon when interviewing participants.[18]

I carried out ethnographic research into the Auckland BDSM scene between 2013 and 2014. After approximately 6 months of getting acquainted with kinksters online, on FetLife,[19] and offline, at various BDSM events,[20] I interviewed 21 people about their experiences with kink. The majority of the interview participants had met me at an event and expressed interest in my research during casual conversation; the remaining 6 interviewees had visited my FetLife profile, read the blurb about my research (I exercised full disclosure and always mentioned my research at every first encounter so that people could make an informed decision about how much information they felt comfortable disclosing to me) and expressed their interest in participating via private messaging online.

Interviews were semi-structured and used open ended questions to allow participants to lead the direction of the conversation. They often commenced with a question like 'tell me a bit about yourself and how you first got into kink,' and then veered towards the topics of conversation that interviewees brought up and wished to pursue. Interview durations spanned from 45 minutes to 2 hours and 15 minutes, with the average interview lasting 1 hour and 30 minutes. One interviewee was located remotely, so a text-based exchange on Google Documents was selected as the medium for interviewing; the remaining

17 Gayle Rubin, 'Studying Sexual Subcultures: Excavating the Ethnography of Gay Communities in Urban North America' *Out in Theory: The Emergence of Lesbian and Gay Anthropology* eds. Ellen Lewin & William L. Leap (USA: University of Illinois Press, 2002), 22.

18 Pranee Liamputtong, *Researching the Vulnerable.* (London: SAGE, 2014), 119–121.

19 www.fetlife.com is a social network site for kinksters.

20 Prior to attending any event I ensured that venue owners and event organisers were aware that I was conducting research and obtained verbal consent from them, or at least an acknowledgement that they knew I was going to be there. They took no issue with my presence and willingly participated.

twenty were interviewed face-to-face. The exchanges were recorded and transcribed by myself after the final interview was completed to ensure participants' anonymity and privacy. Each interviewee was remunerated with a $20 supermarket voucher for their time.

An inductive thematic analysis[21] was conducted with a particular focus on participants' interpretative phenomenological experiences. I utilised the software package CAQDAS NVivo 10 to interpret the arising themes. 9 themes were derived from the analysis, which covered the major facets of participants' experiences. Of these, 3 were concerned with perceptions of BDSM in the public sphere, and will be explored below.

5 Participants' Profiles

Due to the relatively small number of people in the Auckland scene, giving each participant individual profiles would risk identifying them to readers who are members of and/or are familiar with the Auckland scene. As such, only overall information is presented in Figure 8.1.

It should be noted that, compared to previous studies that suggest that BDSM tends to attract greater numbers of people from the well-educated, middle- and upper-class, higher income bracket strata of society,[22] my data shows a lot more variation of socio-economic status, and a mixture of people with different educational levels and professional attainment.

At the time of interviewing, of the 21 participants, 3 resided outside of Auckland, and 2 out of those 3 would infrequently commute to Auckland to attend events. In terms of minority status, two participants belonged to ethnic minority groups and one participant had a visible physical disability.

Participants who are directly quoted in the coming analysis have been assigned pseudonyms. Any personally identifying information disclosed in quotations has been altered or redacted, to ensure anonymity and confidentiality.

21 Virginia Braun and Victoria Clarke, *Successful Qualitative Research: A Practical Guide for Beginners* (London: Sage Publications Ltd, 2013), 175.

22 e.g. Pekka Santtila, N. Kenneth Sandnabba and Niklas Nordling, 'Retrospective Perceptions of Family Interaction in Childhood as Correlates of Current Sexual Adaptation among Sadomasochistic Males,' *Journal of Psychology & Human Sexuality* 12.4 (2001): 72.; Margot D. Weiss, *Techniques of Pleasure: BDSM and the Circuits of Sexuality* (North Carolina: Duke University Press, 2011), 35.

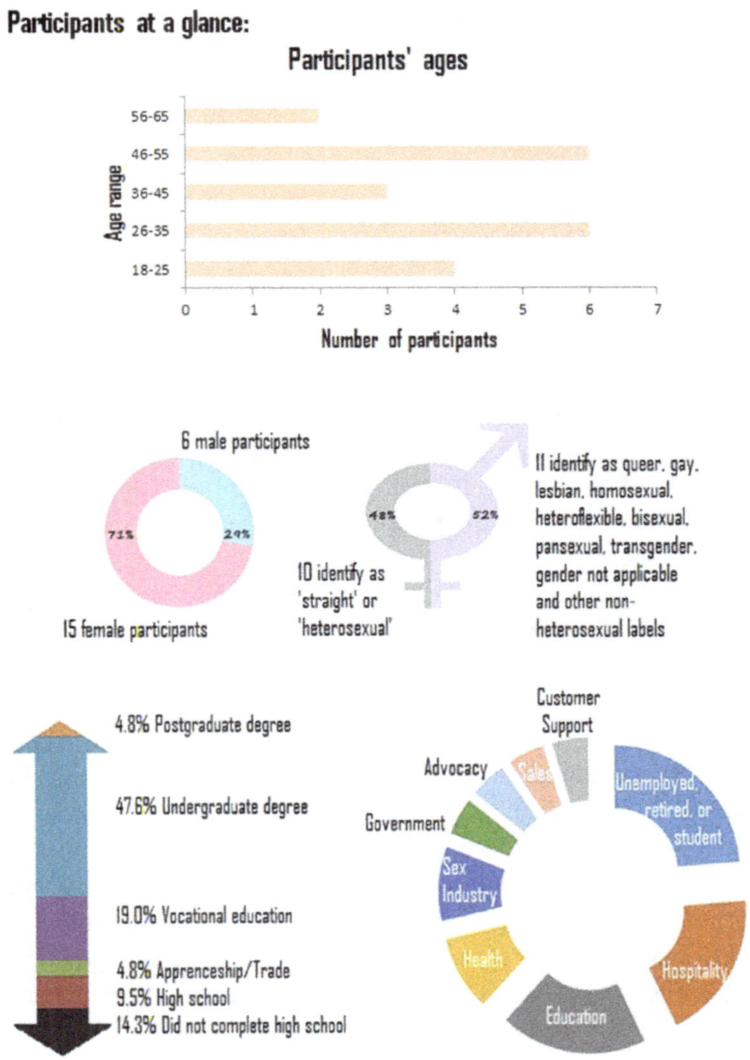

FIGURE 8.1 Visual representation of participant demographic information.
COURTESY OF DEWW ZHANG. © 2015.

6 Perceptions of Kink: Outside, Inside, and In Between

In terms of kink in the public sphere, many interviewees argued that despite maintaining its taboo status, kink had already irreversibly gone mainstream. Though the interviews were conducted before the release of the inevitably controversial *Fifty Shades of Grey* movie and the subsequent reinvigorated publicity it has brought to BDSM, the literary version had already been in circulation for three years. While the rising popularity of BDSM was largely attributed to the *Fifty Shades* franchise, interviewees were particularly critical of these texts, as well as one other artefact, the movie *Secretary*, released in 2002.

Interviewees believed that the negative stereotypes perpetuated by the media have contributed to a distorted portrayal of the kink world. A number of fictional works, as well as documentaries, coverage in the news and tabloid scandals about high-profile individuals involved in kinky activities (including the coverage of seemingly kink-related deaths), have not only stereotyped kink negatively as a practice, but they have also discursively 'fashioned' the *persona* of the kinkster to be an oblique, untrustworthy and mentally disturbed character. According to the media, the 'type' of person more likely to have kinky predilections also displays a host of negative characteristics, such as the inability to maintain long-term relationships, an inclination to violence towards others, and past history of child abuse. This has had the effect of arming the general public with an arsenal of incorrect, misleading and often damaging assumptions about kinksters.

A few interviewees did not consider kink to have become mainstream yet, and instead debated whether kink ought to be steered in that direction. Two participants, Brendan and George, noted that the current event attendee size[23] was optimal, and having too many people at events would have a negative impact. For Brendan, it was important that event attendees were 'going for the right reasons,' which to him meant they had to be interested in exploring kink on their own terms, rather than going to witness 'the circus show' and tell all their friends and family about the 'freaks' they encountered. George added an important consideration: the current event attendance rates made internal community policing a viable option. He pointed out that a community that had swelled to a large number of participants would face increasing difficulties in keeping track of the dangerous elements in the group, the individuals known to be predatory and/or unsafe.

Anne spoke of the 'new *Fifty Shades* crowd' with notable disdain. These individuals would enter the community fresh from reading what was, in her opinion, essentially a 'sexed-up romance novel,' without doing the depth of preliminary research required to know what to expect at 'a real BDSM event,' such as etiquette, safety, consent, and other important facets of 'real-life BDSM.' She believed that a negative incident, involving a 'newbie' ignorant and

23 A range of 40 to 80 people generally attend any given regular public BDSM event from a pool of between 200 to 300 regulars; annual events such as slave auctions and fetish balls can attract up to 120 attendees.

complacent of what would actually take place in the scene, to be imminent, with catastrophic consequences for all involved. Her comments pointed to her resistance to the mainstreaming of BDSM. It poignantly illustrated some of the canvassed kinksters' attitudes: BDSM should be kept out of mainstream and reserved for the exclusive membership of those who 'knew what they were doing.' These arguments were based on the reasoning that only those with 'real' prior experience could ensure the safety for all those involved, through 'proper' play.

In a previous ethnographic study conducted in USA,[24] participants spoke of finding and entering the BDSM community as 'coming home.' Such a description points to the perception that the BDSM community is a place separate from 'the real world' or 'the world out there.' It is a safe space where kinksters are not made to feel as if they are abnormal, depraved perverts who are alone in their desires. The BDSM community cultivates and perpetuates ideals of inclusivity, tolerance and acceptance of all individuals and their inclinations, using techniques such as the mantra 'your kink is not my kink' (henceforth contracted to its acronym YKINMK). YKINMK is often invoked as a reminder or as a means to chastise those who make negative comments about kinks they might personally find strange or repulsive (usually the less common types, such as scat or anything involving the drawing blood). However, as demonstrated by the quotation below, YKINMK is not without its complications:

> Sarah: I would never try anything along the lines of scat? Or urination. Or any of that. Or vomit – I don't even know how that's a fetish. I don't even know how peeing on someone or shitting on someone or vomiting on someone is a fetish. I really don't understand. And I know it's the whole 'your kink is not my kink' but, really? *Really?*[25]

It would appear that YKINMK might hold true only for those activities and fetishes that are 'easier to understand' (by virtue of some unexplained variable such as popularity, or direct relatedness to genital stimulation, perhaps). Or is it simply a politically correct term that holds no inherent significance? A throw-away comment designed to alleviate the fears and anxieties of someone with a rare fetish? Regardless, given the actual lack of validity of the phrase, it is not surprising that one of the critiques that many participants voiced about

24 Staci Newmahr, *Playing on the Edge: Sadomasochism, Risk and Intimacy* (Indiana: Indiana University Press, 2011), 42–44.

25 Sarah, Interview with the Author, 5 February 2014.

the local BDSM scene was that it was very judgemental – to a fault. As noted by Danielle below, even within the seemingly exalted 'pre-*Fifty Shades* crowd,' there exists a division, albeit an unclear one, between those who are known to be predisposed towards the more common, 'vanilla' kinks and the more uncommon, 'extreme' kinks. The non-accepting, judgemental attitude that the non-kinky public is often criticised for, is highlighted by Danielle as a genuine concern within the kink scene itself:

> Danielle: Ah, I mean it's nice- it would be nice if it [*A/N: kink*] was more accepted but there's- there's some- there's some things that won't be. [*Interviewer: Mmm.*] There's just some things in life that won't be accepted. ... I mean you look at all the people who have put [*A/N: on their FetLife profile*] "No bloodplay. I'm not gonna do bloodplay, I'm not gonna do cutting, I'm not gonna do- needles. I'm not gonna do bloodplay." ...but- is that- is that their own perception that it is wrong or painful? Or... unclean or unsafe or is it the- the mass- perception? Because everybody has it in their profiles. That there's something that's not done. It's just something that we don't do.[26]

As kink progressively enters the mainstream realm, even the division between kinky and non-kinky becomes blurred, because everyone who shares the same context – geographically and temporally, inhabiting the same society in the same time period – is subjected to similar overarching discourses and are attuned to similar messages promulgated by the mass media that would guide their judgements and behaviours. Are the tips and suggestions that are offered by any generic popular young women's magazine to 'spice up the bedroom,' or 'reinvigorate your sex life,' considered kinky, or has the modern conceptualisation of sex simply evolved to encompass a greater range of intimate, erotic activities? What might be extremely deviant for one person could hardly be considered erotic to someone else. While participants were able to comfortably talk about their 'kinky journey,' it was assumed that the interviewer and the interviewee shared an understanding of was meant by the nebulous term 'kink,' and none explicitly attempted to define what they meant by *it*, unless they were prompted by the interviewer to consider what they actually meant by the term.

Regardless of whether one could identify the shifting boundaries of kink, some interviewees believed that kink should remain a private, individualised

26 Danielle, Interview with the Author, 19 February 2014.

venture instead of its trajectory towards popularity and commercialisation in mainstream. They thought these had been triggered by the popular franchise of *Fifty Shades of Grey*: and they lamented the fact that the mainstreaming process had 'taken something away' from their personal kink experience. This loss was viewed in terms of the transition from private erotic pleasures to a more public, vocal, activist realm of campaigning on the sexual politics/citizenship front.[27] The allegorical tour buses full of voyeuristic tourists with a passing interest in kink, arriving at BDSM venues and parties, even if just imagined, were already having an irreversible negative, disenchanting impact on the perceptions of 'specialness' of 'real kink' for kinksters, diluting what – albeit exaggerated and romanticised in hindsight – was once a carnal, visceral, authentic experience.

Dora admitted that some of the appeal of kink had stemmed from its transgressive nature, and eventual public acceptance would influence her decision to continue exploring kink:

> Dora: Uhm, but yeah, the internet has been… uhm, good in giving information but I think it's also kind of… vanillarised it a bit or made it- made it very accessible to a range of people which again, is great, but, uh, I guess it's- for me, what I quite liked about uhm… the being- the- the gay- the homosexual law reform thing, when it was against the law there was some sense of underground solidarity?
>
> Interviewer: Yep.
>
> Dora: That was really great?
>
> Interviewer: Mmm.
>
> Dora: And I guess I see that BDSM could go down that track now where it's just become the same as- and what I- what I like about kink is that it, uhm, it can be- it's taboo, it's controversial, it's 'outside of'?
>
> Interviewer: Yep.
>
> Dora: And when I see it being all mainstream, I think, "Ah, I don't know if I want that." [laughter] "To do that anymore." Now that I'm not sure what else there would be to do. Mmm.[28]

Jennifer interpreted her attraction to a transgressive kink in terms of contending with the duality of her 'kinky' and 'real life' self. For Dora and Jennifer, kink

27 John Preston, 'What Happened?' *Leatherfolk: Radical Sex, People, Politics, and Practice* ed. Mark Thompson (California: Alyson Publications, 2001), 210.

28 Dora, Interview with the Author, 1 February 2014.

was inexorably transgressive, non- or perhaps even anti-heteronormative, and while both described the mainstreaming of kink as 'taking something away' from their experience, their understandings of exactly *what* would be taken away or what was going to be lost in the mainstreaming process were very different. Jennifer stated:

> I don't get a kick out of kinky being taboo exactly but I do like having such two such different sides of my character that many people would think was surprising and paradoxical if they knew: the very respectable 'pillar of the community' me and the kinky slutty me. If kink was more widely accepted the paradox would be gone, and that would be a shame.[29]

7 Public (Mis)Representations

Participants expressed ambivalence about the ways in which BDSM was being perceived and consumed in the mainstream. Olivia, for instance, explained:

> I do like the fact that it has opened up- kinky ideas to... to more vanillas. Like [sic] you see more of that stuff in stores. Like [sic] I like the fact that mums are reading it. Just wish it was more... (that) it was better represented.[30]

While interviewees had overwhelmingly negative comments about the fictional narratives of kink that were pervasive in the public sphere, they did mention three positive points that have arisen out of these fictional works. The first has been described as the 'commercialisation' or the 'monetisation' on BDSM; its transformation into a 'Capitalist enterprise.' Where once sex shops were predominantly stocked with BDSM paraphernalia that cost hundreds or thousands of dollars, the popularity of *Fifty Shades of Grey* has ushered in a new wave of mass-produced, low-quality, low-cost equipment that is affordable.

One can now acquire a set of basic bedroom kink items, which could include items like handcuffs, a blindfold, a feather tickler, for less than $50. Specialist equipment, such as custom-made whips and floggers, or BDSM furniture (spanking benches, St. Andrew's crosses, bondage-enhanced beds, and so on), remains expensive and still cost upward of $600. Interestingly, the quality of

29 Jennifer, Interview with the Author, 5 May 2014.

30 Olivia, Interview with the Author, 20 March 2014.

equipment in someone's possession has now become an indirect marker for how 'authentic' of a kinkster the owner of the items is,[31] but the monetary entry level for kink gear is now much lower than it was in the pre-*Fifty Shades* era. The advent of the internet has only facilitated transactions to purchase BDSM equipment, especially now that paraphernalia can be browsed, researched and ordered online, and delivered to one's residence discreetly. This circumvents the need of having to physically set foot in a sex shop, and searching Google can alleviate the anxiety triggered by having to ask the sex shop staff embarrassing questions.

A second effect of the mainstreaming of kink, has been the proliferation of fictional kink narratives that have emerged from its increased visibility as a part of the commercialisation process: kink has been made accessible in a fairly non-threatening way to 'vanilla people.' Again interviewees assumed a shared understanding of what was meant by the vague and ill-defined label of 'vanilla.' The extent to which 'vanilla people' were actually 'vanilla' was rarely something interviewees considered until they were explicitly asked to explain what they meant. Also, the demarcation of the transition from 'vanilla to kinky' was also not clearly elaborated in the narrative of the participants, nor clearly understood. Peter's experiences are illustrative of the proliferation of kink possibilities for 'vanilla' practitioners, and yet makes evident the slippages and ambiguity of the outside/'vanilla'/inside/'kinkster' narratives of the community.

Peter was introduced to kink by women who had read *Fifty Shades of Grey* but felt too intimidated to go to an actual BDSM event, and he credited them for his serendipitous foray into kink which had eventually led him to finding a Mistress whom he was wholly devoted to. For Peter, narratives like *Fifty Shades* presented to the vanilla public alternative possibilities in life that could be explored in a way that would not leave people feeling as if they were abnormal or strange for harbouring seemingly unorthodox fantasies and desires.

For other interviewees, however, these fictional narratives were a double-edged sword, and could even end up normalising a 'version' of kink that was

31 Though it should be noted that there is a pervasive do-it-yourself (DIY) culture in New Zealand, where being able to make or fix something without enlisting third party support, is a valued trait (incidentally it is also one of several problematic defining characteristics of masculinity in New Zealand). Thus, self-made or homemade equipment is often praised for its ingenuity, uniqueness and the counter-capitalist statement it implicitly makes. DIY gear is not looked down upon, or treated with the derision it is subjected to in more affluent communities, previously researched by authors such as Weiss; *Techniques of Pleasure*, 122–124.

downright dangerous. What could end up being normalised was so grossly distorted it might degenerate into non-consensual, oppressive sexual violence rather than 'safe, sane and consensual' BDSM.

As discussed in the previous section, the normalisation process that kink has undergone is also limited in its impact. What is normalised by the media has been termed 'lite' kink, primarily sex-or orgasm-oriented, and pertains to the kind of activities that have been mass-consumed through the franchise of *Fifty Shades,* involving sex toy packages and the use of blindfolds or handcuffs during intercourse. The perception of interviewees is that 'real,' 'proper,' 'extreme,' or 'hardcore' kink, like electrostimulation, impact play (the use of heavy floggers, whips, canes, and so on), anything involving blood (needles, cutting, bloodletting), which are more sadomasochistically-oriented practices, remain marginalised. Kinksters assume that vanilla people continue to think of such practices as bizarre activities, to be relegated to the realm of arthouse/short films, artistic pornography and seedy documentaries, rather than mainstream Hollywood movies.

A final positive aspect to have arisen out of the *Fifty Shades* franchise is the introduction of a common language by which kinksters can engage in dialogue with vanilla people about BDSM. It can be difficult for vanilla people who are willing to engage with kink and kinksters, without any prior exposure or knowledge of the BDSM vernacular and subculture, to participate in any meaningful dialogue about kink. Drawing comparisons to something like the book *Fifty Shades of Grey,* so publicly salient and accessible, enables people to talk and think about kink without having to first learn all the jargon and the nuances involved in important issues such as safety, consent and communication.

> Anya: I think it's [*A/N: the publicity*] helped slightly. I think it has helped. Because it gives people a c-, almost like a context, a context and a language, so if- like [sic] if I did decide to tell my parents, "Oh I'm into BDSM," they might not understand what that meant. But if I said to them, you know, "I'm- I'm into the kind of stuff like in *Fifty Shades of Grey,*" you know, I- they would understand that. It gives people a common language.[32]

Nevertheless, these positive outcomes of how BDSM has been interpreted and represented in the media were overshadowed by an overwhelmingly negative, critical response from the majority of the interviewees. In particular,

32 Anya, Interview with the Author, 22 January 2014.

interviewees were apprehensive about the consequences that would stem from kink being portrayed badly and inaccurately. Outdated views about kink being morally wrong and/or indicative of individual psychopathology are still being disseminated by works like *Fifty Shades* and *Secretary*, and news outlets have a tendency to scandalise and sensationalise any reporting of kink-related activities/deaths. In particular, those who have had direct experiences with the media, such as those who have worked in the media or have been interviewed by journalists, have been dissatisfied with their experiences. Caitlin, quoted below, is a venue owner and event organiser, and has been interviewed by TV and print media journalists numerous times.

> ... media. Yes ... [laughter] from my experience with- *that*, you've got- good representations or- or you've got, you've got media that have ... good, reasons, good [sigh] what's the freaking word.... Good intentions, in terms of *why* they wanna come down and find out about it, why they wanna sit down and interview you... and with all the interviews and everything that I've done, over the years ...I know that Edward [*A/N: her husband*] has got to the point where he's like, "Fuck, if anybody else wants to fucking ask me to be in an article and everything, they can *get fucked.*" Sorry about all the swearing but, because they gleam[sic] out of... they gleam[sic] out of the interview, what they want? Whether it be if they wanna portray it in a good light, then they'll take the good stuff. They wanna slam it? And throw some shit at it? Then they'll pull the- the shit. They wanna, put it down and go, "These kinksters are fucked in the head, they're all mental cases, and... you guys all need to be committed?" Then they'll do that.[33]

Described in the above fashion, the media is perceived to be a manipulative conglomeration of self-interested individuals who reach out to kinksters and pursue their stories with an agenda, an agenda that they are seeking to strengthen through selective, sometimes downright out-of-context usage of interview excerpts.

Above and beyond the impact that BDSM as it is represented in the media would have on kinksters personally, interviewees also expressed concern about the potential consequences that the inexperienced – often pejoratively labelled 'newbies,' 'novices' and 'amateurs' – might face if they engaged in BDSM practices based on what they have seen and read in the media without doing adequate background research. Interviewees describe this as a threefold

33 Caitlin, Interview with the Author, 22 March 2014.

problem: the media's portrayal of kink is unsafe; characters in fictional narratives are in unhealthy, dysfunctional relationships; and the audience is given unrealistic expectations of what BDSM is like in reality. The factor of lack of safety is exacerbated by media portrayals that focus only on the titillating aspects of BDSM, featuring only the apex of BDSM activities rather than the hours of meticulous preparation that is required beforehand, and the wind-down at the end of those activities. People who decide to engage in BDSM activities without doing the necessary checks and preparations beforehand may injure themselves or others in the process.

Ella, who is very involved in the kink scene in terms of organising events, providing resources to newcomers and giving advice to inexperienced kinksters (especially those who are struggling with their polyamorous relationships), eloquently described in the quotation below how she conceptualised her various roles in the community. To her, kink was very 'ordinary,' an activity similar to any other hobby that required event organisation and mentoring. Her community involvement bears little resemblance to how the media portrays BDSM:

Ella: Uh ... Most, things in the media focus on the fun, sexy bits and not on the ... what it's really like? ... so like, you get things like *Fifty Shades of Abuse* and ... even like *Secretary* and things like that.

Interviewer: Yep.

Ella: *Most* of it deals with ... the sensationalist stuff? Like whether someone self-harms or ... whether ... there's contracts and shit involved and all this kinda thing. Where for ... *most* kinksters, it's either a small circumscribed part of their existing relationship, or it's part of the community, just kind of being? Most of the time? You're not really ... doing exciting things and fucking, you're ... having coffee and deciding how you wanna run events and ... it's probably quite similar to Rotary, it's like you know [laughter]

Interviewer: [laughter] That's true.

Ella: But you'd never run a story on Rotary, you'd run a story on, you know, what they did in South Auckland that time. Uhm ... and for us it's, you know, what you did in that South Auckland dungeon that time.[34]

Interviewer: [laughter]

34 South Auckland is notorious for being a dangerous neighbourhood that has high crime rates and an overrepresentation of lower socioeconomic status inhabitants. In this instance, however, there is one prominent dominatrix who has an elaborately-furnished

Ella: Uhm [laughter] Not, you know. Talking to people on FetLife and mentoring them through uhm, the fact that their partner is … may-may not actually be kinky and … [laughter]
Interviewer: Yeah yeah yeah yeah yeah.
Ella: This kinda stuff. Yeah.[35]

In both *Fifty Shades of Grey* and *Secretary*, the heterosexual couples featured are involved in extremely unhealthy relationships. The male protagonists are controlling and coercive: in *Fifty Shades of Grey* he is an invasive, intrusive, persistent presence in the life of the woman he is pursuing. The female protagonists, conversely, are presented as weak and docile, and have characteristics and qualities of characters in literary tragedies. The main female character in the movie *Secretary* in particular, has a history of mental illness and self-harm, and kink is used as a therapeutic avenue to stop her from self-harming.

Another important problem in both mass consumed portrayals of BDSM, *Secretary* and *Fifty Shades*, is the issue of consent, and the actual lack of any meaningful negotiation or discussion of this essential part of kink. There is little evidence of characters' prior research into the activities they are doing, consent is not debated, and despite their romanticisation, the characters and their relationships are deeply dysfunctional. Combined with the unsafe portrayal of kink, the audience ends up taking away extremely unrealistic expectations of what kink is like in reality, if they were to base their expectations and know-how solely on these fictional narratives.

The underlying issue with such narratives is that the focus *is on kink*, which makes it stand out as an unusual trait: the story becomes about an atypical kinky couple, rather than an 'ordinary' couple who happens to have kinky interests. This exacerbates the notions that kink is abnormal, unnatural, and morally problematic, and a problem that needs to be addressed: having kinky predilections is something a kinkster ought to feel ashamed or guilty about. This assumption might potentially contribute to internalised anxiety, and an increased reluctance or resistance for people to discuss their kink with others. The overall sentiment conveyed by interviewees is that due to the way kink has been publicly misrepresented to the public, the media has done more harm than good, essentially creating barriers to the inclusion of kinksters into legitimate sexual citizenship.

dungeon in South Auckland – 'that South Auckland dungeon' refers to a specific location that the majority of local kinksters would be aware of.

35 Ella, Interview with the Author, 25 February 2014.

8 Vanilla Assumptions

In this section, I address how the individuals interviewed described the stereotypes that vanilla people have about kinky people. For most, negative stereotypes stemmed largely from public misrepresentations of kink. Kinksters believed that many non-kinky people assumed they were abnormal, dysfunctional people with histories of child abuse (or alternatively and succinctly termed 'damaged goods'). Additionally kinky events were believed to be highly sexual encounters among strangers, engaging in 'doggy piles' and 'group orgies.' 'Normal,' 'professional' people would not be interested in kink. Interviewees noted that while they had encountered few dysfunctional kinksters in their midst, there were dysfunctional people in any special interest group; these vanilla assumptions made caricatures out of kinksters and BDSM events were grossly caricaturised into something much 'worse' than the actual lived experience. Further, interviewees did not believe that the gulf between vanilla assumptions and kinksters' lives could ever be bridged, because such individuals had no intention of ever attending kinky events or experiencing the real-life *praxis* of kink.

Another noxious stereotype that was discussed by my interview subjects was 'supposed parental inadequacy,' the assumption that kinksters are incapable of being good parents because they are potentially violent and as well as hypersexual. Kinksters are very capable parents, they repeatedly and vociferously stated: most kinksters are 'normal' people with 'normal' lives, 'normal' jobs and 'normal' families. Anyone from any walk of life was equally likely to dabble in kink regardless of their ethnicity, socioeconomic status, gender, physical/mental health status and other characteristics (which kinksters would consider irrelevant). Interviewees also pointed out that while most kinksters might be sexually liberal, some were just as conservative, if not more so, than the average vanilla person in terms of political issues like immigration, social welfare, healthcare, education, and so on.

The nature of kink events were also highly stereotyped and misunderstood, especially with regard to the level of sexual exchange that took place therein. Although kink was widely conceptualised within and outside of the kinky community as being intrinsically sexual, for some interviewees it was not necessarily a sexual experience. Yet, what was meant by 'sexual' was difficult for interviewees to define. If a narrow definition of 'sexual' was adopted – meaning an set of encounters that were orgasm-oriented, requiring physical intercourse involving genitals, and/or foreplay/teasing, leading up to penetrative activities – then these interviewees were adamant that kink was not sexual for them. They might use descriptors such as 'erotic,' 'sensual,' 'intimate' or 'pleasurable,' but they reiterated that this was due to a lack of vocabulary to adequately articulate their experiences.

It is not surprising to find resistance to adopt BDSM vocabulary available to them in general culture: the lived and embodied experiences of BDSM practitioners, in institutional settings and outside of them, have traditionally been explored and framed sexually. The DSM-V, for instance, lumps 'sexual sadism disorder' and 'sexual masochism disorder' together with 'fetishistic disorder' and 'paedophilic disorder,'[36] and in academia BDSM is almost always classified as a branch of sex and sexualities studies. Research tends to approach kink with a sexual filter, for example with questionnaires asking participants about sexual experiences prior to learning about/engaging in BDSM.[37] The extent to which kink is sexual is largely dependent on individuals' perceptions and experiences of kink. Of course, it is likely that BDSM is sometimes sexual for some people if they are sexually attracted to the other kinkster(s) and the mood and the atmosphere is appropriate. BDSM might not be sexual at other times when that sexual attraction is absent. Kink does not necessarily have to be a dichotomous sexual or non-sexual choice. Olivia explains:

> Uhm, right now, kink is sexual for me? I- I choose if I want kink to be sexual for me. ... s ... oh, they're- there're definitely people where, sometimes they do go hand-in-hand just because if I'm really attracted to someone, I do also want that. But ... I've- I've played with people where, it took a long time for us to get sexual, because I wanted to make sure that I was at a level that I was comfortable with? ... kink can totally be not sexual though. Like- Like I said, I've been kinky with people ... that ... I have never had sex with.[38]

Similarly, a previous ethnographic study has questioned in detail the place that sex occupies within BDSM.[39] Sex *could* be scripted into a BDSM scene, BDSM experiences could be experienced sexually in terms of sexual arousal, and if

36 American Psychiatric Association, 'Paraphilic Disorders Factsheet.' *Dsm5.org*, 2013, accessed March 29, 2015,http://www.dsm5.org/Documents/Paraphilic%20 Disorders%20Fact%20Sheet.pdf

37 N. Kenneth Sandnabba, Pekka Santilla, Laurence Alison and Niklas Nordling, 'Demographics, Sexual Behavior, Family Background and Abuse Experiences of Practitioners of Sadomasochistic Sex: A Review of Recent Research,' *Sexual and Relationship Therapy* 17.1 (2002) 43.

38 Olivia, Interview, 20 March, 2014.

39 Newmahr, *Playing on the Edge*, 195..

unscripted, sex could still happen in a BDSM context – but BDSM does not neatly equate with 'kinky sex' and BDSM is not 'all about sex.' Using sex as an explanatory model for BDSM does not sufficiently encompass everyone's experiences. It does not explain why everyone has not become BDSM practitioners by now, nor does it account for those practitioners for whom BDSM is not necessarily related with sexual experiences.

Kink has been alternately described as a hobby, a means of achieving an emotional and experiential 'high,' and as a form of catharsis or release. Particularly for those who have taken up a specialist skill within BDSM (such as learning how to do aesthetic rope bondage, how to crack a single-tail whip, or what is known as fire play which involves putting rubbing alcohol on someone's skin and lighting it on fire as safely as possible), BDSM can be rewarding in terms of mastery, the pure achievement within a specific skillset. BDSM has been previously conceptualised as 'serious leisure,' or a form of leisure activity that is career-like in its progression: it requires a monetary investment from the outset and continues to incur costs over time, involves the gradual cumulative acquisition of specific skills and relevant knowledge over a period of time, and yields durable benefits and rewards in the long term.[40] For people who take up these 'careers' in specific BDSM activities, any sexually gratifying elements of their serious leisure activities may be perceived to be incidental or peripheral bonuses.

In Peter's case, impact play gave him a 'high' which he described below as a release of endorphins in his system. In previous studies this high has also been articulated using the language associated with spirituality,[41] transcendence and healing,[42] but this discourse was very rare among my interviewees.

---

40 D. J. Williams and Gordon J. Walker, 'Leisure, Deviant Leisure, and Crime: "Caution: Objects May be Closer than They Appear",' *Leisure/Loisir* 30.1 (2006): 205.

41 e.g. Joseph W. Bean, 'The Spiritual Dimensions of Bondage,' *Leatherfolk: Radical Sex, People, Politics, and Practice* ed. Mark Thompson (California: Alyson Publications, 2001), 259–260.; Andrea Beckmann, 'The 'Bodily Practices' of Consensual 'SM', Spirituality and 'Transcendence,' *Safe, Sane and Consensual: Contemporary Perspectives on Sadomasochism* eds. Darren Langdridge and Meg Barker (New York: Palgrave Macmillan, 2007), 100–102.; Dianna Vesta, 'Fantasy, Fetish, and the Goddess,' *Leatherfolk: Radical Sex, People, Politics, and Practice* ed. Mark Thompson (California: Alyson Publications, 2001), 270–271.

42 e.g. Alicia D. Horton, 'Flesh Hook Pulling: Motivations and Meaning-Making From the "Body Side" of Life,' *Deviant Behaviour* 34.2 (2013): 120–125.; Tina Portillo, 'I Get Real: Celebrating My Masochistic Soul,' *Leatherfolk: Radical Sex, People, Politics, and Practice* ed. Mark Thompson (California: Alyson Publications, 2001), 49–50.

> Uhm… as a submissive, getting… gently warmed up to a point where you can take heavier and harder hits from different objects, found it releases first adrenaline, and if it goes far enough and you can take enough pain, then the – endorphins release. And one of the first 5 play parties I went to, I was a bit like piggy in the middle, and I took everything I could, and it took me 2 weeks before I even realised how…. Sort of high I was? On the endorphins?[43]

Beyond a physiological chemical release in the brain and throughout the body, some interviewees could also enjoy BDSM for the proverbial emotional and psychological release, which was described as relieving the stress and tension that had built up over the course of a difficult day, or life hardships in general. In this way it was conceived of both as a hobby/leisure activity and as a release.

> Lea: Sir's like "Oh I'll take you to the cross and give you a beating." I was like "Eh. Okay. Whatever." It was just meant to be a normal, you know, beating. After about… 'cause we always play music. … 2 songs into it and I'm like bawling like a baby… and… no idea why. Actually I did have some stuff going on in life and… t- I just let go. And I was just bawling. … And he just knew. And then he just kept going. Didn't stop. And… I felt so much better after it. I was just like… uhm, it was one of those, just, complete releases which I'd never actually had.[44]
>
> Margaret: When I'm, you know, particularly when like, things are crazy at work and I spend all day having, you know, telling people what to do and… you know. Being the- the bad guy and stuff which I don't wanna do. I- that's- I hate that. … So… I find it really quite therapeutic?
>
> Interviewer: Mmhmm.
>
> Margaret: Uhm, to have… quite a- a hard sort of, SM session I suppose. And uhm… I really enjoy uh, crying as well? As… a type of stress relief.
>
> Interviewer: Yeah.
>
> Margaret: Yeah. And it just- makes everything balance out for me [laughter][45]

Some interviewees did not seek a 'higher' explanation for their kinky predilections: they enjoyed BDSM purely because it was fun, and gave responses such

43 Peter, Interview with the Author, 22 March 2014.

44 Lea, Interview with the Author, 28 January 2014.

45 Margaret, Interview with the Author, 5 February 2014.

as 'I do it, I enjoy it, who cares why?'; they rejected the notion that there must always be a logical, rational reason behind every decision.

While there were some who did conceptualise of their preferences as being inherently sexual, and certainly got sexually-related benefits from doing kink, I hope that my discussion has conclusively shown that kinksters perceive and interpret their kink experiences in complex, multi-layered ways. The attempt to portray such experiences by forcing it into a reductive, 'sexual'/'not-sexual' discursive dichotomy does not adequately encapsulate the diversity of these experiences.

9 Conclusion

As with any issue concerning sexual citizenship, the inclusion of BDSM as an alternative, rather than an inferior form of sexuality, is not a straightforward process. Regardless of whether kinksters subscribed to a more essentialist or constructionist paradigm (without excluding those who believed that their BDSM involvement could be attributed to both innate and external reasons), the notion of a 'kinky identity,' as might be employed in identity politics in itself, is fraught with issues in terms of how a 'kinky identity' is defined, interpreted and invoked. By its nature, kink is inherently dynamic, fluid and experimental. There are kinksters who 'don't feel like doing watersports today' or 'went vanilla and monogamous for my ex-partner.' These snippets of conversations are arguably far more common at a BDSM play party than a homosexual proclaiming at a cruise club that s/he 'doesn't feel like doing homosexuality today.'

Though being closeted could arguably be considered as going against the tenets of BDSM, which enshrines open and honest communication, some kinksters no doubt experienced some level of excitement stemming from the secrecy surrounding privately indulged-in kinky activities. Meanwhile, other practitioners preferred BDSM not to lose its 'edge,' its rebellious, transgressive character with its illusion of danger, valuing erstwhile sadomasochists' practices and accoutrements like leather and piercings as anti-authoritative symbols. The concerns stemming from the occasional court case (where consenting to assault was not honoured as a valid legal defence, or a kinky mother lost custody of her children, or the tabloids' kinky sex scandal of the month), have not translated to campaigns to reify anti-discrimination laws against kinksters, to any similar degree as, for example, what the LGBTQ population has accomplished. In fact, it was not uncommon for participants to mention that BDSM in New Zealand currently stood where the LGBTQ movement was 50 years ago.

The media has had a substantial influence on both kinky and non-kinky individuals conceptions of BDSM. Interviewees may not have internalised what they perceived to be the negative presumptions about kinksters that 'vanilla people' had, but many explicitly rejected the notion that kinksters had troubled pasts and were dysfunctional people with dysfunctional relationships. Additionally, interviewees tended to had had sufficient time to grapple with their kinkster identities, and over time had become comfortable with their level of engagement with kink, with their bodies and with what they witnessed and experienced at the events they attended. The most common positive comment interviewees made about how kink had changed their lives was they had acquired enhanced communication skills and strategies since engaging in BDSM, were better able to communicate their wants and needs, which in turn had a positive impact particularly in their romantic relationships.

Public play parties, fetish balls and other kink events bear little resemblance to the media's binary, dichotomous portrayals of either hypersexualised, pornographic, explicitly sexual imagery or dimly-lit dungeons where people are restrained and tortured. The burgeoning popularity of fictional narratives like the *Fifty Shades of Grey* franchise will inevitably change the landscape of this pre-*Fifty Shades* scene, in Auckland, New Zealand and other communities around the world. However, these fictional narratives do not accurately reflect what BDSM and BDSM practitioners are like in reality, and newcomers could potentially be vulnerable to greater physical and emotional risks. While the media could be used to raise awareness about BDSM, encourage people to openly engage in dialogue about kink, and perhaps eventually enable the curious and closeted to explore kink without fear of being judged and discriminated in legal, moral, medical and social realms, narratives about BDSM in their current forms are primarily sexually-oriented – viewing kink as an extension of conventional sex practices. Participants have deemed them to be serving little purpose beyond titillating audiences with fairy tale romances and sensationalist sex scandals.

The different degrees of centrality of one's kinky orientation or desires to one's sense of self has meant that some interviewees were more committed to the lifestyle, immersed in the scene, involved with hosting/organising events, and had more kinky than 'vanilla' acquaintances compared with others. Interviewees spoke of a duality or having to manage dual identities as they distinguished between 'kink' and 'real life' as two separate worlds they inhabited (hence the title 'dungeon lives and daily lies'), and many had vested interest in keeping those two worlds apart from each other, fearing the repercussions for their families, careers and potential legal action that could be taken against them without the consideration of the nuances surrounding consensual 'assault.'

In an ideal situation, fully inclusive sexual citizenship would be attained for all kinksters regardless of what kinds of kinks they were interested in, while simultaneously retaining its 'edgy,' subversive feel with the caveat that kinksters are 'normal, everyday, ordinary people.' The mainstreaming process has 'watered down' kink from being 'weird' and 'painful' to 'naughty' and 'mischievous' activities. The impossible challenge of striking a balance lies in how normalcy and deviancy can manifest together ('Acceptable perverts'? 'Normal deviants'?) within a contemporary limited conceptualisation of sexual citizenship that remains encumbered by setting the privileges accorded to heteronormative relationships as the standard by which all other sexual minorities ought to be able to attain, thereby implicitly promoting practices such as campaigning on the grounds of sexual minorities being 'normal people' with stable identities wanting the same rights that 'other normal people (i.e. a straight married couple with 2.5 children)' have, rather than entertaining the possibilities of transcending beyond the constraints of heteronormative discourses, arrangements, institutions and practices.

Bibliography

American Psychiatric Association. 'Paraphilic Disorders Factsheet.' *Dsm5.org*, 2013. Accessed March 29, 2015.http://www.dsm5.org/Documents/Paraphilic%20Disorders%20Fact%20Sheet.pdf

Bean, Joseph W. 'The Spiritual Dimensions of Bondage.'In *Leatherfolk: Radical Sex, People, Politics, and Practice*, edited by Mark Thompson, 257–266. California: Alyson Publications, 2001.

Beckmann, Andrea. 'The 'Bodily Practices' of Consensual 'SM,' Spirituality and 'Transcendence.' In *Safe, Sane and Consensual: Contemporary Perspectives on Sadomasochism*, edited by Darren Langdridge and Meg Barker, 98–118. New York: Palgrave Macmillan, 2007.

Braun, Virginia and Victoria Clarke. *Successful Qualitative Research: A Practical Guide for Beginners*. London: Sage Publications Ltd, 2013.

Chatterjee, Bela B. 'Pay v UK, the Probation Service and Consensual BDSM Sexual Citizenship.' *Sexualities* 15.5/6 (2012): 739–757.

Creswell, John W. *Qualitative, Quantitative, and Mixed Methods Approaches (4th edition)* London: SAGE, 2014.

Horton, Alicia D. 'Flesh Hook Pulling: Motivations and Meaning-Making From the "Body Side" of Life,' *Deviant Behaviour* 34.2 (2013): 115–134.

Isin, Engin F. and Peter Nyers, eds. *Routledge Handbook of Global Citizenship Studies*. Oxford: Routledge, 2014.

Langdridge, Darren. 'Voices from the Margin: Sadomasochism and Sexual Citizenship.' *Citizenship Studies* 10.4 (2006): 373–389.

Langdridge, Darren and Meg Barker, eds. *Safe, Sane and Consensual: Contemporary Perspectives on Sadomasochism*. New York: Palgrave Macmillan, 2007.

Langdridge, Darren and Trevor Butt, 'The Erotic Construction of Power Exchange.' *Journal of Constructivist Psychology* 18.1 (2005): 65–73.

Lewis, Ellen and William L. Leap. *Out in Theory: The Emergence of Lesbian and Gay Anthropology*. USA: University of Illinois Press, 2002

Liamputtong, Pranee. *Researching the Vulnerable*. London: SAGE, 2014.

MacKendrick, Karmen. *Counterpleasures*. New York: State University of New York Press, 1999.

Newmahr, Staci. *Playing on the Edge: Sadomasochism, Risk and Intimacy*. Indiana: Indiana University Press, 2011.

Plante, Rebecca F. 'Sexual Spanking, the Self, and the Construction of Deviance.' *Journal of Homosexuality* 50.2–3 (2006): 59–79.

Portillo, Tina. 'I Get Real: Celebrating My Masochistic Soul,' *Leatherfolk: Radical Sex, People, Politics, and Practice*, edited by Mark Thompson, 49–55. California: Alyson Publications, 2001.

Preston, John. 'What Happened?' *Leatherfolk: Radical Sex, People, Politics, and Practice*, edited by Mark Thompson, 210–220. California: Alyson Publications, 2001.

Richardson, Diane. 'Constructing Sexual Citizenship: Theorising Sexual Rights.' *Critical Social Policy* 20.1 (2000): 105–135.

Rubin, Gayle. 'Thinking Sex: Notes for a Radical Theory of the Politics of Sexuality.' *Social Perspectives in Lesbian and Gay Studies: A Reader* edited by Peter M. Nardi and Beth E. Schneider, 100–133. USA: Routledge, 1998.

Rubin, Gayle. 'Studying Sexual Subcultures: Excavating the Ethnography of Gay Communities in Urban North America.' *Out in Theory: The Emergence of Lesbian and Gay Anthropology* edited by Ellen Lewis and William L. Leap, 17–68. USA: University of Illinois Press, 2002.

Sabsay, Leticia. 'Sexual Citizenship and Cultural Imperialism.' *Routledge Handbook of Global Citizenship Studies* edited by Engin F. Isin and Peter Nyers, 96–109. Oxford: Routledge, 2014.

Sandnabba, N. Kenneth, Pekka Santilla, Laurence Alison and Niklas Nordling. 'Demographics, Sexual Behavior, Family Background and Abuse Experiences of Practitioners of Sadomasochistic Sex: A Review of Recent Research,' *Sexual and Relationship Therapy* 17.1 (2002): 39–55.

Santtila, Pekka, N. Kenneth Sandnabba and Niklas Nordling. 'Retrospective Perceptions of Family Interaction in Childhood as Correlates of Current Sexual Adaptation among Sadomasochistic Males,' *Journal of Psychology & Human Sexuality* 12.4 (2001): 69–87.

SM International, 'SM International.' *Journal of Homosexuality* 50.2–3 (2006): 263–280.

Thompson, Mark, ed. *Leatherfolk: Radical Sex, People, Politics, and Practice*. California: Alyson Publications, 2001.

Vance, Carol, ed. *Pleasure and Danger: Exploring Female Sexuality*. London: Routledge, 1984.

Vesta, Dianna. 'Fantasy, Fetish, and the Goddess,' *Leatherfolk: Radical Sex, People, Politics, and Practice*, edited by Mark Thompson, 267–275. California: Alyson Publications, 2001.

Weeks, Jeffrey. 'The Sexual Citizen.' *Theory, Culture & Society* 15.3 (1998): 35–52.

Weinberg, Joe. 'The Invisible Closet: Pressure and Difficulties of the 'Fringe-Queer' Community.' *Rupkatha Journal: On Interdisciplinary Studies in Humanities* VI.1 (2014): 18–26.

Weiss, Margot D. *Techniques of Pleasure: BDSM and the Circuits of Sexuality*. North Carolina: Duke University Press, 2011.

Williams, D. J. and Gordon J. Walker. 'Leisure, Deviant Leisure, and Crime: "Caution: Objects May be Closer than They Appear",' *Leisure/Loisir* 30.1 (2006): 193–218.

Wilkinson, Eleanor. "Extreme Pornography' and the Contested Spaces of Virtual Citizenship.' *Social & Cultural Geography* 12.5 (2011): 493–508.

Wright, Susan. 'Survey of Violence & Discrimination Against Sexual Minorities: Fast Facts.' *Ncsfreedom.org*, 2008. Accessed March 29, 2015. https://ncsfreedom.org/resources/bdsm-survey/2008-bdsm-survey-fast-facts.html.

Wright, Susan. 'Discrimination of SM-Identified Individuals.' *Journal of Homosexuality* 50.2–3 (2006): 217–231.

CHAPTER 9

Barebacking as a Form of Homosociality? Notes on *Bottom*

Elly-Jean Nielsen and Todd G. Morrison

Abstract

Bareback sex, the deliberate omission of condoms during anal intercourse between men, is a practice that has faced harsh criticism from social commentators and academics alike. Bareback sex has been routinely stigmatized by some researchers, but others contend that this 'deviant' practice serves an important function among gay men.[1] In this essay, we explore the discourse surrounding bareback sex from the initial monolithic view of this sexual practice as 'dangerous' and 'destructive' to the more multifaceted view of bareback sex as a form of communal bonding and a challenge to gay assimilation and homonormativity. Various theories on barebacking as well as the controversial film text *Bottom*, a pornographic documentary on the barebacking subculture's ritualized sexual endeavours, are used to explore this position. Particular focus is paid to the spoken word among barebackers, namely, their local subcultural vernacular, which highlights the oft-overlooked intersection between homosocial and homosexual.

Keywords

gay men – bareback sex – homosocial – safe sex – pornography – *Bottom*

1 Barebacking as a Form of Homosociality? Notes on *Bottom*

Behind closed doors, in the secluded corners of bars, apartments, bathhouses, gyms, and hotels, in North America's biggest and brightest metropolitan cities,

---

1 See, for example, Tim Dean, *Unlimited Intimacy: Reflections on the Subculture of Barebacking* (Chicago: University of Chicago Press, 2009).

 | DOI:10.1163/9789004392298_011

there exists a subculture of men who have sex with men (MSM) that many would prefer remains clandestine. Around 1997, the practice of intentional condomless anal sex among a community of MSM (including gay and bisexual men) was given a name: barebacking.[2]

Gay men's bodies and sexuality, long burdened with social demonization, face a new demon in our modern times, purposeful contagion.[3] Due to what some theorists call 'sex panic' in the general public, barebackers have attracted a scandalous reputation.[4] There has been no shortage of backlash against the practice of barebacking among a community 'who should know better,' given the recent history of the deadly AIDS virus.[5] Barebackers' 'sexual recalcitrance' is almost unanimously condemned in scholarship and media commentary to date.[6] It seems every article about barebacking, whether the focus is on health or sociocultural factors, perpetuates a singular question: *What makes them do it?*[7]

However, and in contrast to these interpretations, barebacking may also be viewed as a life-affirming practice of contemporary gay male life.[8] In this essay, we further the polemical argument spearheaded by Dean that barebacking subculture requires clearer understanding, and should be viewed through a less moralistic and more affirmative lens. Sexual citizenship, in particular barebackers' homosocial bonds, will be considered a potential source of empowerment for this outlaw community. The film *Bottom*, a gritty, low-budget documentary that follows one New York City self-described 'slut' whose *modus operandi* is mastering 'the art of semen ingestion,' will constitute a critical textual element, and bring this essay into uncharted scholarly terrain.[9]

---

2 Jeffrey Escoffier, 'Sex, Safety, and the Trauma of AIDS,' *Women's Studies Quarterly* 39.1/2 (2011): 133.

3 Byron Lee, 'It's a Question of Breeding: Visualizing Queer Masculinity in Bareback Pornography,' *Sexualities* 17, 1/2 (2014): 101; Michael McNamara, 'Cumming to Terms: Bareback Pornography, Homonormativity, and Queer Survival in the Time of HIV/AIDS,' in *The Moral Panics of Sexuality*, ed. Breanne Fahs, Mary L. Dudy, and Sarah Stage, (New York: Palgrave Macmillan, 2013), 227.

4 McNamara, "Cumming to Terms," 227.

5 Dean, *Unlimited Intimacy*, 2.

6 Gregory Tomso, "Bug Chasing, Barebacking, and the Risks of Care," *Literature and Medicine* 23.1 (2004): 90; Tim Dean, "Breeding Culture: Barebacking, Bugchasing, Giftgiving," *The Massachusetts Review* 49.1/2 (2008): 92.

7 Tomso, "Bug Chasing," 90.

8 Ibid.

9 Dean, *Unlimited Intimacy*, 123.

This essay is organized into eight sections. In the first section, we briefly introduce the film *Bottom*. Next we provide an overview of the semantically unstable terminology surrounding the concept of barebacking. Given that the terminology is inchoate, the third portion of this chapter, is dedicated to a review of the research on barebacking, which highlights the potential problems found therein, tied to the semantic slippages related to the term. In the fourth section, we critically assess disease prevention models and HIV/AIDS discourse, and then go on to reflect upon the health implications and consequences of the practice, with specific attention to the introduction of new drug treatments for HIV, and the effects they have had on the lives of gay men. In the final sections of this essay, we focus on the homosocial bonding evident among members of the barebacking community, as represented by *Bottom*. By highlighting the 'positive' aspects of *Bottom*, we attempt to address the paucity of inquiry on the convergence of homosocial and homosexual. We also call on the subcultural vernacular used in *Bottom* to answer some of the unresolved questions about homosociality in barebacking subculture.

2 *Bottom* and Barebacking

Sceptics might argue that a growing subculture of men who 'fuck freely' without rubber protection is something of an urban legend. What better way to set the record straight than to offer up documentary film footage? *Bottom*, the pithy film title used to describe the receptive role in anal intercourse, is a low-budget documentary on the bareback subculture that follows the conventions of *cinema verité*, but uses pornographic images throughout. The film could also be labelled as ethnographic material, an exposé of sorts, since this film allows a graphic glimpse into a secluded, transgressive subculture.[10]

The documentary's ability to capture underground gay male sexual spaces and culture is impressive.[11] The film follows one New York City 'bottom' whose only *modus operandi* is being a 'cum dump': to collect as many 'loads' as he can internally (through his anus) in a decidedly short period of time, either through bareback sex or by collecting semen from used condoms. His

10 Paul Hockings, *Principles of Visual Ethnography*, (Berlin: De Gruyter Mouton, 2001), vii.

11 It should come as no surprise that the community remains underground, since barebacking by HIV-positive men is a criminal act in 36 U.S. states: Timothy Frasca, Gary W. Dowsett and Alex Carballo-Diéguez, "The Ethics of Barebacking: Implications of Gay Men's Concepts of Right and Wrong in the Context of HIV," *International Journal of Sexual Health* 25.3 (2013): 208.

ceaseless quest for more semen is signified through a recurring close up shot of the bottom's handheld tally counter that numerically increases in real time and acts as an obvious symbol for the number of loads acquired in the recent past. The anonymous bottom is readily involved in barebacking subculture; at the onset of the film, he openly acknowledges that he is dissatisfied with his job, he does not have much of a social life, and his interests lie exclusively in being the recipient in unprotected, 'raw' gay sex.[12]

There is a curious lack of passion in the character of the bottom, which borders on nihilism. Indeed, the anonymous bottom's 'nihilistic hedonism' appears acute.[13] He seems devoid of emotion and to care little for his sexual partners. He is HIV-positive, but at one point in the film, announces that he wished he had lied about his serostatus in order to have sex with an HIV-negative man who had caught his eye. There is something uniquely realistic and, thus, transgressive about the pornographic scenes in *Bottom* since the characters do not struggle with a barrier of shock or disgust during unconventional sexual practices. The viewer cannot identify the characters in the film, as their voices have been altered and their faces concealed. The narrative on queer sexuality in this film may be deemed nihilistic, hedonistic, and countercultural, but its unconventionality deserves closer reflection, as does the discourse surrounding the practice of barebacking.

3 Barebackers, a New (and Semantically Unstable) Erotic Identity

There is a new primacy given to sexual subjectivity in our postmodern world. Gay male sexual identity is not a homogenous category and the advent of HIV/AIDS brought about multiple new categories of identities and intersections with other modes of being. The emergence of a sexual subjectivity of barebackers in our contemporary Western world supports the idea that sexual minority groups unsettle ordered erotic categories. As Weeks asserts, 'boundaries dissolve, and new ones have to be hastily assembled.'[14] For example, various

12 In addition to the many depictions of bareback sex, numerous scenes show the bottom participating in Internet chat room interactions, colloquially known as 'cybercruising': Michael Shernoff, "Condomless Sex: Considerations for Psychotherapy with Individual Gay Men and Male Couples Having Unsafe Sex," *Journal of Gay & Lesbian Psychotherapy* 9.3/4 (2005): 150. The bottom cannot remember the last time he met someone in a bar or nightclub, asserting that he meets partners online or at sex parties exclusively.

13 bell hooks, *Reel to Real: Race, Class and Sex at the Movies*, (New York: Routledge, 1996), 81.

14 Jeffrey Weeks, 'The Sexual Citizen,' *Theory, Culture & Society* 15.3/4 (1998): 41.

sexual practices (e.g., barebacking), sexual roles (e.g., top, bottom), sexual types (e.g., bear, cowboy), and serostatuses (e.g., poz, neg) have recently emerged.[15] These new forms of belonging represent the most intimate elements of personal life and are often sequestered away from the public gaze.[16]

To better understand the practice of intentional unprotected anal intercourse between men, both the practice (i.e., barebacking) and the identity (i.e., barebackers) require scrutiny. The term barebacking comes from the equestrian world, based on the thrills of riding dangerously without the barrier of a saddle.[17] In line with queer theory, bareback sex registers as the discursive inverse of safer sex, and similarly, HIV-positive is the deviant *Other* to HIV-negative.[18] The practice of unprotected anal sex, however, is not *a priori* irrational or risky.[19] Junge and other scholars have drawn attention to the instability of the inchoate terminology on barebacking and deem it as 'emergent, semantically unstable, and contested construction of sex and sexual identity.'[20] Halkitis and colleagues found that both gay and bisexual men in the New York metropolitan area are far from unanimous on what the term means. Remarkably, only one of 227 men was able to name every definitional aspect of the term, calling it 'anal sex, no condom, on purpose.'[21]

Circa 1997, Gendin was one of the first activists to publically voice the perks of sex between 'poz men,' and O'Hara, who is known as the discursive initiator of the term 'barebacking,' got 'HIV positive' tattooed on his shoulder – an act that embraced, re-appropriated, and transformed the dangerous cultural and

15 Dean, "Breeding Culture", 84;Gust A. Yep, Karen E. Lovass and Alex V. Pagonis, "The Case of 'Riding Bareback': Sexual Practices and the Paradoxes of Identity in the Era of AIDS," *Journal of Homosexuality* 42.4 (2002): 3.

16 Weeks, "The Sexual Citizen," 35.

17 Tomso, "Bug Chasing," 93.

18 McNamara, "Cumming to Terms," 227; Yep, Lovass and Pagonis, "The Case of 'Riding Bareback.' ", 3.

19 Thomas Haig, "Bareback Sex: Masculinity, Silence, and the Dilemmas of Gay Health," *CanadianJournal of Communication* 31.4 (2006): 872; Shernoff, "Condomless Sex," 162.

20 Benjamin Junge, "Bareback Sex, Risk, and Eroticism: Anthropological Themes (Re-) Surfacing in the Post-AIDS Era," in *Out in Theory: The Emergence of Lesbian and Gay Anthropology*, ed. Ellen Lewin and William L. Leap (Chicago: University of Illinois Press, 2002), 190; Christien Garcia, "Limited Intimacy: Barebacking and the Imaginary," *Textual Practice* 27.6 (2013):1036; Perry N. Halkitis, Leo Wilton and Paul Galatowitsch, "What's in a Term? How Gay and Bisexual Men Understand Barebacking," *Journal of Gay & Lesbian Psychotherapy* 9.3/4 (2005):43.

21 Halkitis, Wilton and Galatoitsch, "What's in a Term?" 40.

physical status of having a positive serostatus.[22] Thus, originally, barebacking was used to describe HIV-positive men who intentionally engaged in unprotected sex; however, current research has confirmed that barebacking is a phenomenon that cuts across demographics and serostatus.[23] Therefore, the practice cannot be reduced to the conceptualization that younger generations are ignorant to the AIDS-related suffering of the 1980s, nor to the idea that people from a particular social class (here assumed to be hierarchically inferior, or lower class) are more likely to take sexual risks.[24]

Bareback sex has always existed, but the emergence of, and allegiance to, the identity-label of 'barebacker' is a comparably new phenomenon.[25] Although, much like barebacking, the definitions of a barebacker are shifting and ambiguous, the label has been commonly employed by scholars in the area as well as practitioners of this sexual practice. Researchers have cautioned that the concept of 'identity' is mired in constructionist and essentialist notions that limit and parameter the self.[26] Hypothetically, for example, a monogamous gay couple who intentionally engage in unprotected anal sex technically could be considered barebackers. However, our present understandings point to the fact that barebackers form a community of men who embrace both the practice

22 Stephen Gendin, "Riding Bareback: Skin-on-Skin Sex--Been There, Done That, Want More," *Poz Magazine* 24 (June 1, 1997): 64; Scott O'Hara, *Autopornography: A Memoire of Life in the Lust Lane* (New York: Haworth Press. 1997), 196; Haig, "Bareback Sex," 861; David O. Harvey, "Calculating Risk: Barebacking, the Queer Male Subject, and the De/ formation of Identity Politics," *Discourse* 33.2 (2011):169. Another tattoo seen on barebackers is the biohazard symbol (e.g., various porn stars from the controversial company Treasure Island Media [TIM] display it.); Matthew Halse, "Biohazards and the Queer Sexual Imagination," *The Word Hoard* 2.7 (2013): 19; Lee, "It's a Question,"113. Despite claims made that barebackers are often heavily inked, there is a curious absence of tattoos in *Bottom*;Dean, "Breeding Culture," 85; Escoffier, "Sex, Safety," 135. Nonetheless, the unmarked main character does have both nipples pieced and a 'Prince Albert' (i.e., a penile piercing).

23 Jeffrey T. Parsons and David S. Bimbi, "Intentional Unprotected Anal Intercourse among Sex who Have Sex with Men: Barebacking – from Behavior to Identity," *AIDS and Behavior* 11.2 (2007): 279; Dean, "Breeding Culture," 84; Perry N. Halkitis, Leo Wilton and Jack Drescher, "Introduction: Why Barebacking?" *Journal of Gay & Lesbian Psychotherapy* 9.3/ 4 (2005): 3.

24 Dean, "Breeding Culture," 84; Dean, *Unlimited Intimacy*, 38.

25 Parsons and Bimbi, "Intentional Unprotected Anal Intercourse,"283.

26 See, for example, Tim Edwards, *Erotics and Politics: Gay Male Sexuality, Masculinity and Feminism* (New York: Routledge, 1994), 153.

and the identity-label; thus, to a certain degree, the label must be collectively- and self-imposed.

Harvey asserts that the organization of barebackers as a group is political: their erotic dissidence is contrary to the rest of the gay community.[27] As some assimilationists continue the 'fight for neoliberal inclusion in the normative national body,' barebackers may be seen as adopting an anti-homonormative stance.[28] Although the claim that condoms lessen sensation is a particularly well-known narrative, Escoffier opines that the organized subculture of barebackers focuses more on transgression than on pleasure per se.[29] Indeed, to Cohen, the emergence of an identity – a socially imposed categorization – is to assert 'difference' and resist dominant ways of being.[30] The sexual preferences of a group of individuals can sustain an identity, and Edwards has put forth that gay male sexuality in the context of HIV/AIDS has been a particularly ripe context to pave the pathway to 'more positive' identity developments.[31]

A voice-over scene from *Bottom*, where the main character reads off his blog a heated dialogue between himself and a previous attendee of a 'party,' proves a fitting example of the bottom's allegiance to solidified sexual identity. The exchange is fairly acidic in tone as the top argues that he caught an STI from the bottom. In retaliation, the bottom exclaims that he 'gets tested regularly.' Like other scenes of the film, the bottom's eagerness to display his expertise on barebacking subculture is apparent. He belittles those who are naïve enough to put faith in harm-reduction techniques, such as strategic positioning (i.e., topping to avoid infection). In this short clip, the bottom presents himself as a sexual professional, an expert in *Eros*, and a pioneer in the erotic avant-garde.[32] Though shrouded in anonymity, his master status as barebacker – and more specifically, as a bottom – is an all-consuming mode of being.[33] Given the importance and centrality – yet inchoate and unstable nature – of the label

27 Harvey, "Calculating Risk," 157.

28 McNamara, "Cumming to Terms," 228; Dean, *Unlimited Intimacy*, 9.

29 Escoffier, "Sex, Safety," 135.

30 Ed Cohen, "Who Are 'We'? Gay 'Identity' as Political (E)Motion (a Theoretical Rumination),"in *Inside/Out: Lesbian Theories, Gay Theories*, ed. Diana Fuss (New York: Routledge, 1991),73.

31 Edwards, *Erotics and Politics*, 133.

32 Dean, *Unlimited Intimacy*, 39.

33 As further evidence, when cruising or blogging online, the bottom refers to himself as 'bb cunt,' that is, a bareback cunt.

barebacker, existing research approaches and findings on the topic require critical assessment.

4 Research (Concerns) on Barebackers

How have barebackers been positioned in academic scholarship? Tomso points out that science is yet another form of discourse, which has serious implications for the way barebackers are (mis)understood. Accounts of barebackers are highly sensationalized, often focusing on the identities of 'bug chasers' (i.e., HIV-negative barebackers who actively seek seroconversion) and 'gift givers' (i.e., HIV-positive barebackers who seek to seroconvert others).[34] Despite the hyperbole, both are relatively new modes of gay self-expression and are overwhelmingly rare within the bareback community at large.[35]

More problematically, the very basis of existing scholarship in the area seems to petulantly ask '*why do they do it!?*' as opposed to making a concerted effort to understand barebackers' experiences. Much of the health-related scientific work on the bareback community discusses the Internet or illicit drugs as catalysts for risky sexual practices/desires.[36] For example, Parsons and Bimbi found that self-identified barebackers were more likely than other gay men to report crystal methamphetamine use.[37] Interestingly, although drugs are not entirely absent from *Bottom*, at one point in the film the anonymous bottom launches into a discussion on how he sternly turns away hard drugs like 'crystal,' since they can impair sexual proficiency.

Unsurprisingly, numerous analysts on the practice of barebacking convey a dramatic, chastising tone. The harsh criticism comes from both conservative thinkers and well-known (and 'out') commentators and scholars on gay issues.[38] Stall, for one, equates the practice of bareback sex among urban gay men to the coping mechanisms of 'forgetfulness' for war trauma, and compares it to the way people went on with their everyday lives in Europe despite the damage experienced in long-term military conflict.[39] That is, Stall implies

34 Tomso, "Bug Chasing," 88.

35 Dean, *Unlimited Intimacy*, 17; Harvey, "Calculating Risk," 166; Tomso, "Bug Chasing,"88.

36 Tomso, "Bug Chasing," 98; Yep, Lovass and Pagonis, "The Case of 'Riding Bareback,' " 7.

37 Parsons and Bimbi, "Intentional Unprotected Anal Intercourse," 283.

38 See, for example, Andrew Sullivan, Dan Savage (Tomso, "Bug Chasing," 100) and Kevin Alderson (Garcia, "Limited Intimacy," 1048).

39 Ronald Stall, "Preface: Psychosocial and Public Health Approaches to Barebacking," *Journal of Gay & Lesbian Psychotherapy* 9.3/4 (2005): xxi-xxiii.

that in spite of the considerable loss and trauma inflicted upon individuals during the HIV/AIDS 'pandemic,' the practice of bareback sex suggests that gay men have amnesic coping strategies. Concerns also have circulated that barebackers will jeopardize the great strides made in acceptance of the queer community as well as financial support for HIV/AIDS research, treatment, and education.[40]

Unable to see any liberatory aspects of seroconversion, the 'moral rhetoric of anti-barebacking' insists that engaging in this practice is a death-sentence, physically, psychologically, and socially.[41] With this line of thinking, there is no room for reflections on how barebacking subculture might be contributing to dialogue on sexual freedom, or challenging the deep-rooted stigmas associated with HIV/AIDS. In line with Patton's earlier understanding, Dean cautions that researchers' tendency to pathologize barebackers as 'irresponsible' and 'self-destructive' is refusing the ethical challenge to understand a new erotic practice.[42]

While most see barebackers as having a *penchant* for self-destructive, erotic excess, others appeal to the 'powerful acts of political resistance to conventional sexual morality and scientific orthodoxy.'[43] Regardless of the subtle or more overt homonegativities involved within existing scholarship, Harvey maintains that the eruption of barebacking into discourse is, in the end, beneficial, and marks the first steps toward frank affirmation.[44] If one were to listen to those from the bareback community, might one hear the 'positive values and emotions' associated with their identity and sexual preferences?[45] What differences might one see in research results if subtle discursive alterations were made

40 Dean, *Unlimited Intimacy*, 10.

41 Tim Dean, "Bareback Time," in *Queer Times, Queer Becomings*, ed. Ellen L. McCallum and Mikko Tuhkanen (New York: State University of New York Press, 2011), 83; Richard Parker, "Critical Intersections and Engagements: Gender, Sexuality, Health, and Rights in Medical Anthropology," in *Medical Anthropology at the Intersections: Histories, Activisms, and Futures*, ed. Marcia C. Inhorn and Emily A. Wentzell, (London: Duke University Press, 2012), 214.

42 Cindy Patton, "Safe Sex and Pornographic Vernacular," in *How Do I Look?: Queer Film and Video*, ed. Bad Object-Choices (Seattle: Bay Press, 1991a) 45; Cindy Patton, "Visualizing Safe Sex: When Pedagogy and Pornography Collide," in *Inside/Out: Lesbian Theories, Gay Theories*, ed. Diana Fuss (New York: Routledge, 1991b) 384; Dean, "Bareback Time," 77.

43 Tim Dean, "The Erotics of Transgression," in *Cambridge Companion to Gay and Lesbian Writing*, ed. Hugh Stevens (Cambridge: Cambridge University Press, 2010) 67; Tomso, "Bug Chasing," 88.

44 Harvey, "Calculating Risk," 176.

45 Yep, Lovass and Pagonis, "The Case of 'Riding Bareback,'" 6.

to current approaches, such as viewing barebacking not as a social *problem* but as a social *phenomenon*?[46] Furthermore, how have researchers' and medical practitioners' efforts to bridge the gap between 'us' and 'them' fared so far? Does the rhetoric of sexual health appeal to underground sexual communities, such as barebackers?

5 The Context and Status of HIV/AIDS Discourse

While volunteering this summer at the local sexual health centre, I look up and across from me is a plain looking poster to promote condom use. It states, 'Think condoms spoil the fun? Think again.' *It contains no images, no graphics, no puns, no punch line, no novel health-related research findings, and no evidence on how the fun isn't spoiled. The words are in large block letters, front and centre, contained within a large shaded cut-out of a man's head. Sex itself seems prudishly obscured by this poster as do the myriad reasons someone might choose to forgo condoms. Being in the midst of writing a manuscript on bareback sex, I think to myself: such non-compelling and redundant safer-sex advertisements are the perfect example of empty, paternalistic statements that are likely to have little impact on a bonded, coherent subcultural population such as barebackers. Am I correct?*[47]

As this 'condomocracy' advertisement shows, the messages HIV prevention programs provide to MSM have remained relatively unchanged.[48] The ad also implicitly communicates anxiety about sexual discourse, as if an open and direct discussion of sex need always assume a certain amount of risk. A 'state-of-emergency' approach can actually be counterproductive and increase, rather than decrease, rates of infection.[49] The 1980s 'safer sex' campaigns not only were ineffectual, but created a powerful backlash in some gay male communities.[50] Public service announcements, such as the one analyzed above, beg the question if one is bound to fail the mantra of 'use-a-condom-every-time,' why not abandon the mission altogether?

---

46 Harvey, "Calculating Risk," 167.

47 The 'I' in this autoethnographic passage refers to the primary author.

48 Eric Rofes, "Barebacking and the New AIDS Hysteria," *Stranger* 8.29 (April 8, 1999), 16; Richard J. Wolitski, "The Emergence of Barebacking among Gay and Bisexual Men in the United States," *Journal of Gay & Lesbian Psychotherapy* 9.3/4 (2005),22.

49 Rofes, "Barebacking and the New," 17.

50 Tomso, "Bug Chasing," 98.

Safer sex campaigns and slogans have been considered gauche at best, and prudish and anti-sex at worse. Patton reminds us that safer sex is a cultural intervention that cannot be imposed without making participants feel ridiculed and attacked.[51] Safer sex discourse permeates our culture and has a stranglehold on our consciousness.[52] However, the value of this discourse may be questioned. For instance, in her oft-cited 2002 public health work, Ann O'Leary of the CDC acknowledges that long-term condom use is daunting and dubious for virtually everyone.[53] Further, Rofes notes: 'gay men don't need more brochures, more programs to improve our supposedly sagging self-esteem, or more sound bites and marketing messages... [We] need a multi-issue, multicultural gay men's health movement.'[54]

Does *Bottom* constitute filmic resistance to safer sex discourse and omnipresent compulsory heteronormativity? The effects of the AIDS virus have clearly made a mark on gay erotic life; indeed, as Dean argues, 'It is hardly surprising that some men opt for the assertion of anticipated certitude that comes with high-risk sex.'[55] Greater sexual risks may be taken due to safer sex burnout, or 'condom fatigue,' as well as the introduction of highly active antiretroviral drug therapies, which slow the course of HIV.[56] It is reasonable to imagine that *Bottom*, being filmed in a time of antiretroviral therapies, displays the exhaustion felt by some members of the gay community with safer sex discourse and the policing of their sexuality.

6 Health Implications of Barebacking

Dorothy's arrival in Oz is a climatic and transformative moment, but not for her alone. As viewers of the film, we are scarcely aware of the plight of the Munchkins prior to Dorothy bumping off the Wicked Witch of the East. Glinda the Good Witch assures the Munchkins to 'come out' for a miracle has occurred. Slowly, the Munchkins begin to show their faces again. They appear from behind the houses and bushes – they even emerge out of the sewer. The extensive, high-spirited welcome song and dance Dorothy then receives solidifies

51 Patton, "Safe Sex," 33.

52 Patton, "Visualizing Safe Sex," 375.

53 Ann O'Leary, *Beyond Condoms: Alternative Approaches to HIV Prevention* (New York: Kluwer Academic Publishers, 2002), xi.

54 Rofes, "Barebacking and the New," 17.

55 Dean, "Bareback Time," 85.

56 Shernoff, "Condomless Sex," 151.

that a major shift has taken place in Munchkinland. Indeed, the Munchkins come to realize, the wicked witch really is dead ...

Though certainly not a flawless allegory for the introduction of protease inhibitors, this landmark in time can be likened to the accidental murder, and the end of the reign of the Wicked Witch of the East. The variety of new, antiretroviral treatment options that became available during the mid-1990s for those who were HIV-positive had substantial impacts on men's health, including their physicality.[57] AIDS mortalities among MSM steadily declined in the U.S. and, thus, the motivations to be consistent in condom use were challenged.[58] There undoubtedly exists two temporalities of the plague: that of HIV as a sure-fire death sentence, pre mid-90s, and HIV as a chronic manageable illness, post mid-90s. With the emergence of combination therapies, Dean makes an interesting argument about such timelines in relation to bareback subjectivity.[59] After decades (an eternity?) of policing gay men's sexuality, protease inhibitors have ushered in 'altered realities' in gay men's sexual decision-making.[60] This altered reality, in all its glory, can be seen in the Munchkins' parade of merriment, or, analogously, in the epic resurgence of sexual activity among MSM, including activities without condoms.

But surely the bareback sex community understands the potential for a medical backlash; that is, a figurative rain on their figurative parade? What are the risks of 'acquiring a multidrug-resistant strain of HIV'?[61] Do the risks of becoming sicker outweigh the powerful source of camaraderie found through bareback subculture? With little agreement among medical professionals on the chances of re-infection with a more virulent and dangerous strain of HIV, the fear of 'superbugs' – or, in medical jargon, 'medication resistant/untreatable HIV mutant variants'– is of little concern for many HIV-positive barebackers.[62] According to Dean most HIV-positive barebackers are not fazed by such

57 Haig, "Bareback Sex," 867; Junge, "Bareback Sex," 192. The bodily juxtaposition of the ultra-thin and lesion-riddled AIDS body during the initial years of the virus outbreak and the contemporary buff and scarred HIV-positive body (partly from accompanied testosterone prescriptions. Dean, *Unlimited Intimacy* 83; Garcia, "Limited Intimacy," 1034; Lee, "It's a Question," 102) is telling enough. The recent visual depiction of muscular male bodies in the film *Bottom* illustrates this claim.

58 Haig,""Bareback Sex," 862.

59 Dean, "Bareback Time," 76.

60 Dean, *Unlimited Intimacy*, 31.

61 Shernoff, "Condomless Sex," 174.

62 Rofes, "Barebacking," 17; Halkitis, Wilton and Drescher, "Introduction," 4; Dean, *Unlimited Intimacy*, 64.

risks, and instead mention the annoyance of a few extra infections and the hassle and expense of medications.[63] Results from a recent qualitative study with a diverse sample of gay men living in the New York City area by Frasca, Ventuneac, Balan, and Carballo-Diéguez showed that 'they accepted the risks involved as the cost of sexual fulfilment.'[64] Or, perhaps, could it be the homosociality, the crucial sense of community and belonging, that outweighs the risks of infection?

7 Homosocial Bonding and Desire: the Barebacking Brotherhood

What does a concurrently homosocial and homosexual film look like? Who are its characters and what do we know of their lived experience – their shared struggle, their jouissance, and their modes of interaction? Men's homosociality has been artistically represented extensively, through poetry, literature, drama, and film, and thus appears to be a particularly powerful and widely shared discourse.[65] Although male bonding is studied quite extensively as well, the majority of this research investigates male solidarity in heterosexual contexts. Though often overlooked, homosexual texts may in fact communicate 'pure,' unadulterated homosociality, since male bonding is said to occur par excellence without the interference of heterosexual attraction.[66] Might the highly ritualized, erotic activities among the men featured in *Bottom* be assessed as homosocial bonding?

Dean considers bareback sex on video to be 'a subcultural ritual rather than merely a manifestation of unbridled lust.'[67] Thus, if we look beyond the sexual content of *Bottom* and focus on the interactions and community between men – the male solidarity, in line with an 'old boys club,' or the mentality of a fraternity, – a new light is shone on bareback subculture and this cinematic text.[68] For one, the 'dynamic of competition and initiation – how much can

---

63 Dean, *Unlimited Intimacy,* 87.

64 Timothy Frasca, Ana Ventuneac, Ivan Balan and Alex Carballo-Diéguez, "Inner Contradictions Among Men Who Bareback," *Qualitative Health Research* 22.7 (2012): 949.

65 Scott F. Kiesling, "Homosocial Desire in Men's Talk: Balancing and Re-creating Cultural Discourses of Masculinity," *Language and Society* 34.1 (2005): 696; Justin Wyatt, "Identity, Queerness, and Homosocial Bonding: The Case of Swingers," in *Masculinity: Bodies, Movies, Culture,* ed. Peter Lehman, (New York: Routledge, 2001), 52.

66 Kiesling, "Homosocial Desire,"696.

67 Dean, *Unlimited Intimacy*, 128.

68 Kiesling, "Homosocial Desire," 695.

you take? – that characterizes membership in exclusively male groups such as fraternities' is present in the film.[69] The anonymous bottom is determined to take as many loads as he can and he 'gets by with a little help from his friends.' Further, the astute viewer can detect the communal bonds evident in the ways the men treat each other with the utmost respect before, during, and after a sexual transaction. In one illustrative scene a 'friend' helps the bottom acquire loads by bringing and installing a hard metal 'ass-parting device' and injecting the ejaculate contained in used condoms. The medical gaze in this scene subtly eroticizes semen injection, in which 'transmission, not sexuality, becomes the object of voyeurism.'[70] The event comes across as highly ritualized and they thank each other kindly post-op.

Since barebacking cuts across demographics, it is unsurprising that the main character in *Bottom* has sex with men from all ages and backgrounds. Dean notes that barebackers are as racially diverse as the U.S. at large, a finding that is mirrored in the film where the bottom fetishizes the racial identity of his diverse sexual partners.[71] What is potentially perplexing is that the anonymous bottom pledges vocally – both to the viewer/filmmaker and on his blog – that he engages in 'mercy fucks' (i.e., has sex with men who are aging, unattractive, or have small cocks). The bottom is in fantastic physical shape and certainly could be much fussier about his sexual partners. Although he comments on his partners' sexual proficiency and physical appearances post-sex, he is not guided by these factors; instead, what matters most is the absence of condoms and the presence of semen.[72] This democratic aspect of the barebacking brotherhood is at least surprising (if not laudable), for the main character eschews the normative selective practices based on ageism and beauty embedded in the gay scene, as well as entrenched ideals based on physicality, such as an insistence upon the 'youthful clone look.'[73] The bottom's welcoming of all sorts of men attests to the kinship structure that is outside 'the heterosexual matrix that otherwise determines relational intelligibility.'[74]

Bareback 'gang bangs,' depicted in the film *Bottom*, have been deemed by participants as an empowerment zone, where there is no stigma for being HIV-positive. The camaraderie found at the parties may have considerable benefits

69 Dean, *Unlimited Intimacy*, 139.

70 Dean, *Unlimited Intimacy*, 172; Patton, "Visualizing Safe Sex," 381.

71 Dean, *Unlimited Intimacy*, 40.

72 Dean, *Unlimited Intimacy*, 53.

73 Barry D. Adam, "Constructing the Neoliberal Sexual Actor: Responsibility and Care of the Self in the Discourse of Barebackers," *Culture, Health & Sexuality* 7.4 (2005): 333.

74 Dean, "Breeding Culture," 90.

for those involved. This point is illustrated in the testimony of one man quoted by Shernoff, who states that he leaves these parties feeling self-confident, and compares this experience to the feelings of inadequacy felt when leaving the bar/club scene, places where HIV status is highly stigmatized.[75] Gang bangs are regulated by a system of rules, such as 'only one bottom at each party,' with versatility strictly forbidden. Dean draws attention to united 'witnessing' – that is, 'the desire to be witnessed when undergoing meaningful sexual rituals' – as being central to bareback gang bangs.[76] The countercultural representation of a bareback gang bang in *Bottom* shows how information to participate must be 'learned on-site… and the learning process is continuous,' since the participants are expected to adhere to an orchestrated tradition with specialized clothing brought to the event (e.g., a jock strap).[77]

In *Bottom*, the viewer does not witness any violence and, although rules and restrictions are enforced (e.g., cuddling is strictly forbidden), the participants are verbally gracious for their sexual encounters. For example, in one memorable scene, the anonymous bottom has to politely ask the top fucking him to leave and come back in 10 minutes since another top is coming over. The request is completely understood by the top and is carried out with no intragroup conflict, social disturbances, or hierarchical shifts.[78] Additionally, the unforgettable scene explored above in which a 'friend' helps the main character take more inside himself than seems physiologically possible, is markedly non-erotic and the two do not engage in coitus after the deed is done; rather, they thank each other pleasantly. Although the film demonstrates homosexual desire, perhaps more keenly it demonstrates homosocial desire, the need for friendship, and non-erotic affection toward building a fortified subcultural community. Language serves as the primary means through which these needs and desires are conveyed.

8 'Verbal, My Favourite': Language and Mythology

> Indeed, it is the Word, it is language that really reveals to man that world which is closer to him than any world of natural objects and

75 Michael Shernoff, *Without Condoms: Unprotected Sex, Gay Men and Barebacking* (New York: Routledge, 2006), 173.

76 Dean, *Unlimited Intimacy*, 129.

77 William L. Leap, *Word's Out: Gay Men's English* (Minneapolis: University of Minnesota Press, 1996), 114; Dean, *Unlimited Intimacy*, 104.

78 Clifford Geertz, "Deep Play: Notes on the Balinese Cockfight," *Daedalus* 101.1 (1972): 5.

> touches his weal and woe more directly than physical nature. For it is language that makes his existence in a community possible; and only in a society, in relation to a "Thee," can his subjectivity assert itself as a "Me."[79]

What would the bareback community be without the spoken word? How are the homosocial bonds seen in *Bottom* strengthened through idiosyncratic verbal discourse? Cassirer has drawn attention to how verbal structures can appear as mythical entities, and that 'the Word' has a primary force in culture.[80] According to Leap, acquiring 'Gay English' is a vital part of gay socialization as well as the coming out process. For the queer subject, acquiring gay references is not a way to pass the time, but fulfils a crucial social function. Leap argues that Gay English text-making is a subversive act in spite of prevailing, hegemonic discourses: through Gay English, gay experience is expressed in its own terms.[81]

The all-male environment, a factor contributing to mythology in Mercer, is the dream for homosocial community.[82] The 'glorious, lost quality of the homosocial bond' can be seen in a nostalgic yearning for some paradise lost, the 'golden age' or mythic state of men's friendships during youth/adolescence.[83] In the social arena, the idea of eternal return is attached to speech, quite plainly: 'I like to talk and I want this pleasure to come again.'[84] Idiosyncratic communication translates the beliefs and habits that make up the group mythology. In short, speech – in particular, colloquial diction – strengthens the social group.

According to Haig, efforts to talk run counter to bareback sex culture.[85] However, the masculine norm of silence thought to be influential in the bareback community requires scrutiny. In recounting a client's experience, psychotherapist Shernoff noted: 'Even when an uninfected man chooses not to go

---

79 Ernst Cassirer, *Language and Myth* (New York: Harper and Brothers Publishers, 1946), 61.

80 Cassirer, *Language and Myth*, 45.

81 Leap, *Word's Out*, 5.

82 John Mercer, "In the Slammer: The Myth of the Prison in American Gay Pornographic Video," in *Eclectic Views on Gay Male Pornography: Pornucopia*, ed, Todd G. Morrison (Binghamton: Harrington Park Press, 2004), 155.

83 Kiesling, "Homosocial Desire," 702; Paul Ricoeur, *From Text to Action: Essays in Hermeneutics, II* (Evanston: Northwestern University Press, 1991), 322.

84 Paul Zumthor, *Oral Poetry: An Introduction* (Minneapolis: University of Minnesota Press, 1990), 23.

85 Haig, "Bareback Sex," 859.

home with him, he only feels disappointed and not crushed, since he knows he can always go to Brandon's parties and talk about these experiences with other understanding men and always find sexual playmates.'[86] As this man's account suggests, some bareback sex parties do include talk; moreover, open discussion with other men can be a source of self-confidence and solidarity. Sexual vernaculars are argued to be the identifying characteristic of liminal sexualities, and it is only when a vernacular is reaching hegemony that it sounds natural or coherent.[87]

In simple terms, the local vernacular heard in *Bottom* is definitely far from having reached master status, and nowhere near hegemony. The central figure in *Bottom* repeatedly states that he is turned on by 'verbal' sexual partners. Near the opening of the film, he states wryly and wickedly 'verbal, my favourite,' when recounting a particularly delectable sexual experience. He is also verbal, often mentioning how his 'ass is loaded up and oozing with cum.' The discourse in *Bottom*, though arguably jarring, may be more typical than it appears. In order to establish an elective kinship bond, the ostensibly heterosexual term 'breeding' is used among barebackers.[88] Although this erotic language emphasizes kinship, which may be read as 'mirroring the meaning ascribed to (hetero) sexual reproduction,' the queerness remains primary.[89] The use of breeding is an 'elaborate discourse surrounding HIV transmission.'[90] Returning to the idea of bareback sex as a form of resistance, Dean argues that when barebackers fetishize 'poz cum,' they gain a sense of mastery over viral transmission – something that, for many, was originally transmitted without their awareness or consent.[91] Semen containing HIV has developed a positive connotation as a good object to be incorporated, rather than something negative to be kept 'outside.'[92] As can be seen in *Bottom*, the main character's lust for

86 Shernoff, "Condomless Sex," 173.

87 Patton, "Safe Sex," 45.

88 Dean, "Breeding Culture," 82; Escoffier, "Sex, Safety," 135; Yep, Lovass and Pagonis, "The Case of 'Riding Bareback,'" 5.

89 Garcia, "Limited Intimacy," 1034.

90 Dean, *Unlimited Intimacy*, 138.

91 Dean, "Bareback Time," 91.

92 Dean, "Breeding Culture," 85; Dean, *Unlimited Intimacy*, 53. In bareback porn, especially TIM films, the transfer of ejaculate via the mouth, anus, etcetera is the climax moment rather than the act of ejaculation itself (Lee, "It's a Question," 107). Since internal ejaculation is needed to 'plant the seed' – to use barebacking parlance – the sexual practices in *Bottom* point to what Dean calls the eschewing of 'hard core's conventional money shot in favor of other forms of verisimilitude;' Dean, *Unlimited Intimacy*, 170. In the final scene

poz cum over the phallus shows that semen 'containing HIV is radioactive with significance.'[93]

How can fortified, well-established communities, such as barebackers, properly function in silence? Furthermore, might silence on a topic mean shame? Although it is argued that at local bareback sex parties members are to remain silent about HIV status, illness, or medicine, during nearly every sex scene in *Bottom* HIV is routinely eroticized though various verbal utterances (e.g., 'I love verbal poz breeders,' 'AIDS cum,' 'breed this cunt,' 'dirty fucking load,' 'toxic load,' etc.). While silence over one's serostatus may be erotized at certain game-like sex parties, it is erroneous to assume this is unequivocally the case. Dean posits that a 'colourful vernacular' is part of the erotic appeal in pornography, which can certainly be seen in *Bottom*.[94] In this film, viewers are privy to the 'online lexicon specific to bareback sex,' which acts as a ritualized source of bonding.[95] It is even worth suggesting that the idiosyncratic verbal discourse acts as subcultural glue, bonding men to one another in the process.

9 Conclusion: Final Thoughts and Notes on the Film Text

Sex is foundational to gay male identity and community.[96] Men who fuck each other without rubbers are no longer merely outlaws; they are members of an outlaw culture.[97] The subculture of barebackers points to the reality that seropositivity is no longer a death sentence, nor is it a social death.[98] The label

of the film, the bottom performs a 'reverse money shot'; that is, in a close-up, maximally visible display, he expels the semen from inside his anus into a bowl below.

93 Dean, "Breeding Culture," 85. Kristeva's early understanding of the abject – of corporeal waste (excrement and its equivalent) – is that it represents ourselves/our bodies and we are at once repulsed by, and yet identify with and long for, these excrements. Matter which has just traversed the boundary of our body remains symbols of ourselves, and thus, they take on puzzling complexities; Julia Kristeva, *Powers of Horrors: An Essay on Abjection* (New York: Columbia University Press, 1982) 3. Bodily fluids are defined and regulated culturally, but they are not only matter; they may be ripe with meaning and a source of fun. (Garcia, "Limited Intimacy," 1041; Lee, "It's a Question," 111). Read through a Kristevian lens, the recurring images of men's semen in *Bottom* offers an alternative reading to the more pedantic view of barebacking practice as shocking or disgusting.

94 Dean, *Unlimited Intimacy*, 82.

95 Haig, "Bareback Sex," 863.

96 Yep, Lovass and Pagonis, "The Case of 'Riding Bareback,'" 2.

97 Dean, *Unlimited Intimacy*, 38.

98 Ibid; Parker, "Critical Intersections," 214.

'barebacker' itself is a source of pleasure. As the main character in *Bottom* articulates, his sexual partners who utter 'bareback' while fucking are his 'favourite,' and he notes that even the words 'raw' or 'bare' are less titillating than 'bareback.'

Will gay men, or anyone for that matter, ever be as conservative in their sexual practices as prevention advocates would like them to be? Our understandings of HIV prevention need to be reframed in light of new modes of identity and the increased survival rates that have accompanied new treatments.[99] It is reductionist to pathologize sexual risk-takers as self-destructive, suicidal, homicidal, or damaged, as it perpetuates the oppressive tradition of considering gay men to be purveyors of negativity.[100]

In her pivotal work on homosociality, Sedgwick commented that nonsexual love between men is superior to both heterosexual and homosexual sex.[101] Dean argues that the communal bond among barebackers is gaining steam, as they forge their own identity, rituals, and iconography.[102] Thus, it comes as no surprise that the homosocial bonds in *Bottom* are perhaps more significant than the homosexual ones. These ideas are expressed vividly through the polysemic medium of film. Without this cinematic text we would know little of the lived experience of an underground gay male subculture.

The idiosyncratic vernacular used among participants of bareback subculture has a kaleidoscope of meanings. The barebackers' unique mix of cordial and crude language marks the overlooked intersection of homosocial and homosexual semiology. The argument that silence in bareback culture is part and parcel of a highly masculine sexuality also has been scrutinized, since what is spoken among those involved is vital. Following from Cassirer's early theorizing, language may be regarded as the main tool used to bond people within communities and to understand the other, and hence the self, in deeper and richer terms.[103]

New subjectivities and identities, such as 'barebacking' and 'barebackers,' are cultural creations. The collective narratives of barebackers are invented and reproduced, and create new circumstances and possibilities.[104] If individuals

99 Junge, "Bareback Sex," 210.

100 Shernoff, "Condomless Sex," 163; McNamara, "Cumming to Terms," 228; Patton, "Safe Sex," 45; Garcia, "Limited Intimacy," 1035.

101 Eve K. Sedgwick, *Between Men: English Literature and Male Homosocial Desire* (New York: Columbia University Press, 1985), 2.

102 Dean, *Unlimited Intimacy*, 1.

103 Cassirer, *Language and Myth*, 61.

104 Weeks, "The Sexual Citizen," 46.

open their minds to barebacking, they open themselves to alterity. Dean's words are hard to forget: in approaching homonormativity, barebackers 'keep their sex outside the pale of bourgeois respectability… [and] within the sphere of transgression.'[105] We will do well to notice the positive aspects of cinematic depictions of transgressive queer sexual citizenships, lest we forget that queer sex can never be removed from the heteronormative gaze.

Bibliography

Adam, Barry D. "Constructing the Neoliberal Sexual Actor: Responsibility and Care of the Self in the Discourse of Barebackers." *Culture, Health & Sexuality* 7.4 (2005): 333–346.

Bad Object-Choices, ed. *How Do I Look?: Queer Film and Video.* Seattle: Bay Press, 1991a.

Cassirer, Ernst. *Language and Myth.* New York: Harper & Brothers Publishers, 1946.

Cohen, Ed. "Who Are 'We'? Gay 'Identity' as Political (E)motion (a Theoretical Rumination)." *Inside/Out: Lesbian Theories, Gay Theories*, ed.ited by Diana Fuss, 71–92. New York: Routledge, 1991.

Dean, Tim. "Breeding Culture: Barebacking, Bugchasing, Giftgiving." *The Massachusetts Review*, 49.1/2 (2008): 80–94.

Dean, Tim. *Unlimited Intimacy: Reflections on the Subculture of Barebacking.* Chicago: University of Chicago Press, 2009.

Dean, Tim. "The Erotics of Transgression." *Cambridge Companion to Gay and Lesbian Writing*, edited by Hugh Stevens, 65–80. Cambridge: Cambridge University Press, 2010.

Dean, Tim. "Bareback Time." *Queer Times, Queer Becomings*, ed. ited by Ellen L. McCallum and Mikko Tuhkanen, 75–99. New York: State University of New York Press, 2011.

Edwards, Tim. *Erotics and Politics: Gay Male Sexuality, Masculinity and Feminism.* New York: Routledge, 1994.

Escoffier, Jeffrey. "Sex, Safety, and the Trauma of AIDS." *Women's Studies Quarterly* 39. 1/2 (2011): 129–138.

Fahs, Breanne, Dudy, Mary L., and Sarah Stage, eds. *The Moral Panics of Sexuality.* New York: Palgrave Macmillan, 2013.

105 Dean, *Unlimited Intimacy*, 85. For more on the concept of gay assimilation and homonormativity see Nick Mulé's chapter "Constituting Queer Citizenship in Canada's Shifting Civil Society," in this volume.

Frasca, Timothy, Gary W. Dowsett and Alex Carballo-Diéguez. "The Ethics of Barebacking: Implications of Gay Men's Concepts of Right and Wrong in the Context of HIV." *International Journal of Sexual Health* 25.3 (2013): 198–212.

Frasca, Timothy, Ana Ventuneac, Ivan Balan and Alex Carballo-Diéguez. "Inner Contradictions Among Men Who Bareback." *Qualitative Health Research* 22.7 (2012): 946–956.

Fuss, Diana, ed. *Inside/Out: Lesbian Theories, Gay Theories.* New York: Routledge, 1991.

Garcia, Chistien. "Limited Intimacy: Barebacking and the Imaginary." *Textual Practice* 27.6 (2013): 1031–1051.

Geertz, Clifford. "Deep Play: Notes on the Balinese Cockfight." *Daedalus* 101.1 (1972): 1–37.

Gendin, Stephen. "Riding Bareback: Skin-on-Skin Sex--Been There, Done That, Want More." *Poz Magazine* 24 (June 1, 1997): 64–65.

Haig, Thomas. "Bareback Sex: Masculinity, Silence, and the Dilemmas of Gay Health." *Canadian Journal of Communication* 31.4 (2006): 859–877.

Halkitis, Perry N., Leo Wilton, and Jack Drescher. "Introduction: Why Barebacking?" *Journal of Gay & Lesbian Psychotherapy* 9.3/4 (2005): 1–8.

Halkitis, Perry N., Leo Wilton, and Paul Galatowitsch. "What's in a Term? How Gay and Bisexual Men Understand Barebacking." *Journal of Gay & Lesbian Psychotherapy* 9.3/4 (2005): 35–48.

Halse, Matthew. "Biohazards and the Queer Sexual Imagination." *The Word Hoard* 2.7 (2013): 17–28.

Harvey, David O. "Calculating Risk: Barebacking, the Queer Male Subject, and the De/formation of Identity Politics." *Discourse* 33.2 (2011): 156–183.

Hockings, Paul. *Principles of Visual Ethnography*. Berlin: De Gruyter Mouton, 2001.

hooks, bell. *Reel to Real: Race, Class and Sex at the Movies*. New York: Routledge, 1996.

Inhorn, Marcia C., and Emily A. Wentzell, eds. *Medical Anthropology at the Intersections: Histories, Activisms, and Futures*. London: Duke University Press, 2012.

Junge, Benjamin. "Bareback Sex, Risk, and Eroticism: Anthropological Themes (Re-) Surfacing in the Post-AIDS Era." *Out in Theory: The Emergence of Lesbian and Gay Anthropology*, edited by Ellen Lewin and William L. Leap, 186–221. Chicago: University of Illinois Press, 2002.

Kiesling, Scott F. "Homosocial Desire in Men's Talk: Balancing and Re-creating Cultural Discourses of Masculinity." *Language and Society* 34.1 (2005): 695–726.

Kristeva, Julia. *Powers of Horrors: An Essay on Abjection*. New York: Columbia University Press, 1982.

Leap, William L. *Word's Out: Gay Men's English*. Minneapolis: University of Minnesota Press, 1996.

Lewin, Ellen, and William L. Leap, eds. *Out in Theory: The Emergence of Lesbian and Gay Anthropology*. Chicago: University of Illinois Press, 2002.

Lee, Byron. "It's a Question of Breeding: Visualizing Queer Masculinity in Bareback Pornography." *Sexualities* 17.1/2 (2014): 100–120.

McCallum, Ellen L. and Mikko, Tuhkanen, eds. *Queer Times, Queer Becomings.* New York: State University of New York Press, 2011.

McNamara, Michael. "Cumming to Terms: Bareback Pornography, Homonormativity, and Queer Survival in the Time of HIV/AIDS." *The Moral Panics of Sexuality*, edited by Breanne Fahs, Mary L. Dudy, and Sarah Stage, 226–244. New York: Palgrave Macmillan, 2013.

Mercer, John. "In the Slammer: The Myth of the Prison in American Gay Pornographic Video." *Eclectic Views on Gay Male Pornography: Pornucopia*, edited by Todd G. Morrison, 151–166. Binghamton: Harrington Park Press, 2004.

O'Hara, Scott. *Autopornography: A Memoire of Life in the Lust Lane.* New York: Haworth Press. 1997.

O'Leary, Ann. *Beyond Condoms: Alternative Approaches to HIV Prevention.* New York: Kluwer Academic Publishers, 2002.

Parker, Richard. "Critical Intersections and Engagements: Gender, Sexuality, Health, and Rights in Medical Anthropology." *Medical Anthropology at the Intersections: Histories, Activisms, and Futures*, edited by Marcia C. Inhorn and Emily A. Wentzell, 206–237. London: Duke University Press, 2012.

Parsons, Jeffrey T. and David S. Bimbi. "Intentional Unprotected Anal Intercourse among Sex Who Have Sex with Men: Barebacking – from Behavior to Identity." *AIDS and Behavior* 11.2 (2007): 277–287.

Patton, Cindy. "Safe Sex and Pornographic Vernacular." *How Do I Look?: Queer Film and Video*, edited by Bad Object-Choices, 31–64. Seattle: Bay Press, 1991a.

Patton, Cindy. "Visualizing Safe Sex: When Pedagogy and Pornography Collide." *Inside/Out: Lesbian Theories, Gay Theories*, edited by Diana Fuss, 373–386. New York: Routledge, 1991b.

Ricoeur, Paul. *From Text to Action: Essays in Hermeneutics, II.* Evanston: Northwestern University Press, 1991.

Rofes, Eric. "Barebacking and the New AIDS Hysteria." *Stranger* 8.29 (April 8, 1999): 15–19.

Sedgwick, Eve K. *Between Men: English Literature and Male Homosocial Desire.* New York: Columbia University Press, 1985.

Shernoff, Michael. "Condomless Sex: Considerations for Psychotherapy with Individual Gay Men and Male Couples Having Unsafe Sex." *Journal of Gay & Lesbian Psychotherapy* 9.3/4 (2005): 149–169.

Shernoff, Michael. *Without Condoms: Unprotected Sex, Gay Men and Barebacking.* New York: Routledge, 2006.

Stall, Ronald. "Preface: Psychosocial and Public Health Approaches to Barebacking." *Journal of Gay & Lesbian Psychotherapy* 9.3/4 (2005): xxi-xxiii.

Stevens, Hugh, ed. *Cambridge Companion to Gay and Lesbian Writing*. Cambridge: Cambridge University Press, 2010.

Tomso, Gregory. "Bug Chasing, Barebacking, and the Risks of Care." *Literature and Medicine* 23.1 (2004): 88–111.

Weeks, Jeffrey. "The Sexual Citizen." *Theory, Culture & Society* 15.3/4 (1998): 35–52.

Wolitski, Richard J. "The Emergence of Barebacking among Gay and Bisexual Men in the United States." *Journal of Gay & Lesbian Psychotherapy* 9.3/4 (2005): 9–34.

Wyatt, Justin. "Identity, Queerness, and Homosocial Bonding: The Case of Swingers." *Masculinity: Bodies, Movies, Culture*, edited by Peter Lehman, 51–66. New York: Routledge, 2001.

Yep, Gust A., Karen E. Lovass and Alex V. Pagonis. "The Case of 'Riding Bareback': Sexual Practices and the Paradoxes of Identity in the Era of AIDS." *Journal of Homosexuality* 42.4 (2002): 1–14.

Zumthor, Paul. *Oral Poetry: An Introduction*. Minneapolis: University of Minnesota Press, 1990.

Filmography

Bottom. Directed by Todd Verow. Bangor: Bangor Films, 2012. DVD.

Index

www.ingramcontent.com/pod-product-compliance
Lightning Source LLC
Chambersburg PA
CBHW071435230926
51846CB00001B/238
* 9 7 8 9 0 0 4 3 9 2 2 8 1 *